WA 1067693 7

D0618905

12.99

The making of an
English 'underclass'?

The making of an English 'underclass'?
The social divisions of welfare and labour

KIRK MANN

Open University Press
Milton Keynes · Philadelphia

1067693 7

305.56
MAN

For my Mother and Father

Open University Press
Celtic Court
22 Ballmoor
Buckingham MK18 1XW

and
1900 Frost Road, Suite 101
Bristol, PA 19007, USA

First Published 1992

Copyright © Kirk Mann 1992

All rights reserved. No part of this publication may be
reproduced, stored in a retrieval system or transmitted in
any form or by any means, without written permission from the
publisher.

British Library Cataloguing-in-Publication Data

Mann, Kirk
    The making of an English 'underclass'?:
    The social divisions of welfare and labour.
    I. Title
    305.50942

    ISBN 0–335–09719–7
    ISBN 0–335–09718–9 pbk

Library of Congress Cataloging-in-Publication Data
Mann, Kirk, 1952–
    The making of an English 'underclass'? : the social divisions of
    welfare and labour / Kirk Mann.
        p.   cm.
    Includes bibliographical references (p.   ) and index.
    ISBN 0–335–09719–7 (hardback)—ISBN 0–335–09718–9 (pbk.)
    1. Public welfare—England.   2. Poor—England.   I. Title
HV249.E89M36   1991
305.5'6'0942—dc20   91–16475CIP

Typeset by Inforum Typesetting, Portsmouth
Printed in Great Britain by Biddles Limited, Guildford and Kings Lynn

27/4/93

Contents

Acknowledgements

I am indebted to a great many people going back to the early 1970s. Gerry Whitehouse, Jenny Mann, Wendy Frankcom and Andy Metcalf all helped me form my ideas and to survive the 1970s. At university, Sarah Fildes, Alan Deacon and Malcolm Harrison provided intellectual food for thought and some elementary English lessons. Alan and Malcolm were also crucial in providing support, ideas and criticism during my PhD marathon from which this book is drawn. Other people who have commented on this book, at various times and in different forms, were Moira Ashley, Chris Hunt, Geof Mercer, Lucy Aspinall, Tony Novak, Paul Bagguley, Judith Anstee, Alan White, Chris and Jane Dunne, John Skelton and Peter Craig. Jim Kincaid and Ian Gough forced me to tidy up my ideas and Peter Taylor-Gooby's support at the draft stage is much appreciated. I would like to thank all my colleagues in the department of Social Policy and Sociology at Leeds for their support. Adrian Sinfield deserves special thanks because he has, in the best academic tradition, responded to unsolicited chapters, proposals and queries. I should also like to thank all the students I have taught on my third-year option for their constant flow of criticism and interest. Carolyn Weaver, Liesel Carter, Margaret Gothelf and, more than anyone, Debbie Hook have assisted with typing and the idiosyncrasies of the word processor. Sven Kleinschmidt and Maunagh Frankcom have had to put up with my changes of temper over many years and I would like to thank them for being so tolerant. Linda is owed a debt that I cannot express in words, nor adequately repay.

Finally, in case I have missed anybody out, and in the best Radio One tradition, I would like to thank 'anyone else who knows me'. The comments and criticisms I have received have sometimes been negative, humorous or mutually incompatible. However, I have chosen who to take note of and who to ignore. This means, of course, that I cannot blame anyone but myself for the final product.

List of abbreviations

AEU	Amalgamated Engineering Union
AUEW	Amalgamated Union of Engineering Workers
ASE	Amalgamated Society of Engineers
DHSS	Department of Health and Social Security
DSS	Department of Social Security
GMWU	General and Municipal Workers Union
GSWT	Genuinely Seeking Work Test
LEC	Local Employment Committee
NCB	National Coal Board
NGA	National Graphical Association
NUM	National Union of Mineworkers
NUWM	National Unemployed Workers Movement
PAC	Public Assistance Committee
RAL	Reserve Army of Labour
SDW	Social Division of Welfare
TUC	Trades Union Congress
UAB	Unemployment Assistance Board

*one*_____

Introduction

Ours has become a divided society. Millions are excluded from
society's benefits and they now amount to an underclass; bitter,
resentful and angry Mrs Thatcher has created a divided nation (Gerald
Kaufman, Labour Party Shadow Home Secretary, talking on BBC
Television 3 days before the 1987 general election).

Who can civilize the yobs?

How to civilise the masses – that great preoccupation of our Victorian
forebears ought once again to come to the fore of public debate
(Peregrine Worsthorne, *Sunday Telegraph*, 3 November 1985).

We live in the age of the yob. Whatever they don't understand, whatever isn't protected, the yobs will smash, and spoil it for everybody
else. Did you notice the traffic bollards on the way here?

"It's unemployment that's responsible", said Robyn.

"Thatcher has created an alienated underclass who take out their
resentment in crime and vandalism. You can't really blame them."

"You'd blame them if you were mugged going home tonight", said
Vic (David Lodge, 1988, p.241).

There are many ways to identify an underclass. I will concentrate on
three phenomena . . . illegitimacy, violent crime, and drop out from
the labour force (Charles Murray, 1990, p.4).

This book is concerned with a fairly simple issue: the development and
maintenance of social divisions and their relationship to the provision of
welfare. The focus will be on some of the poorest members of society and I
shall ask why it is that they are so often seen to be segregated from the rest
of the working class.

Social divisions may not have replaced class as the principal obsession of
British social scientists but they have certainly moved very close to the top of
the academic agenda. Although social divisions can take a variety of forms, I

am concerned here with divisions within what can broadly be defined as the working class. Political and social scientists have made mention of social divisions for many years. Thus terms such as 'the underclass', 'marginalized groups/stratum', 'excluded groups', 'reserve army of labour', 'housing classes', 'the pauper class', 'the residuum', 'relative stagnant population', and, more obviously, the poor, have all been used to describe a section of society which is seen to exist within and yet at the base of the working class (see Rex, 1971; Giddens, 1973; Jordan, 1973; Marx, 1976; Gough, 1979; Jessop, 1979; Parkin, 1979; Sinfield, 1981; Byrne and Parson, 1983; Mann, 1984, 1986; Stedman-Jones, 1984; Dahrendorf, 1988; Field, 1989; Murray, 1990).

Few of the terms used are located within any coherent theory of social divisions and most are, even descriptively, rather vague. It might be argued that many of these terms are used as a form of shorthand, a way of referring briefly to a social phenomenon with which we are all familiar. It is simply a matter of commonsense, after all, to acknowledge that the working class has within or below it a stratum that fares particularly poorly. Unfortunately, commonsense views tend to be riddled with the observer's own prejudices. Thus, for example, it is doubtful if there is any agreement over the bases of social division or what to do about them. Adding to the diverse views of academics have been those of a number of politicians, journalists and writers. As the quotes above illustrate the idea of an underclass, currently the most fashionable term, is used by some incompatible bedfellows.

One of the most recent and contentious pieces has been Charles Murray's (1990) polemic on *The Emerging British UNDERCLASS* (emphasis in original). His account will be discussed in Chapter 6, but what is most remarkable about Murray's version of the underclass is how easily he has been able to disseminate his ideas. Few academics can have had the opportunity of explaining their views at length in Rupert Murdoch's *Sunday Times*. Indeed, his research in Britain was sponsored by the News International Group. In this respect, he represents a long tradition of commentators (Chadwick, Booth and the Webbs would be some of the most notable) who have observed a stratum of hopeless degenerates. By following that tradition Murray, like his predecessors, panders to middle-class fears of the yob.

What Murray does illustrate is the fact that it is all too easy to slide from the identification of a social group who suffer social problems, into the position where the victims are regarded *as* the social problem. Often the claim that there is a sub-stratum beneath the working class proper is linked to the provision of public welfare. One of the reasons why this book considers intra-class divisions more seriously, was a sense of unease regarding the use of such *terms* as 'underclass'.

A second reason for considering the relationship between welfare and social divisions is more straightforwardly academic. The various terms employed are simply confusing and lack any explicit historical or theoretical location. Without wishing to make any grand claims, it is hoped that this book will at least provoke a more considered theoretical perspective on intra-class divisions. My contribution is an attempt to provide both a historical and theoretical framework within which social divisions and their relationship to welfare can be examined.

The third reason for putting finger to keyboard relates to my own experiences. As an activist during the first half of the 1970s, in Claimants Unions, Squatters groups and later as an AEUW convenor, I was often baffled by the attitudes of many working-class people to others who were, as far as I was concerned, part of their class. Racism and sexism were complemented by a contempt for 'dossers' and 'scroungers'. Despite my view at the time of a unitary working class I was often confronted with the opinion that there was a class of undeserving people who lived off state welfare (even though such views were often challenged by other workers and were rarely articulated by those who had any experience of poverty).

Looking from 'the bottom up'

It was this experience that ensured that my perspective on social divisions is informed by a *bottom up* approach. That is, I consider social divisions to be *made* by a host of social processes, but not least by the working class itself. The claim is that those at the bottom of the class system are active agents of change and try to influence the world in which they live. Intra-class divisions may be reinforced by legislation, they may be economically or politically advantageous to capital at particular moments, but looked at from the bottom up it is impossible to ignore the part played by the working class and its organizations. This is not to deny that other social processes may be vitally important if a different perspective is adopted, but the concern here is to examine the part the working class has played in its own *making*. However, before expanding any further, it might be as well to clarify what this study does not do.

The part played by the state in setting and maintaining social divisions is given very little attention. In part, this is because it is claimed that the state does not create social divisions but builds upon those that already exist. A further reason for neglecting the state is that analyses which take the state as their starting point tend to emphasize the structural restraints, the fiscal crisis and the political economy of the welfare state. Instead, it will be shown here that the making of social divisions has to be explained (Kaye, 1984). Too often the existence of intra-class divisions is dismissed or reduced to some key function they perform for 'capital'. Why some groups rather than others should consistently perform this function tends to be ignored. Nor are the processes by which some are assigned this function adequately explained. For example, it may suit employers to have a cheap, readily available source of labour, usually referred to as the reserve army of labour, but precisely how this is created tends to be ignored. To assert that it is in the interests of capital and that the state acts to assist capital does not tell us how, over time and in a variety of settings, the reserves are selected. Since no team sheet appears with the names of the reserves listed, what stops them getting onto the field of play?

Moreover, there are already enough books, many written by Marxists, which locate the state and its welfare activities at the heart of their analysis (O'Connor, 1973; Ginsburg, 1979; Gough, 1979; Novak, 1988). These have certainly added a richness and depth to studies of welfare and its development, but they do not satisfy the need for a history from below. Despite class being a major concern of these approaches, they tend to focus more on the requirements of the capitalist class and the state. For most of these accounts, Marx's assertion that 'people make history' brings forth the strident retort, 'BUT NOT UNDER CONDITIONS WHICH THEY CHOOSE' (Mann, 1986).

There is, however, another Marxist tradition which takes a class struggle, or a bottom up, perspective. Kaye (1984, p.233) has stated that:

> The British Marxist historians examine classes as historical relation-ships *and* processes. Implicit in their work, and occasionally explicitly stated, . . . is the analytical and historical priority given to class struggle, out of which, in specific historical circumstances, class – in the full sense – has emerged or been 'made'.

My argument is not that the state is irrelevant, far from it, but that it has already had enough attention. The structural requirements of capital may restrain people and classes but the concern here is with how classes have struggled, and not with the chains that restrained their movement (Mann, 1986; Wetherly, 1988).

Nor will the reader find a detailed account of specific social divisions. However, numerous examples of how specific groups have been excluded and restricted in their attempts to escape the trench of dependency are provided. For example, sexual divisions are a constant theme and numerous examples of the way in which women have been excluded are given. However, it was not possible to make the in-depth and detailed research necessary to address sexual divisions properly. The account here is a general account and a theory of social divisions. As such, it is likely to antagonize the specialist. That is simply one of the penalties of generalizing.

The approach advocated here is heavily influenced by three intellectual strands, which I have tried to synthesize. The first being the ideas presented by Titmuss (1958) in his essay on the social division of welfare. The second is what Kaye (1984) has called 'class struggle analysis,' which is most closely associated with the work of Thompson but which can be regarded as part of a tradition in which a number of British Marxist historians have played a part. Thus the argument attempts to apply a Marxist perspective to the social division of welfare. However, it is a far from orthodox brand of Marxism which is applied. A more accurate, but still rather clumsy, label for the approach might be Libertarian Marxism, although I appreciate that many will claim that these two intellectual traditions are in opposition and cannot be combined. The third significant influence has been the labour process debate initiated by Braverman (1974). These ideas are all considered in a critical light, and none of them escapes without some modification or revision. Mention has already been made of what a class struggle analysis involves, but it might benefit the reader to have the other key concepts explained in a little more depth before I outline the structure of this book.

The social division of welfare

Titmuss wrote his essay on the Social Division of Welfare (SDW) as a defence of the early post-war welfare legislation. The importance of the essay lies in the fact that it provides a better description of the constituent elements of the welfare state, and the possibility of a more informed theory. By the 1950s, a number of critics of *the* welfare state argued that the middle classes were effectively subsidizing the working classes. Not only was this extremely unfair, in the view of the critics, but it would also undermine the moral fabric of the nation. Titmuss replied that they were wrong on both counts.

Titmuss argued that many of the benefits that the middle classes received were not defined as 'welfare' by the Treasury, whereas the benefits provided for the poor were defined as welfare and appeared, therefore, as a cost to the middle-class taxpayer. The problem of defining a social service, or the welfare state, made it difficult to know whether or not the critics were including the services that had a large middle-class clientele. Titmuss was particularly keen for the tax system to be considered a social service, which in his view it had to be since it had played an increasingly significant part in the distribution of income since 1907. If the tax system was defined as part of the welfare state, then features of that system could be seen to benefit the middle classes more than the working classes.

Once the definition of a social service was shown to be problematic, Titmuss went on to show that there were different systems of welfare that operated in different social spheres to meet similar needs. He argued:

> Considered as a whole, all collective interventions to meet certain needs of the individual and/or to serve the wider interests of society may now be broadly grouped into three major categories of welfare: social welfare, fiscal welfare, and occupational welfare. When we examine them in turn, it emerges that this division is not based on any fundamental difference in the functions of the three systems (if they may be so described) or their declared aims. It arises from an organizational division of method, which, in the main, is related to the division of labour in complex, individuated societies (Titmuss, 1958, p.42).

By social welfare Titmuss meant those publicly provided funds and services which commonsense notions of *the* welfare state might consider to be the only welfare activities of the state. Social security, local authority housing, the National Health Service (NHS) and the personal social services are perhaps the examples that most readily spring to mind.

For Titmuss, 'social welfare' met similar needs and dependencies to the other two elements of the SDW: fiscal and occupational welfare. Fiscal welfare consists of: 'Allowances and reliefs from tax, [which] though providing similar benefits and expressing a similar social purpose in the recognition of dependent needs, are not, however, treated as social service expenditure' (Titmuss, 1958, p.44). In recent years, the tax allowances to those purchasing their home with a mortgage have been the focus of considerable attention (Forrest and Murie, 1983; Goodin and Le Grand, 1987). The Conservative governments since 1979 sought to reduce expenditure on local authority housing while at the same time the Treasury has lost vast sums due to mortgage interest tax relief (estimated at £7 billion in 1990 by the Inland Revenue). The subsidies paid to local authority tenants are highlighted as a burden on the economy and yet the effective subsidy to purchasers is not portrayed as burdensome. Thus similar needs are met through different welfare systems, but one is more 'acceptable' than the other.

The third system of welfare, occupational welfare benefits, were described as follows:

> They include pensions for employees, wives and dependants; child allowances; death benefits; health and welfare services; personal expenses for travel, entertainment, dress and equipment; motor cars and season tickets; residential accommodation; holiday expenses; children's school fees; sickness benefits; medical expenses; education and training grants; cheap meals; unemployment benefit; medical bills and an incalculable variety of benefits in kind ranging from 'obvious forms of realizable goods to the most intangible forms of amenity' (Titmus, 1958, pp.50–1).

A major reason for the growth in these occupational welfare benefits was, Titmuss observed, '*The drive to "buy" good human relations in industry*' (1958, pp.52–3: emphasis added). This point will be referred to on a number of occasions throughout the book, since it underlines the relationship between the SDW and industrial relations. Titmuss recognized that, although these benefits were administered through the occupational system and were the responsibility of particular employers, it was the Exchequer which, in the main, bore the costs, because most of these benefits were deductible against tax due (Titmuss, 1958, p.50). Consequently, although the three systems of welfare are distinct in the form in which they are delivered to recipients, they all depend upon state legislation and/or sanction. This does not mean that the three elements are seen by Titmuss as flowing in some mechanistic fashion from the state. Rather the state is seen by him to recognize the multitude of services as 'needs'.

Since the 1950s, the SDW has been further developed, and in such a way that it has built on existing social divisions. New schemes have excluded particular groups, and older forms of welfare have been adapted in such a way as to reinforce the isolation of those who rely on public welfare. The redundancy payments scheme, occupational pension schemes, private health insurance and a host of new 'fringe benefits' have reinforced Titmuss's case. The unemployed are obviously not recipients. Occupational welfare is only available to those with an occupation. Nor are most of the lowest paid, the less well-organized, part-time and precariously employed workers able to get many 'fringes'. Indeed, it would appear that the higher up the income and occupational ladder a person climbs, the greater are the occupational benefits (Field, 1981, 1989; Green *et al.*, 1984; Lonsdale, 1985, pp.165–6).

These three elements to the SDW – social, fiscal and occupational welfare – provide a useful starting point for an analysis of social divisions. It has to be admitted here that fiscal welfare will receive considerably less attention than social/public and occupational welfare. This is because my concern is with divisions within the working classes, for whom, in general, fiscal welfare is less significant than occupational or social/public welfare. The three elements of the SDW are related by Titmuss to the division of labour in society, increased labour specificity and industrial relations practices. These points will be developed in the next chapter; however, I shall argue that they have to be revised to take account of class struggle and the labour process.

Class struggle and the labour process

The importance of class struggle has already been mentioned briefly, but it needs to be stressed that it is interpreted very broadly. It is, for example, recognized that class struggle arises on a day-to-day basis (Beynon, 1973). One of the most important locations for class struggle is the workplace, where contests over the labour process are common (Stark, 1982). When, for example, employers complain about trade union 'restrictive practices', they are bemoaning their lack of control over the labour process. On the other hand, whenever the organization of work is transformed and, usually following redundancies, a more flexible pattern of work (from the employer's perspective) is established, the employer has probably won a victory in the battle over the labour process. The labour process refers, therefore, to the organization of work and the control and definition of skill. This too is explained in more detail in the next chapter. Put very simply, the claim, first made by Marx and revived by Braverman (1974), is that the way that work is performed is a crucial aspect in the construction of divisions between workers.

Tool-makers in engineering, for example, are usually paid more than machine minders. There are a number of reasons for this but the most obvious are their claims to be more skilled, and the fact that they have always been paid more than machine minders. In order to become a tool-maker, it is normal to have completed an apprenticeship of 3–5 years. Although there are now many government and company training schemes, it remains the case that apprentices are usually trained 'on the job'. Even with day release to college, the most important source of knowledge for apprentices is the tool-makers who train them. Entry to the trade has historically been restricted, and it is common for the tool-room, despite current legislation, to be a closed shop. Although tool-makers may be set times for completing particular tasks, and the attempt by employers to control the labour process has encroached on the autonomy of the tool-maker, they retain a degree of discretion over their pace of work. This measure of control is denied to most other workers in the industry.

If employers were somehow able to obtain and codify the knowledge that tool-makers possess, it would be possible to challenge the control the tool-maker has, by introducing new working practices. In the past, this has usually meant breaking the tasks down into more detailed elements. It is not easy to do this in the case of tool-makers, but it has been possible to do so for many other types of work. Each time a task is disaggregated, the detailed division of labour becomes more complex and control of the labour process passes from the worker to the employer. Moreover, together with this loss of control, the workers will also experience a loss of self-esteem: their relationship to work has been demeaned and they will feel more vulnerable, which of course they are because they can now be replaced. Nor are such issues confined to engineering workers. Cousins (1987) has applied a similar analysis of the labour process to workers in welfare organizations. Along with privatizing public utilities, there has been a drive to introduce 'efficiency' and the principles of the private sector into the public sector.

Consequently, where a person is located, in both the social and the detailed division of labour, is vitally important to their material well-being. The best organized trades or industries, and those with more control over the labour process, will be more likely to gain access to occupational welfare. The more control workers can exercise over entry to their trade, and over the labour process, the less likely it is that they will have to rely on public welfare.

This brief outline of how the labour process interacts with the SDW is far from complete. In particular, it fails to acknowledge how workers contest their location, and how specific groups are excluded from the more privileged places in the labour market. Nevertheless, it touches on some of the points which will be used to construct an alternative model of the SDW.

The structure of the book

In Chapter 2, the reader will be asked to take a critical, but still appreciative, look at Titmuss's original thesis and subsequent treatments of that essay. The labour process debate will also be returned to.

One of the major flaws in the SDW thesis, outlined in Chapter 2, has been the lack of any historical context within which to locate the theory. Chapters 3–5 are not intended to provide a comprehensive account, but an outline of the history of the SDW. They detail how the SDW was made in the struggle to avoid the debilitating effects of capitalism, and how control over the labour process was vitally important if workers were to escape the clutches of the Poor Law. For example, in Chapter 3, it is shown that there were social divisions in feudal England, and that there was also a crude SDW. It is argued that some of these older ideas and divisions impacted with the emergent capitalism. Chapter 3 then proceeds to show how, as organized labour adjusted to the prevailing economic and social conditions of capitalism, the SDW was redefined.

Exclusionary practices, which were common among mid-nineteenth-century trade unions, provided one of the few means by which sections of the working class could collectively avoid poverty. Only by keeping their labour scarce could workers hope to improve wages and, thereby, their welfare. It is the form and direction that class struggle has taken which has been so important in promoting the SDW. Pragmatic acceptance of the limits within which class struggle takes place has encouraged sectionalism, and this in turn promotes social divisions. A further feature of Chapter 3 will be the response of middle-class commentators to the evidence they saw of social divisions. It will be shown that this evidence was used and, in some cases, subsequently built into social legislation. Chapter 3 concludes by looking at the Liberal reforms of 1906–1912 and how these lay the foundations of the SDW.

Chapter 4 covers the period from the beginning of the First World War to the end of the Second World War. The inter-war years are frequently associated with mass unemployment. The use of administrative solutions to political problems, most notably that of how to remove the issue of unemployment from the political agenda, had profound effects for the SDW. Chapter 4 explores further the continuing theme of how the adoption by the labour movement of a strategy of pragmatic acceptance, influenced the form taken by the SDW. It will be shown that the the growth of occupational welfare, overtures towards the state, contests over the labour process, economistic and sectional industrial struggles, and political sectarianism, all shaped the administration and provision of welfare.

The impact of the Second World War and, in particular, the involvement of the trade union leadership in a much closer relationship to the state, had the effect of redrawing the boundaries of the SDW. Chapter 5 is the last to cover the history of the SDW. Despite the supposed consensus on universalism in the immediate post-war period, it will be argued that the seeds of contemporary social divisions were sown during this time. Corporatism in the post-war period necessarily involved the exclusion of certain interests. Throughout the 1960s, the great problem for British industry, as far as the media and some politicians were concerned, was the 'restrictive practices' pursued by sections of the trade union movement. Shop floor militancy, largely over wages, working practices and demarcation lines, often prevented management from pursuing 'rationalization' and investment plans. The 1960s also saw employers hoard labour, which further increased the sectional bargaining power of the well-organized workers during a period of almost full employment. Labour shortages and government policy encouraged people from the Indian sub-continent and the West Indies to emigrate to Britain. Simultaneously, the numbers of married women in the labour market increased markedly. However, the new recruits to the labour market were seldom able to gain admission to those trades which provided the best wages and conditions. The strategy of exclusion may have increased the ability of some workers to challenge their employers, by maintaining homogeneity within the workplace, but it closed avenues of opportunity to other members of their class. Parkin (1979; see also Chapter 6) refers to this as 'dual closure', a strategy of the organized labour movement which both challenged the privileges of dominant groups but also served to reinforce social divisions. These divisions were in turn reflected in the SDW by the 1970s.

Chapter 5 also takes the reader through the 1980s and the return of mass unemployment. Simultaneously, there was increased consumer spending, often fuelled by a boom in house prices and easy credit, which saw social divisions taking on a harder edge. Patterns of consumption, previously associated with the middle classes, combined with divisions based on access to fiscal and occupational welfare had, by the 1980s, spread to significant sections of the working class. At the same time, the realm of industrial relations was being redefined. Workers who had previously been able to exert considerable industrial muscle were defeated by a government intent on breaking their hold on key industries, and in newer industries some commentators began to talk of a division between 'core and peripheral' workers (Atkinson and Gregory, 1986). Along with an increase in the service sector and the sale of public utilities, the labour movement found itself on the defensive. Once again, a more pragmatic and sectional strategy emerged which abandoned any class-wide struggle and, in the process, social divisions appeared firmer than ever. Indeed, by the late 1980s, there was considerable talk of an *underclass*.

Chapters 6 and 7 turn to the theoretical problems associated with social divisions and welfare, and tackle the strengths and weaknesses of existing accounts of social divisions. Non-Marxist approaches are examined in Chapter 6, the concepts of housing classes (Rex, 1971, 1973), dual labour markets (Barron and Norris, 1976), consumption cleavages (Dunleavy, 1986; Preteceille, 1986; Saunders, 1986) and social closure (Parkin, 1979; Murphy, 1988) being addressed in turn. Although there are a number of criticisms made of these concepts, it will be argued that there are also some attractions, the most significant of which is that they are not bound to the concept of a homogeneous working class, defined in relation to the means of production.

In Chapter 7, Marxist approaches are considered. Marxism will be shown to have uncritically adopted too many of the assumptions and prejudices associated with Marx's and Engels's work. The idea of a lumpen proletariat is firmly rejected and the concept of the reserve army of labour (RAL) criticized and qualified. Likewise, the chapter goes on to discuss the political marginalization of the poorest sections of the working class by Marxism. Two elements of Marx's work which are treated more favourably are his discussion of dependency creation, through the purchase and sale of labour, and the theory of alienation.

Chapters 6 and 7 set the scene for Chapter 8, where the central components of a Libertarian, but still (I think) Marxist, perspective of the SDW are assembled. Thus the discussion focuses on how a Marxist theory of alienation explains the isolation and dependence of workers within a capitalist labour market. These ideas are linked to others which emphasize the divisive effects of the labour process. Thus, it will be shown that capitalism encourages sectional competition and economistic class struggles. These, in turn, promote intra-class divisions which the SDW comes both to reflect and at the same time enhance.

Finally, the ambitious nature of this project has to be admitted. To claim that a new perspective upon the SDW is possible, and that this provides exciting insights into social divisions, is likely to antagonize current orthodoxies, both Marxist and non-Marxist. Likewise, the failure to stay within the confines of a particular academic discipline may tread on the toes of the specialist. Whatever the shortcomings of this attempt, there is a desperate need for a general account of social divisions which does not patronize the poor. This book tries to locate the experience of poverty in the context of a class society, but does not reduce this to an economic function of capitalism. There are few excuses offered, nor many condemnations, for the attitudes and behaviour of sections of the working class in pursuing their pragmatic and sectional interests. It is clear, I hope, that I wish it were different, but I do not feel well placed to be casting any stones. Irrespective of my wishes, the form and direction which class struggle has taken has served to reinforce the SDW, and to ensure that social divisions are likely to continue to be a feature of the 1990s.

two

The social division of welfare: a suitable theoretical framework?

Are those on the left caught between the bankrupt orthodoxies of the Fabian tradition and the utopian recipes of the neo-Marxist approach? (Lee and Raban, 1988, p.1).

Students of social policy all too often assume that theoretical considerations should be left to political scientists and sociologists. Like Mr Gradgrind in Dickens' *Hard Times*, it is supposed that facts somehow speak for themselves. Theory is implicit, normative, or the task of some other discipline. It would, though, be misleading to suggest that it is only undergraduates who persist with such views. Taylor-Gooby (1981) has suggested that 'arthritic empiricism' is almost congenital within social administration, with Chadwick, Rowntree, Booth, the Webbs, Beveridge and Donnison infecting their intellectual offspring. In this chapter, it will be argued that Titmuss, one of the 'founders' of social policy and, since the Second World War, probably its most influential intellectual figure, provided one of the more interesting opportunities for developing a theory of social divisions. Chapter 1 touched on the SDW and indicated that this had to be revised. I now want to provide a more thorough exposition and critique of Titmuss's approach. This will be followed by a consideration of Sinfield's Weberian revision of the SDW thesis. The chapter will conclude by outlining in more detail the manner in which welfare, the social division of labour and the labour process interact. Thus it will be shown that a class struggle perspective on the SDW relates the study of welfare to some of the central theoretical concerns of the social sciences.

The social division of welfare

The SDW was initially outlined by Richard Titmuss in 1955, and subsequently published in 1956, and again in 1958 as part of his collection of writings in *Essays on the Welfare State*. Since the 1950s, the essay has become a standard text for undergraduates and a frequently cited source in publications. There can be little doubt that Titmuss 'remains a massive presence in the study of the welfare state' (Kincaid, 1984, p.114), and, arguably, his essay on the SDW is a principal reason for his continuing influence.

Titmuss insisted that his essay on the SDW had to be read in the context of the social and political climate of the 1950s. He felt that there was a concern with the social well-being of the nation, which went beyond the cost of the newly established services. There was, implicitly, a fear that state intervention was undermining the moral fibre of the nation; indeed this was on occasion the explicit criticism. In short, Titmuss (1958, p.36) felt that the critics of the welfare state were portraying a future in which 'a decaying, over-worked and anxious middle class' supports a working class that does not really need the benefits for which the middle classes are paying. In the 1950s, with the Conservatives in power and a moral panic about juvenile delinquency in the press, it may have seemed that a period of reaction would reverse the gains of the 1940s. It was against this social and political backdrop that Titmuss wrote his essay on the SDW. He never intended his essay to be read as a theoretical model of social divisions, but as a polemical retort to what we would now call the selectivists.

Titmuss sought to show that (a) the welfare state did not redistribute resources from the middle class to the working class, (b) that the welfare state consisted of not one but three systems of welfare and (c) that the development of these three systems of welfare was related to 'the division of labour and the search for social equity' (1958, p.38).

He addressed the first point by querying the definition of the welfare state used by its critics. Titmuss was especially keen to emphasize the less visible benefits provided to the middle classes. This led him to identify his three systems of welfare: fiscal, occupational and social welfare. The term social welfare, however, is slightly misleading, because the other two elements of the SDW are also obviously social. It might be better to describe social welfare (following Sinfield, 1978) as *public* welfare. It is public in the sense that it is visible and in so far as the public (in general of course) identify this element with *the* welfare state. Indeed, the visibility of public welfare services means that they are the ones most frequently singled out for criticism.

With the exception of Sinfield (1978), whose revision of Titmuss's theory we shall turn to shortly, there has been a peculiar reluctance to treat Titmuss's theoretical, as opposed to his descriptive, framework seriously. The fact that the theoretical implications of the SDW have been neglected is especially significant given that the concept is so frequently employed by students of social policy.

The division of labour

For Titmuss, the key to understanding how and why the three systems of welfare had developed was in the growth of needs and dependencies, . . . which, in the main, is related to the division of labour in complex, individuated societies' (1958, p.42). Following his critique of the selectivists and his definition of the SDW as three related divisions, Titmuss went on to devote considerable space to what he saw as the major determinants of the SDW.

First, he identified the growth of 'states of dependency,' which he felt had been 'defined and recognized as collective responsiblities' (1958, p.42). Titmuss acknowledged certain 'natural' dependencies, such as child-bearing, childhood and extreme old age but he argued that in the creation of dependency, *'the dominating operative factor has been the increasing division of labour in society and, simultaneously, a great increase in labour specificity'* (Titmuss, 1958, p.43: emphasis added).

In pointing to the division of labour and labour specificity, Titmuss made considerable use of Durkheim's (1933) sociological study *The Division of Labour in Society* and he concluded by pointing the reader towards Durkheim's work (Titmuss, 1958, p.55). It is true that Durkheim was not the only influence upon Titmuss's thinking, and that his Fabianism, humanism and moral individualism were capable of embracing a disparate body of thought. There is certainly plenty of evidence to show that Titmuss's work, as a whole, did not slavishly follow Durkheim. Despite these necessary qualifications, in his essay on the SDW, and particularly where he wanted to relate the SDW to the division of labour, labour specificity and the growth of dependency, Titmuss relied heavily upon Durkheim.

The significance of this point is that Titmuss misleads the reader as to the nature and historical development of the division of labour, and therefore its relation to the SDW. Titmuss, like Durkheim, had a deep concern with moral individualism. Thus he was quick to identify what he saw as the state's responsibility for welfare provision but, at the same time, he was very reluctant to urge the state to take coercive action against those interests that promoted dis-welfare. The state, therefore, had a duty to relieve dependency by providing health care through the NHS, but it ought not to nationalize the pharmaceutical industry since this restricted individual freedom (Kincaid, 1984). The delicate balancing act that the state has to perform is complicated, Titmuss believed, by the social forces of industrial society. Of these forces, the division of labour is regarded, by both Titmuss and Durkheim, as the most significant.

The importance of the division of labour, for Titmuss, was that it served to individuate society. That is, as tasks become more detailed, more specialized and impersonal, so too does society. Titmuss appears to accept Durkheim's view that, unless carefully held in check by his or her attachment to social norms and values, the individual will experience anomie, i.e. normlessness. For Durkheim, the result of anomie was a rise in the rates of suicide, as well as nervous and psychological disorders. If there were a more general lack of social norms, the result would be higher levels of crime, social disorder and eventually anarchy. For Titmuss, and once again he was roughly in line with Durkheim, the moral regulation of society is necessary as a means of overcoming the isolation (anomie) generated by the division of labour. However, 'individual dependencies and their social origins and effects' (Titmuss, 1958, p.44) are gradually recognized, with the growth of organic solidarity. That is to say, the process of individuation also encourages 'the inter-dependence of individuals or groups in systematic relations of exchange with one another' (Giddens, 1978, p.25). But this interdependence is not confined to the economic sphere. Interdependence also encourages a respect between individuals for the autonomy and dignity of others leading to moral individualism. The growth in the SDW is, therefore, a function of, and a response to, the dependencies created by the division of labour.

The development of the SDW reflected Titmuss's (1958, p.53) view that '. . . man [sic] is not wholly responsible for his dependency'. Since he saw the three aspects of the SDW performing a 'similar social purpose', i.e. meeting needs and dependencies created by the division of labour, Titmuss went on to argue that there ought to be equity between the three systems of welfare. Clearly, if it is accepted that society promotes dependencies, it is unjust, in Titmuss's eyes, for the needs of some to be resolved on more favourable terms than others. Put most simply, Titmuss argued that if the needs that society created were the same for everyone, it was unfair for some people to be given more generous treatment simply because they had access to a different system of relief.

The tendency for critics of the welfare state to ignore the more generous treatment of those in receipt of fiscal and occupational welfare was, therefore, unjust. Worse than this, by treating the same needs differently, as the SDW did, the state was likely to encourage sectional solidarities and social disharmony. The result could all too easily be an ethos of 'I'm all right Jack'. (This was also the title of a Peter Sellars film which appeared at about the same time and seemed to be making some similar points.) Any further social differentiation added to the process of dependency and individuation by provoking further sectional demands. This cycle of dependency and individuation made the individual '. . . more aware of his [sic] dependency, more liable to failure, more exposed to pain' (Titmuss, 1958, p.55).

It has been necessary to explain both the background to Titmuss's essay and its central themes, because they provided the backdrop against which the argument in this book was set. Titmuss's work in general, but arguably the SDW most of all, has been a central plank in the defence of the welfare state in the 1980s (e.g. Walker, 1984; Goodin and Le Grand, 1987; Johnson, 1987). It is rare, however, to find the theoretical, as opposed to the descriptive or polemical, aspects of the SDW being outlined (e.g. Harrison, 1986). It would be comforting to feel that the neglect of Titmuss's theory was due to a considered critique, but it is more probably a desire to ignore theory.

A critical assessment

The core of Titmuss's essay can be stated crudely as follows:

1 'The Welfare State' is not a unitary whole, and cannot be assumed to be only those services and resources made available to the working classes.
2 The middle classes gain from a variety of welfare measures which are concealed by the fact that they are distributed by different methods to those provided for the working classes.
3 The different systems of welfare distribution fall roughly into three categories – fiscal welfare, social welfare and occupational welfare.
4 These different elements of the welfare state meet similar needs and dependencies.
5 The state has a duty to meet these dependencies because in the main they arise from social and cultural forces beyond the control of individuals.
6 The major determinant of these dependencies is the division of labour and the increasing specialization of work as a result of technological and industrial change.
7 Simultaneously, there is an awareness of dependency, and of the injustice of the state meeting similar needs differently, which is likely to lead to further estrangements.
8 The net result is a society that promotes self-interest, individuation, sectionalism and social conflict.

As an argument to counter critics of the post-war reforms, Titmuss's essay on the SDW has much to commend it. It was almost as if Titmuss was pointing out to the critics that they failed to understand the scope of the welfare state, its importance for social order and its part in providing a variety of less visible benefits for the middle classes. In contrast to Titmuss's carefully argued and presented case, the critics could be portrayed as crude and naive. For the Fabian supporters of the welfare state, the essay represented a call for an extension of the state's welfare activities along more equitable lines.

There is also much to admire in the analytic possibilities that the essay provides. Unfortunately, as Sinfield (1978, p.131) suggests:

> Others who have employed the concept have generally confined themselves to illustrating the division of welfare and have shown little concern for exploring it further and in particular investigating its causes and its relation to the division of labour.

Part of the reason may be that within a few years of the essay's publication, the sociological foundations upon which Titmuss had based much of his argument were being undermined. The explosion of radical sociology in the 1960s and early 1970s was not concerned with the empirical issues that Titmuss addressed. By the late 1960s, Titmuss was also more closely identified with the conservative forces of academic life than in the 1950s. Moreover, Durkheim was seen as one of the founders of the functionalist and positivist schools of sociology and had little, or nothing, to offer the new radical tradition. In citing Durkheim, Titmuss was unlikely to win many supporters within sociology. Despite the considerable value of the original analysis in linking the development of welfare to the development of the division of labour, there are a number of assumptions made by Titmuss which have to be questioned. Three of the most important and questionable assumptions relate to (1) the nature of the state, (2) the bases of dependency and (3) the determinants of the division of labour.

The state

The first feature of Titmuss's approach that needs to be critically examined is his concept of the state. By claiming that the state comes to recognize dependencies, Titmuss implies that need is a major factor in the development of social policies. Of course, he accepts that similar needs are met by different policies, and that the form of welfare a person has access to will depend upon his or her position in the social division of labour. On the other hand, he does not consider whether the state may act in the interests of a particular group, but claims that:

> All collectively provided services are deliberately designed to meet certain socially recognized "needs": they are manifestations, first, of society's will to survive as an organic whole and secondly, of the expressed wish of all the people to assist the survival of some people (Titmuss, 1958, p.39).

The difficulty with this view of the development of welfare is that we have no evidence that 'society' makes the sort of decisions Titmuss suggests, nor that 'people' are consulted about whether they want to help others. By claiming that 'society' wants to survive as an organic whole, Titmuss seems to accept Durkheim's view of society as a functional organic unit.

Rather than being a functioning unit, society could be portrayed as a highly stratified, conflict-ridden, sectional, hierarchical system that survives in its present form due to the power of the privileged to manipulate the state (Miliband, 1973). Titmuss did regard the ability of the state to structure the SDW as crucial, but he did so from a Fabian perspective. He considered the state a tool that could be used to bring about more equal treatment within capitalism. This optimistic view of how the state could represent the interests of the poor *might* have been understandable in the early 1950s, following the reforms of the post-war period, but it is harder to sustain in the harsh light of the 1980s.

Dependency and determinism

Secondly, Titmuss tends to portray the growth of dependency-creating circumstances as inevitable. Industrialization is portrayed as being capable, without any other influence, of creating needs. Why the ability to produce more goods and more food and to deliver produce to consumers very rapidly should create needs rather than satisfy them is not explained. That industrialization was accompanied by the establishment of a capitalist class system is not considered significant by Titmuss. As Sinfield (1978, p.134) has observed, the discussion of quite how dependencies and needs are generated is not developed by Titmuss and he remained 'closer to the "industrialisation" thesis, with its implications of technological determinism'. We shall see in subsequent chapters more clearly how capitalism, rather than industrialization, was a major factor in the creation and promotion of dependency.

The division of labour and the labour process

Thirdly, the discussion of the division of labour is restricted by the framework within which Titmuss locates it. By accepting the inevitability of the division of labour and the increasing specificity of labour, Titmuss conceals the intense conflicts that have accompanied this process. For example, Titmuss does not provide a framework within which we can account for changes in the detailed division of labour. Titmuss refers to this as an increase of labour specificity without really explaining why the process of work should become more specific/detailed. In order to clarify the issue we need to return to the labour process and expand on some of the points made in Chapter 1.

Braverman (1974) has argued that the increasing specifity of labour is a creature born of capitalism. For Braverman, it is necessary first to distinguish between the general division of labour, which arises in all societies, and the subsequent subdivision of labour, that occurs within capitalist societies. He points out that whereas a worker in pre-capitalist society (he gives the example of a tinsmith) may have divided the various operations he or she performed in the making of a number of items, the planning and execution of all of these operations would have remained the responsibility of one person. Thus, for example, when producing funnels, a tinsmith would have designed the funnel, cut and rolled the sheet metal and then undertaken the riveting and seaming of the funnels. In the process, the tinsmith may have designed fixtures and templates to make the process easier, more accurate and faster. The amount of time spent analysing the work and designing special equipment, would have varied with the quantity of funnels (or whatever else he or she was making). Throughout the process, control still rested with the craftsperson. However, with the advent of capitalism, the control exercised by the worker was rapidly assumed by the employer. Each task was broken down and, from the planning stage to the finishing and inspection of the work, particular workers performed very narrowly defined tasks which were previously the responsibility of one worker. As Braverman (1974, p.78) puts it:

The worker may break the process down, but he [sic] never voluntarily converts himself into a lifelong detail worker. This is the contribution of the capitalist, who sees no reason why, if so much is to be gained from the first step – analysis – and something more from the second – breakdown among workers – he should not take the second step as well as the first. That the first step breaks up only the process, while the second dismembers the worker as well, means nothing to the capitalist, and the less since, in destroying the craft as a process under the control of the worker, he reconstitutes it as a process under his own control.

Edwards (1979) has pointed out that the move from control over the labour process by the craftworker to control and management of the worker by the capitalist is accompanied, as a rule, by intense conflict and struggle. Reducing people to measurements of labour necessary for production, something which is forced upon the individual capitalist by the requirement to compete within the market, has led to strikes, demarcation disputes and trade union 'restrictive practices'. This last phrase – restrictive practices – sums up the desire employers have to eradicate any aspect of control that workers might exercise over the labour process. It also highlights the extreme difficulty capitalism has had in gaining complete control of the labour process over the last 200 years.

It is vitally important at this stage to note that the significance of the labour process for Braverman lies in the alienation of the worker from the act of production, and from the product of his or her labour. The importance of the labour process in promoting alienation and dependency will be expanded upon in the last chapter. However, there is a further aspect of the division of labour that deserves attention in the context of this critique of Titmuss's claim that dependency arises as a result of industrialization *per se*. In Braverman's view, the breakdown of crafts does not take a random or unpredictable form. The employer ensures that each operation, once removed from the control of the craftsperson, is assigned to the most suitable labour. Suitability in this instance means the cheapest and most amenable labour. Where strength is likely to be the desired quality, the employer will seek fit young labour. Using the example of the breakdown of the tinsmith's craft, strength might be required of the person whose sole task is to lift and carry the sheet metal. The planning of the work will be carried out, most probably, by a skilled or trained worker, the cutting by a semi-skilled worker, the rolling by an unskilled worker, etc. Each of the workers will be paid according to their grade and the rates may vary quite significantly. The employer gains from this aspect of the division of labour because (a) the number of 'skilled' workers is reduced and (b), it serves to divide the loyalties of workers according to their 'skill' or grade. It is this second feature whereby workers are segregated from one another by grade and skill, which historically has underpinned the SDW. It has promoted sectionalism and differential wage rates. The sectionalism of the workforce can backfire on the employer, in the shape of inter-union disputes, demarcation disputes, etc., but it more frequently makes the task of the socialist trade union activist more difficult (Braverman, 1974, pp.77–83).

The social division of labour and the increasing specificity of labour is not, therefore, an outcome of industrialization, but of capitalism. The development and use of new technology is not an inevitable consequence of abstract social forces but, in very large measure, a development designed to provide particular capitalists with an advantage over their competitors. Although changes in technology may arise because of marketing pressures, or managerial decision making (McLoughlin and Clark, 1988), the principal motive is the reduced labour costs associated with increased control over the production process.

There are, though, social divisions which, while related to capitalist production relations, cannot be reduced to them. For instance, the sexual division of labour and racial divisions are profoundly influenced by the way that white male workers have sought to defend their positions against changes in the labour process. Frequently, the language and practice of the labour movement has drawn on patriarchal and racist ideas. Thus the form and direction class struggle takes may be designed to exclude other members of a broadly defined working class. Braverman acknowledges these divisions but underemphasizes the part the working class has played in making them. Consequently, the manner in which social divisions, particularly sexual divisions, are seen to be generated in Braverman's account has provoked some criticism (Knights and Wilmott, 1986a; Cousins, 1987). Throughout this study, it will be demonstrated that capitalists and the labour movement have both sought to exploit the ideologies of social division at certain historical moments.

The point that needs to be emphasized is that, irrespective of the flaws in Braverman's work, he highlights the fact that Titmuss obscures the forces that have promoted the detailed division of labour. Titmuss therefore misleads the reader as to the source of social divisions. Provided the shortcomings in Titmuss's original essay are recognized, it should be possible to use the perceptive and potentially exciting analysis that the SDW offers. Indeed, a number of scholars have used Titmuss's idea of a SDW, and a number of others have touched on many of the same themes (e.g. Korpi, 1978; Reddin, 1982; Walker, 1984; Castles, 1985; Johnson, 1987; Field, 1989; Esping-Andersen, 1990). The most sustained and sophisticated attempt to revise Titmuss's SDW thesis has been provided by Sinfield (1978), and it is to his Weberian account which I shall now turn.

Sinfield's revision

Sinfield does not state that he wants to revise Titmuss's account, but that is in effect what he does. For Sinfield it is necessary to combine a number of key sociological concepts with the SDW theory. With more than a shade of understatement, Sinfield (1978, p.144) points to 'three other issues that received less attention from Titmuss – power and the state, time and security, and the institutions of capitalism'. Moreover, Sinfield has earlier written into the thesis a consideration of class, has highlighted and rejected the apparent technological determinism of the original essay and has skilfully turned Titmuss's concern with social integration into an analysis of legitimation (1978, pp.134, 141–3).

Legitimation

The process of legitimation is a subtle one, but it can be illustrated by the example of the deserving/undeserving distinction. The greater visibility of public welfare (what Titmuss called social welfare) can have two effects. First, the 'undeserving' are given considerably more media attention than, for example, tax evaders (Golding and Middleton, 1982; Cook, 1989). In the 1970s, 'scroungerphobia' in the press was followed by increased surveillance of social security claimants. The less visible, but arguably more significant in terms of cost to the Exchequer, abuse of the tax system is treated somewhat differently. The press, when they do refer to tax evasion, tend to portray surveillance as an infringement of the individual's rights. As Golding and Middleton (1982, pp.98–9) observed: 'Such concern for the tender susceptibilities and civil rights of tax evaders has rarely been extended to people under investigation for the usually rather smaller sums involved in social security fraud.' Thus, the first effect may be to legitimate the view that 'scrounging' is not only a major problem but it must be rooted out with whatever punitive measures are necessary (Cook, 1989).

Secondly, the 'welfare state' can be portrayed as the acceptable face of capitalism. If the 'deserving', however they might be defined, are provided with benefits by the state, even though these benefits may be worth considerably less than those obtainable through the fiscal and occupational systems, capitalism can be seen to 'care'. It is unlikely that the recipients will regard 'the system' as any fairer, but for the bulk of the population it may serve (at times) this legitimating function (O'Connor, 1973). Public welfare may serve to draw a *cordon sanitaire* around those who would otherwise be the visible reminders of the penalties of failure in a capitalist economy (Jones, 1983, p.63). Simultaneously, therefore, the state giveth and the state taketh away. If, as appears to be the case, the least stigmatized benefits go to those higher up the stratification ladder, while those at the bottom experience public welfare as demeaning, support for public welfare is likely to be undermined. Moreover, those in receipt of occupational and fiscal welfare benefits are likely to regard their benefits as 'earned' and therefore deserved. Thus the stratification system is not only reflected in the social division of welfare, but it may well gain ideological support from it (Taylor-Gooby, 1985).

Class, power and the state

The relationship of the SDW to the class structure of society is also demonstrated by Sinfield in his discussion of power. He states: 'The greater power

of certain classes or organisations to influence the allocation of scarce resources is a central issue for any analysis of the social division of welfare'
(1978, p.149). Although Sinfield's account recognizes the inadequacy of
Titmuss's discussion of power, it does not go much further than stating the
need for power to be a more central aspect of the SDW thesis. There is also a
peculiar vagueness about Sinfield's discussion of the relationship between
the state, power and the SDW. He emphasizes the unintended consequences
of state activities and calls for a more 'sustained critique of the role of the
state in the development of the social division of welfare' (1978, p.145).
Nevertheless, he does not go on to provide this much needed critique. In
part, this may have been due to the widespread sense of confusion many
felt when confronted with the debate about the nature of the state in the
late 1970s. There will no doubt be many who sympathize with Sinfield's
scepticism regarding the usefulness of much of the literature on the state
(Althusser, 1969; Clarke, 1977; Holloway and Picciotto, 1978). Too often
the debate is divorced from any empirical base and fails to explain adequately how the state and welfare interact. Where welfare provisions are
discussed, they tend to be described as the structural accompaniments of
capitalism tying down the working class. In the work of Althusser (1969)
and his adherents, it was possible for anyone who did not share their view to
detect an unacceptable sub-text of bondage. Welfare legislation was almost
invariably portrayed by this strand of Marxism in a restrictive fashion – the
bonds or chains which prevent the working class appreciating the 'real'
relations between classes (Mann, 1986).

For Sinfield (1978, p.155) it is possible to accept the obstacles to reform,
including the influence of capitalism upon the institutions of the state, without resorting to a Marxist model. Unfortunately, apart from making it clear
that he feels a non-Marxist analysis of the state, power and the SDW is a
possibility, and one that is needed, Sinfield does not attempt the task
himself.

The approach advocated here acknowledges the power and effect of the
state at significant historical moments (see, e.g. Chapters 4 and 5), but it is
argued that the context within which the state operates has been neglected.
Crucial for any contextualization of the state is the form and direction that
class struggle takes. The focus will be on the manner in which class struggle
is conducted, and how this is popularly experienced and interpreted by
different sections of the working class. Thus experience will be shown to be
more important than is allowed for by theories of the state. Sinfield also
appears to appreciate the need to locate explanations of welfare development at the level at which they are experienced and contested. He has no
objection to identifying the effect the state has; rather, he is sceptical of the
abstraction and rarefication in much of the theorizing on the state. There
will be no argument here with this point, but it should be borne in mind that
the part played by the state is not fully addressed in this book.

Time and security

In his discussion of time and security, Sinfield provides an insight into the inegalitarian method of service delivery that the three divisions of welfare conceal. He draws on another of Titmuss's (1962) essays to show the insecurity of living on public welfare, in contrast to the security of benefits paid through the fiscal and occupational systems of welfare. The tax system, for instance, makes long-term planning easier for the very wealthy, occupational benefits like pensions (assuming that they are in a 'good' scheme) similarly make it easier for recipients to plan many years ahead, but public welfare tends to generate insecurity, because it demands planning on a daily basis.

Living on the poverty line ensures that simple matters like cooking the evening meal requires thought about what can be purchased cheaply. This will, in turn, consume time and energy in finding the shops that are the cheapest for each item. Likewise, the convenience foods that 'make time' for other activities are too expensive for the low-paid and the poor. Anyone who has 'signed on' and been sent from the Department of Social Security (DSS) to the Department of Employment and then perhaps back again, will testify that time, the only resource they appear to have in abundance, is perversely consumed by the very conditions which make it available. The attitude appears to be that the unemployed have nothing better to do and therefore what does it matter if they are made to wait? The services provided through the fiscal and occupational systems of welfare on the other hand, are less time-consuming and less stigmatizing. They also provide a greater sense of continuity, and thereby security. In the discussion of time and security, Sinfield is not really adding any new conceptual features to the SDW thesis. Rather, he highlights another aspect of inequality that flows from social divisions within the three systems of welfare.

One of the main points to note in Sinfield's revision is the emphasis he places on changes in the SDW. Sinfield makes it quite clear that changes in the provision of welfare have to be linked to changes in the wider capitalist society. He suggests that welfare may be used as a tool for changing economic or political features of society contrary to many commonsense opinions. For Sinfield (1978, p.154), it appears that the sharp increase in the rate of unemployment in the early 1980s was a means of reducing the influence of the trade unions and is, therefore, a class weapon. Likewise, change may, in itself, provide opportunities for certain businesses, irrespective of other features of that change. For example, privatization may encourage the service sector by making a previously public sector open to market forces. This type of change may occur irrespective of any measured 'efficiency', but may rely on such notions, in discussion in the media for example, to legitimate change.

Sinfield (1978, p.155) does not claim to have provided a comprehensive theoretical position. The aim is simply to develop and expand upon Titmuss's original essay, and to draw out aspects of that essay which might provide the basis for a more critical social policy, which is not necessarily indebted to Marxism. There is a temptation to regard Sinfield's revision, and it has to be seen as a revision and not merely an exposition, as the Weberian answer to the implicit Durkheimian account provided by Titmuss. Certainly, the central concerns of Sinfield's essay are class, status and power, three elements most usually associated with a Weberian analysis. Moreover, there is a long and respectable tradition within Weberian sociology which concentrates on intra-class divisions (see Chapter 6).

The attraction of Sinfield's version of the SDW is that it introduces, explicitly, a link between the class system and welfare divisions. Power and the state are acknowledged as important features in the development of the SDW, but the tendency to reduce these to necessary variables in an overall capitalist economic equation is avoided. Written at a time when the fashion was for elaborate and rarefied theories of the state, Sinfield's revision was a reminder that it was possible to take a critical stance, without taking on board the baggage that accompanied structural Marxism. Unfortunately, Sinfield's main contribution was simply to identify the questions that needed to be answered and the issues that had to be addressed. He did not go on to provide the answers, and no-one has really taken up the challenge. The only other significant contribution on the nature of the SDW has been provided from a different perspective, that of feminist scholarship.

A sexual division of welfare?

An attractive feature of Titmuss's thesis on the SDW was that it challenged commonsense definitions of welfare. Subsequently, it has ensured that discussions of welfare focus on questions of power, inequality and the division of labour. While Sinfield has demonstrated that the SDW is integrally concerned with key sociological concepts, and particularly the stratification system, for Rose (1981, p.479):

> The Titmuss concept of the 'Social Division of Welfare' with its potential openness for the examination of the contradictions of race, age and sex as structured by social policy offers a tradition of empirical enquiry which refuses the automatic reduction of all oppressions to that of class.

Rose suggests that the means for detailing the sexual division of welfare rest within 'the Titmuss paradigm' and she does not regard the essay on the SDW as singularly useful. Drawing on Titmuss's general work, Rose argues that it provides a means of counterbalancing the macro accounts of 'the new social policy'. She identifies Piven and Cloward (1977), O'Connor (1973), Gough (1979) and, from a different political perspective, Donnison (1979) and Wilensky (1976) as examples of, what was 10–15 years ago, the 'new' social policy. More recently, the work of Esping-Andersen (1990) could be seen as an example in the same tradition. Applauding the achievements of the new approach, in particular the location of welfare within the totality of political and economic relations, Rose is nevertheless concerned that the 'micro' aspects of welfare should not be lost in the more general overview. Although the new social policy legitimately asks questions about the functioning of the economy and locates welfare within it, Rose points out that questions about day-to-day events can highlight the taken-for-granted part that women play in the production and reproduction of welfare relations. In this context, Rose (1981, p.496) asks: 'Who cooks the dinner?'.

Answering this question raises further questions about the part women play in domestic labour, caring and the sexual division of labour. Likewise, the distribution of incomes within the family highlights the sexual inequalities that are too easily obscured when the focus of research is at the macro level. Thus Rose provides a view of the division of welfare that is specific to the maintenance of sexual divisions. While the development of the social division of labour may be the basis of class inequalities, Rose points to the development of the sexual division of labour to account for sexual inequalities within the sexual division of welfare.

Rose's essay represents the case for not dissolving specific forms of inequality and exploitation within any simple unitary cause. In terms of the SDW thesis, the significance of Rose's 're-reading of Titmuss' is two-fold. First, it stresses the need for any theory to treat specific forms of oppression as integral to the theory. Consequently, it is not enough to add a general qualification about women's part in the development of welfare. For Rose, the sexual division of welfare developed alongside, and as a part of, the SDW. The danger of subsuming sexual inequalities is avoided, in her approach, by asking questions that raise issues specific to women. Such questions, however, are not afterthoughts, but integral to the general question of inequality. Secondly, Rose points to the part the early labour movement played in the establishment of a sexual division of labour. This, in turn, she sees as laying the basis for the sexual division of welfare. The acceptance of patriarchal ideology and its infusion into the early labour movement is illustrated in more detail in Chapter 3, but it needs to be stated here that there is a strong case for a study that deals specifically with the development of a sexual division of welfare.

Furthermore, the questions posed by Rose highlight the inadequacies of a three-fold conception of the SDW. Within a definition of welfare as fiscal, occupational and public, where are we to locate the welfare tasks performed, on an unpaid and unrecognized basis, by millions of women in the family? At the same time, caution needs to be exercised in case we construct so many divisions of welfare that they lose any explanatory power they might have had. There are also grounds for arguing that these tasks are not strictly welfare, but forms of diswelfare. By diswelfare I mean that the work women (for it is overwhelmingly women who perform these caring roles) do is a factor in creating and maintaining their dependency. The trouble with such a line of argument is that it makes a distinction between the public and private caring roles that women perform, simply on the grounds that one is paid and the other is not. It is rather difficult to claim that NHS nurses provide public welfare, whereas women caring for sick children or relatives are experiencing diswelfare.

On the other hand, there is a desperate need to highlight those welfare tasks which are the least visible and most often taken for granted, by designating them as 'informal', 'domestic' or 'private'. Each of these terms has drawbacks, however, since informal welfare implies a certain casualness, which is entirely inappropriate in the context of child-rearing, cleaning, cooking, shopping, etc. These tasks require careful planning and thoroughness in execution, and the term 'informal' seems misplaced. Similarly, the notion of 'domestic' has two connotations which are both negative. It can imply passivity or an employee who does the tasks. Nor is the term 'private' welfare appropriate because it is associated with the market for welfare services, e.g. private health care and private education.

I shall refer to a sexual division of welfare but accept that this too is problematic. The difficulty is that we confuse the services with the service providers. Moreover, there is a sexual division of welfare within each of the systems of fiscal, occupational and public welfare. Lastly, in relation to the definitions and categories used, once the definition refers to the characteristics of the recipients or the providers, it has to be accepted that there is also a case for identifying a racial division of welfare, an age division and other specific divisions based on the failure of welfare to cater for the needs of the various and disparate groups which constitute the poor. Consequently, although the idea of a sexual division of welfare is used, it is felt to be rather ambiguous and ought, I would argue, to mean only those services that are unpaid and concealed within, in the main, the home.

Another feature of Rose's essay on the sexual division of welfare worth highlighting is where she points to 'a bargain struck between labour and capital' (1981, p.497). By emphasizing this point, her reading of Titmuss and the possibilities he provides for a more sensitive account of social divisions, is similar to the approach advocated here. However, Rose does not expand on how a historical study of the development of welfare might proceed. Nor does Rose attempt to provide a coherent method for the study of social policy. This is not to suggest that she has no method; rather, she is more concerned with rendering visible the inequalities that a sex-blind theory obscures. She concludes by stating: '. . . until we have a transformative theory of a social formation which is both patriarchal and capitalist it is too soon to abandon the painstaking documentation of inequalities in the relations of production' (Rose, 1981, p.501). Once again it is easy to agree and the issues raised in this chapter have re-emphasized the need for such a theory.

Summary

Titmuss's essay laid the basis for thinking about welfare in a broader and more challenging fashion. The fact that he did not take up the challenge is to be regretted, but in Sinfield's revision of the original thesis the potential is made plain. Despite the modesty Sinfield exhibits, he has, by his refusal to be confined within an 'arithmetic empiricism', shown the radical possibilities of the SDW thesis. The explicit consideration of class, power and the way these articulate with welfare legislation, ensures that social policy (as a discipline) is concerned with the mainstream issues of British social science.

In contrast to Titmuss, it has been argued that social divisions do not arise as a consequence of industrialization but are profoundly affected by the form and direction of class struggle. In this context, the labour process was shown to stress the manner in which work within a capitalist society promotes dependency and sectionalism and how a revised version of the SDW thesis needs to locate the labour process at its heart.

In Rose's exposition of the Titmuss paradigm, we are reminded of the need to avoid economic and class reductionism. She also points to the manner in which sexual divisions have been made historically and the need to develop our understanding of the processes involved. The point is given even more weight when it is remembered that Sinfield (1981, p.149) identified the need for a '. . . sound historical base' to the SDW. This will be the task of the following three chapters.

Finally, this chapter has pointed to both the attractions and the problems associated with the SDW thesis. It has been shown that neither Titmuss's functionalist approach nor Sinfield's Weberian revision are adequate. Whether we can resolve all these inadequacies is doubtful. Nevertheless, the enduring attraction of Titmuss's original essay, and the advantages of it over other approaches, suggests that it might be worthwhile to attempt the task.

*three*_____

The making and re-making of the social division of welfare

The artisans are almost to a man red hot politicians. . . . The unskilled labourers are a different class of people. As yet they are as unpolitical as footmen (Mayhew, 1862, p.243, cited in Thompson, 1968, p.266).

I cares nothing about politics neither: but I'm a chartist (street scavenger cited by Mayhew; taken from Thompson, 1968, p.266).

In this chapter, we shall look at the historical development of social divisions and the SDW. Starting in the pre-industrial period, we shall travel at an alarming speed through history up to the outbreak of the First World War. The chapter clearly does not provide a comprehensive history of social divisions over such an enormous time-span; rather, it touches on some of the most important landmarks. Beginning with sexual divisions in feudal England, the aim is to illustrate the links between the control of the labour market, the labour process, the form and direction of class struggle, social divisions, middle-class observations and welfare.

Pre-capitalist sexual divisions

The sexual division of labour, and the patriarchal ideas which have supported it, pre-date capitalism but were profoundly altered by it. In agriculture, the work that men and women performed was, in general, different, but there was a considerable measure of overlap. Men undertook work that was often carried out by women and vice versa (Middleton, 1979, p.153). There was a clearer sexual division of labour in respect of the most remunerative trades and crafts. Most of these were carried on in the towns and were regulated by the guilds. Metal-working crafts tended to be reserved for men and the more status a craft had, the more likely it was that it would be 'man's work'. Likewise, when women worked as day labourers, which was less common than it was for men, they were frequently less well rewarded for their labour. It appears that if men and women performed the same tasks they were usually paid the same rate but, since the tasks were divided between the sexes, low pay was a common feature of women's work. Even within one trade, there were likely to be clear sexual divisions. Spinning, for example, was women's work, but the men generally controlled the looms. Other types of work for which women were largely responsible could be carried out from home. Brewing beer was one such activity for which a woman could gain a local reputation, which was not always appreciated by the magistrates. Women were also more likely to be involved in 'informal' sectors of the economy. These activities, by far the most numerous for both men and women, can be loosely defined by the fact that they were not regulated by the guilds. The work of servants, huckstering (street trading), nursing, searching the dead and laundering were commonly performed by women. Men might work in both the informal and formal sectors, but women were virtually excluded from the latter (Charles and Duffin, 1985).

At certain times, the employment of women was prohibited by guild masters, but why female employment was regarded as unacceptable is less clear. As Charles points out, this may have been due to pressure from apprentices or journeymen to protect their future prospects – what the nineteenth- and early twentieth-century skilled male worker subsequently called 'female dilution'. Whatever the reason, there was clearly a desire to exclude women from certain trades, to pay them less than men in general and to ensure that there was a distinction between men's work and women's work (Charles and Duffin, 1985, pp.5–19).

Despite the evidence of a sexual division of labour in pre-capitalist and pre-industrial England, it has to be stressed that it was by no means as rigid as it was to become. There were many tasks which were performed by both sexes and in the rural environment, in which the overwhelming majority of the population was located, there was considerably more overlap than in the towns. Even in the towns women could gain access to that most exclusive of organizations, the guild. They tended to do so as the wives, often the widows, of guild members, and their activity in the guild may have been heavily circumscribed in practice. Nevertheless, they could play a prominent part in the guilds and girls were enrolled as apprentices, albeit in far fewer numbers than boys (Middleton, 1979; Wright, 1985).

This sexual division of labour suggests that the following two points have to be borne in mind. First, a sexual division of labour based on patriarchal ideas of women's natural place in society pre-dates capitalism (Walby, 1986). Neither Titmuss's claim that social divisions arise as a consequence of industrialization, nor the view that it is the advent of capitalism that serves to divide work between the sexes, can be sustained. Secondly, we can see that certain patriarchal values have been carried over from this earlier period into the present day. As far as the discussion here is concerned, the

most significant feature of a pre-capitalist sexual division of labour is the
intimate link it has with the provision of welfare.

Organized welfare before 1800

In so far as there was a division of welfare within the labouring population,
it existed between those who had access to the guild, the Friendly Society
and the tramping system, and those who had to rely on their family or the
local parish. The fact that women were largely excluded from those trades
which had the highest status, ensured their exclusion from those forms of
welfare which these trades organized. However, it was not only sexual
divisions that were manifest in pre-capitalist Britain. Organizations that
provided some type of welfare were usually formed around common ethnic
origin, region, religion, position in the division of labour and/or gender. The
history of the guilds, the Friendly Societies and the tramping system all
highlight the impact pre-industrial, and in many instances pre-capitalist,
social divisions had upon subsequent developments.

The guilds have a long history and can be traced back as far as the twelfth
century. In 1388, in Norfolk alone there were 160 different guild organizations. Guilds were based in particular towns and were trade organizations,
in the main, but some were primarily religious bodies. Not surprisingly, the
guilds underwent change between 1400 and 1800. Rather than the guild
representing everyone in a particular trade, a distinction began to emerge
between the 'Masters and Merchant Guilds' on the one hand and the 'Journeymen and Artisan Guilds' on the other. It was the latter which were to
change still further, in some cases developing into trade unions (Hobsbawm,
1968).

Virtually all the guilds offered some form of welfare benefits. Members
were asked to contribute regular subscriptions to cover them in the event of
illness. It was common for the guild to provide donations to the widows of
members, and to ensure members received a proper burial. In addition,
guilds provided alms to the deserving poor. It is also important to note that:

> . . . they belonged to the new towns, where industry and a division of
> labour developed, they were monopolists who sought to control their
> monopoly by excluding interlopers and by obliging all of the same
> craft and city to join their guild; they controlled their crafts by roughly
> similar organizations; they sought to maintain high standards of
> workmanship and service; and they exercised exclusive control over
> all workers in their craft (Gregg, 1976, p.127).

This theme of control over the organization of work, the labour market,
entry to the trade and relatively privileged access to welfare, is one which
will be reiterated time and again. Gregg also provides evidence of another
feature of the social division of welfare having a history that predates capitalism, i.e. exclusion. Certain guilds excluded people thought to be 'un-
desirables'. For example, bondmen, that is men who were bound to their

Lord or landowner, were frequently prevented from joining guilds. They excluded 'aliens', principally Irish, Dutch, French and Jewish immigrants, but this could include people migrating from one town to another. The Irish were most frequently excluded, and there appears to have been an almost uniform attempt to prevent Irish labour joining guilds as early as the fifteenth century.

As the towns grew, so did the welfare role of the guilds. Schools were established and some of the earliest hospitals were paid for by the guilds. These welfare services were only available to members, and by the eighteenth century the mutual self-help offered by the guilds came to resemble that provided by the newer Friendly Societies (Gregg, 1976, pp.125-36). It should be noted that the guilds only made provision for a small percentage of the population. They were trade-based, parochial and there was considerable variation throughout the country. Practices in one town might not apply in a town some distance away.

Tramping

Tramping was a rather ambiguous benefit for recipients, since it was only likely to be provided in circumstances which were quite desperate. By sending men – and it was a system only provided for men – out on the road in search of work, societies were acknowledging the desperate situation in their locality.

In brief, the system served to support the craft control of the guilds. When there was a slump in trade or when there were too many craftsmen employed locally, the unemployed would be despatched to more prosperous districts. En route, hostelries would provide beer, a meal and a bed for the night. In the morning, the tramp would be taken around the workshops in search of work in the locality. If there was no work in the area, the tramp would be given a penny or so and sent on to the next town. Many of the early trade unions used the symbol of the tramp – being assisted in the pursuit of work by people who were brothers in the society but strangers to each other – as a symbol of fraternal support and mutual aid. Although the tramping system is identified by Leeson (1980) as having been in operation since the fourteenth century, it continued right up until the 1930s, when Orwell (1970) claimed to have met men who were tramping in much the same manner.

It would be misleading to overstate the value of the tramping system, but it deserves attention because it operated as an early form of labour exchange. Women, in so far as they did tramp, trudged along behind their husbands. Thomas Hardy, in The Mayor of Casterbridge, described the tramping system, and how appallingly women could be treated by their husbands. Like the guild upon which it was based, tramping provided an option denied to non-members, and it was closely tied to a person's place in the division of labour.

The Friendly Societies

The Friendly Societies were a more recent development than the guilds, but they certainly existed from at least the seventeenth century (Gosden, 1973). Their members might be entitled to a range of benefits including money during spells of unemployment (although this was rare before 1800), sickness benefits, widow's benefit, death and funeral grants and, occasionally, small loans to cover exceptional short-term needs (Gosden, 1973). The importance of funeral and burial grants is perhaps difficult to appreciate today. Three hundred years ago, however, great store was placed on having a proper burial. To be buried by the parish without a headstone – a pauper grave – was a prospect dreaded by many of the poor.

The stigma of pauperism, therefore, clearly predates the 1834 New Poor Law, and the ability to join a friendly, or burial, society was consequently highly valued. As we shall see, the Friendly Society was better suited to industrial capitalism as an organizational form than the guilds or the tramping societies. By 1803, it was estimated that nearly 8 percent of the population of England and Wales were society members and over 9000 societies existed. Like the guilds, they were exclusive welfare organizations which provided an alternative to the parish.

Exclusion of women and aliens was not uncommon, but the main obstacle to membership tended to be the cost. Only the best paid workers could expect to join, or form, a Friendly Society. Many of the organizations formed by 'lesser trades' collapsed when members most needed them, because demands for relief exceeded the funds available (Hobsbawm, 1968; Gosden, 1973; Henriques, 1979).

The guilds, Friendly Societies and tramping systems were not sophisticated welfare agencies. They were simple, elementary forms of welfare for only a minority of the population. They operated exclusive practices, and used their place in the division of labour to their advantage. Nor were they uniform or consistent in their practices. Indeed, there were so many variations and different practices, the synopsis above must be treated as partial. In some respects, they appear to be the forerunners of more modern forms of organization, such as trade unions and specifically welfare-oriented societies, but in many others they are distinctly pre-capitalist – their oaths, ceremonies and benefits were designed for, and belonged to, a different age. They give the lie to the idea that welfare divisions and divisions of labour are features of a specifically industrial or capitalist system of production. At the same time, it should be emphasized that these early organizations were radically changed by the impact of industrial capitalism (Hobsbawm, 1968; Gosden, 1973; Leeson, 1980).

Continuity and change

Thus far it has been important to establish that social divisions pre-date industrial capitalism, that they were related to the social division of labour and to welfare provisions. It is not being argued that this crude form of the SDW has simply persisted until today.

The benefits provided by the guilds, Friendly Societies and tramping societies do not correspond with the SDW as we know it. It could be argued that an occupational division of welfare existed, but this would be stretching a point beyond credibility. Control over the labour market certainly enabled some artisans and journeymen to establish a degree of protection for themselves. However, the tramping system, the guilds and the early Friendly Societies were organized by the members for the members. They were not benefits provided by employers in order to, as Titmuss put it, 'buy good human relations in industry'. Likewise, the concept of public welfare would be inappropriate for the period before 1800. For example, the significance of the obligations that the aristocracy had for their poor does not translate into the language of the twentieth century (Stedman-Jones, 1983). Local systems of relief varied enormously, and a person's parish of birth was often as important in affecting their welfare as any other factor. Alternatively, even before 1834, poor relief might have meant the workhouse (Henriques, 1979; Crowther, 1981; Fraser, 1984). Nor can we identify a fiscal system of welfare that can be compared to the complex system of today.

Nevertheless, and having acknowledged the differences, there are significant similarities between the pre-capitalist division of welfare and present-day practices. Women were largely dependent on the parish or their husbands. The pre-capitalist sexual division of labour served to exclude women from those trades which were the gate to some form of welfare other than public welfare. Likewise, immigrants, whether they were from the countryside or the Continent, were unable to gain admission, in general, to the trade and benefit societies of the indigenous worker. These themes of exclusion, location in the labour market and the development of the SDW will now be examined in the light of the period after 1800.

The making of a divided working class: 1800–1850

The formation of the English working class in the first half of the nineteenth century has exerted a hold over social historians that is easily understood and justified. The bravery, originality and unity that were displayed in the making of an identifiable working class is astounding. Simultaneously, it has to be recognized that, as the working class wrestled within the chains which restrained its activity, it generated its own 'peculiarities' (Thompson, 1978). Pragmatism, conservatism, sectionalism and division have to be set alongside inventiveness and combativity. The making of a working class, and the way it made itself, in the period before 1850 set the pattern for the next 150 years.

As Thompson (1968) states in his study of the development of the English working class, the terms 'making' and 'made' are appropriate, since they describe a process. The working class was in one sense 'made' by the demands of capitalism: the discipline of factory life, the thundering command of the clock, the compulsion to work, the control of work, and the sale of labour power. Of course, these demands were, and are, supported by the rule of law and the state's defence of property. The control and ownership of the means of production is clearly a major determinant of the social relations of production. Once the means of production are controlled by a minority, and there are no social obligations to assist those without property, then the conditions for the creation of a working class are established.

It is the creation of a nominally free labour market which for Marx (1976, p.274) is one of the definitive features of capitalism:

> It is different with capital. The historical conditions of its existence are by no means given with the mere circulation of money and commodities. It [capitalism] arises only when the owner of the means of production and subsistence finds the free worker available, on the market, as the seller of his [sic] own labour power. . . . Capital, therefore, announces from the outset a new epoch in the process of social production.

The fact that workers have to go to work in order to 'make a living', or – to put it in Marxian language, workers have to sell their labour power in order to subsist, is a central element of Marxist theory. While workers are told that they are free to come and go as they please, most know that this is a myth. The fear of the sack or redundancy acts as a major restraint on the behaviour of workers. Without a job, the worker is always in danger of falling into poverty. It is in this context that distinctions within *the* working class have to be explained.

Unfortunately for capitalism, the working class did not passively accept its allotted role in the new order of things. It also 'made' itself, and remade itself over time. It contested every restraint, sought to establish its own vision of the future, challenged property rights, organized against the owners of the means of production and, in so doing, changed the world at the very same time as it experienced it. As Thompson (1968, p.8) puts it, 'The working class did not rise like the sun at an appointed time. It was present at its own making'.

Central to the making of the working class was the struggle over the social division of labour. The social and detailed divisions of labour are continually being redefined and contested by employers and workers. At the forefront of this contest has been the 'skilled' worker (Harrison and Zeitlin, 1985, p.7). From the first, trade unions sought to exclude certain types of worker from competing with them in particular trades. The ability to escape subsistence living depended upon the degree of unity workers could muster in their struggle with employers. Unity alone, however, was seldom enough. It had to be linked to control of the labour process. Hobsbawm (1959, p.109) claims that:

> Broadly speaking, social differentiation within or between crafts

produced organizations modelled on the pattern of the older guilds or fraternities, but expressing the specific interests of particular sections, notably the journeymen, and a good deal of the traditional pattern was subsequently taken over (in a somewhat different form) into the first trade unions.

In those trades where subcontracting of work was common, the 'gaffer' – the worker who supervized and in some cases hired the subcontracted labourers – had a more powerful position from which to organize than those (it was invariably men who were gaffers) he supervized. Skilled workers, generally, had to control entry to their trade if they wanted to retain control of the labour process. Failure to do so would in all probability result in them losing their status as skilled workers. Once the employer could dictate who should, or should not, be admitted to the trade, the employer would be able to either disseminate the skills of the worker so that many 'semi-skilled' workers performed what had been skilled work, or reduce the wages of skilled workers once the competition for work was more intense (Braverman, 1974, pp.59–69).

What stands out is not the fact that there were distinctions within the newly formed working class – these had always existed – but that changes in the organization of work, or the technology used, provided the basis for such distinctions. Intra-class divisions hinged on the ability of workers to control any changes in the labour process so that they retained a measure of control over entry to the trade. Where changes were dramatic, previously 'skilled workers' could all too easily find themselves among the ranks of the poorest labourers (Thompson, 1968, p.273). Where a trade was superceded by a new invention or the move to factory production, as in the case of the handloom weavers, there was little value in controlling entry to the apprenticeship. Workers had to ensure that their 'skill', their knowledge of the labour process, was not broken down by employers. If they succeeded, they could maintain a measure of 'social closure' (Parkin, 1979; see also Chapter 6). If they failed, they were as vulnerable as the rest of their class to abject poverty.

For the 'lesser trades', the control of the labour process exercised by the more organized/skilled workers often posed further problems: 'Entry to a whole trade might be limited to the sons of those already working in it, or might be bought only by a high apprenticeship premium'(Thompson, 1968, p.265).

For working-class women and the poorest sections of the working class, the opportunities for combining were more limited. When they tried to adopt similar tactics to the skilled (male) workers, they were always more likely to be sacked and replaced by other unskilled labour. Moreover, and despite the attempts of the Grand National Consolidated Trade Union, mixed sex unions, the ideas of Methodism, socialism and Owenism, women and the unskilled were excluded from the more privileged places in the social division of labour which might have enabled them to adopt the same strategy.

Unfair female competition

The first half of the nineteenth century is one of the points in history when patriarchy and capitalism appear to have operated hand in glove to either exploit or exclude women. For many of the early trade unions 'the woman problem', as it was called, hinged on the substitution and dilution of labour. By this they meant the replacement of men by women and children. The new production techniques offered employers the ability, especially in the textile trade, to replace certain skilled jobs with unskilled – and consequently poorer paid – labour. While some trade unions admitted women as members, and in some industries women formed their own unions, it was far more common for male trade unionists to argue that women should be kept in their 'proper sphere', i.e., the home. As the Journeymen Tailors Society put it in 1811:

> Have not women been unfairly driven from their proper sphere in the social scale, unfeelingly torn from the maternal duties of a parent and unjustly encouraged to compete with men in ruining the money value of labour? (quoted in Drake, 1984, p.4)

This neatly catches both the economic argument and the moral tone that epitomized the male trade unionists' attitude. When Lord Shaftesbury claimed that it was indecent to have men and women working alongside one another, male trade unionists were not slow to exploit the argument. This was most common in the mines, where men and women worked together, often as a family unit, but, because of the heat, both sexes were semi-clad. The image of men and women together in the bowels of the earth conjured up the fears of the middle classes. Such images could be exploited to argue for the exclusion of women and children whose natural purity, it was argued, might be corrupted by the men. The following appeal of the potters union in 1845 played on these concerns:

> To maidens, Mothers and wives, . . . we say machinery is your deadliest enemy. Of all sufferers by mechanical improvements you will be the worst. It is a systemized process of slow murder for you. It will destroy your natural claims to home and domestic duties, and will immure you and your toiling little ones in over-heated and dirty shops, there to weep and toil and pine (quoted in Drake, 1984, p.6).

Of course, none of the rhetoric could prevent women taking whatever work they were offered. Poverty dictated that they risk their health and their reputations by entering industry in droves. For example, in Oldham, by the 1850s, one in three women were employed in the mills; indeed, more women than men were employed in textiles. The toll they paid was heavy with, for instance, one in eight women in Oldham between the ages of 24 and 34 dying of tuberculosis (Foster, 1974, p.92).

In comparison to the working-class women of London, the mill workers were fortunate. They at least had, for the most part, regular employment.

(Although this may sound like the Monty Python team when they said: 'Luxury we used to dream of dying of tuberculosis'.) Alexander (1976, p.108) points out that in London women were competing by hand with the northern manufacturing districts; as a result, '. . . many women's employments merged almost imperceptibly into the many partial and residual forms of work which were the mark of poverty or even destitution'.

Working women in London were excluded from the early labour movement, for the most part, by their reliance on domestic work, the 'sweated trades' and the precarious nature of the London labour market. Here only a relatively small number of craftsmen and 'artisans' were capable of escaping the clutches of poverty. For women in the capital, this meant that:

> Prostitution or the workhouse were imminent and real threats to the unsupported woman without a trade in periods of economic distress, and prostitution was often the chosen, desperate alternative to the workhouse (Alexander, 1976, p.108).

The skilled trades that might have provided women with employment were dominated by men. Most of the emergent metal trades, building trades, printing and the honourable (i.e. organized) sections of the garment and tailoring trades were men's work. As in the guilds of pre-industrial times, women were only very rarely permitted entry to any of the apprenticed trades.

As Rose (1981) has noted, a further argument used to exclude women was the call for a family wage. Male trade unionists began to argue in the 1840s for a wage that would enable them to support a wife and children (Rose, 1981). Employers were urged, on the one hand, to exclude women and, simultaneously, to pay them less than men. Cheap female labour suited the employers who were reluctant to accept the first demand but were seldom slow to adopt the second. It can be no surprise that women who had to sell their labour power did so at rates below those which men would accept. There were attempts at mixed-sex unions, but the influence of patriarchal values inherited from the pre-capitalist era undermined any unified struggle.

The Irish

The Irish could, with some justification, claim to have provided the bulk of the first true proletariat. It was their labour which, in large measure, was used to build the canals, railways and factories of the first industrial nation. Although there were a number of craftworkers, from Belfast and Dublin especially, the vast majority of the immigrant population was unskilled. Indeed, most had left abject rural poverty in Ireland for the squalid, but relatively rich cities of northern Britain (Treble, 1968; Swift and Gilley, 1985). However, Irish labour was seldom given a warm welcome by the host workers. One reason that has been suggested is that the Irish were used as strike-breakers. But the claim that 'Irish hordes were bidders here, our half paid work to do', made by Ebenezer Elliot (cited in Treble, 1968, p.78), ignores the fact that in many cases the Irish had little opportunity to pursue more remunerative employment (Swift and Gilley, 1985, pp.21–3). Thus, any attempt to dismiss the hostility of indigenous workers towards the Irish 'hordes' by simply pointing to the employers' divisive strategies has to be heavily qualified. Anti-Irish and anti-Catholic sentiments (the two are not easily separated) have a very long history and certainly date back as far as Guy Fawkes.

Language, desperate poverty and culture all served to distinguish the English worker from the Irish. The Irish lived in some of the worst conditions that could be found in the major cities of Britain. Overcrowding, open sewers, cesspools, an appalling diet, a lack of adequate clothing, pauperism, disease, alcoholism, casual domestic and street violence and, on a lighter note, the keeping of livestock, all served to mark the Irish ghetto. Not that all, or any, of these factors were the preserve of the Irish immigrant. These were features common to all poverty-stricken rural migrants to the cities – English, Scottish and Irish. The Irish were more numerous and more visible simply because they were much poorer in the first place (Treble, 1968; O'Tuathaigh 1985).

There is less evidence of overt discrimination against the Irish immigrant on the part of the British working class and its organizations in the 1830s and early 1840s than later in the century. Exclusion from trade unions would have been a consequence of one of a number of factors: the immigrants' lack of skills, insufficient resources to pay an apprenticeship or union membership fees, and, in some cases, an adherence to the Pope's call for good Catholics not to join trade societies. As Belchem (1985, pp.85–95) argues, the period 1815–1848 witnessed a decline in the anti-Popery and anti-Irish attitudes of the English working class. Belchem also shows that, in many respects, the major political movements of this period saw the Irish and English working class combining. Radicals in England called for reforms in Ireland that would improve the lot of the Irish, while simultaneously calling for the adoption of the Charter. There was, then, the possibility of unity and, in some cases, this was realized. However, any unity was short-lived and extremely fragile (Rude, 1980; Hunt, 1981).

It is no accident that the Irish were, for the most part, confined to the most physically demanding types of work. Canal digging and railway employment were frequently the only work the Irish were offered. The all-male gangs, the nature of the work and the competition for work which the gangs engaged in, made fighting and drinking part of their experience of work. It also served, of course, to reinforce the stereotype of the Irish labourer. Thus the Irish were 'rough' men, ill-mannered and squanderous. When they had work they drank their earnings, when they did not have employment they applied to the poor law. There was some truth in this stereotype, but it failed to consider the social and economic conditions which produced such behaviour.

Of course, the middle classes witnessed the behaviour of 'the roughs', whether Irish or English. What they saw were divisions within the working class between those who tried to escape dependence on the parish and those who did not. Not surprisingly, it was argued that it was necessary to encourage the independent labourer and to punish the pauper.

Independent labourers and paupers

Throughout the nineteenth century, the Friendly Societies and the Poor Law were the two principal forms of relief available to the working classes. The Friendly Societies provided a range of benefits and services and they were a major social institution around which working-class life focused (Gosden, 1961, 1973). Friendly Societies were fiercely independent and distinctly working class. A great many societies either refused, or failed, to register for the first three-quarters of the nineteenth century. In the first half of the century, there was a genuine fear that the state might confiscate their funds, but this suspicion of the state persisted long after any real threat existed. It should be remembered that hostility to the establishment, and particularly the state, was reinforced by the fact that, under the Combination Acts (in operation from 1799 to 1824) and the Correspondence Act of 1797, society membership could result in transportation to the colonies. For a sizeable section of the population, the Friendly Societies were the main form of welfare provision. If the impact of industrialization, urbanization and a capitalist labour market was as severe as most historians suggest, then it was also felt more severely by those who were unable to join a society. Access to Friendly Societies was, therefore, an indication of success in the labour market and, not surprisingly, exclusion from one was often a result of exclusion from the other.

Women were seldom admitted to Friendly Societies and when they were, it was usually as 'affiliates' of their husbands. The specific needs of women were not catered for even when they were given some form of membership. Pregnancy and childbirth, for instance, disqualified women from any benefits. It was their meagre income, a consequence of the sexual division of labour, that was the major obstacle to forming or joining a Friendly Society. The cost of joining a Society involved a considerable weekly outlay. Many societies that had tried to keep the costs of membership low, while still offering reasonable benefits, collapsed as soon as the trade cycle took a downturn. Only those societies with a fairly high subscription rate could expect to survive during difficult times. Given that women were, because of the sexual division of labour, excluded from those forms of employment which enabled them to earn enough to put aside some part of their income, they were automatically unable to afford Friendly Society membership. The family wage, women's exclusion from certain trades and patriarchal ideas of women's natural dependencies combined to establish a sexual division of welfare (Rose, 1981).

Likewise, the Irish immigrant, unable to earn more than a subsistence living, and the bulk of the unskilled would have found the costs of Friendly

Society membership prohibitive. While direct discrimination in the first half of the nineteenth century does not appear to have been the norm, it is the case that where a person stood in the division of labour played a key role in providing access to Friendly Society benefits. If you were a woman or an unskilled worker, it was unlikely that trade union provisions existed (Thompson, 1968; Drake, 1984).

The independent labourer, a term that gained currency at the turn of the century, was recognized by the rate-paying middle classes as a model that, it was hoped, the rest of the working class would adopt. As dissatisfaction with the Poor Law became more common among the middle classes, discussion turned to alternatives. Of these ideas, Curwen's plan for a national Friendly Society deserves particular attention. Like the National Insurance proposals put forward by the Liberals nearly 100 years later, the plan was that employers and employees would fund two-thirds of the cost of relief. The Poor Law would provide the other third (Henriques, 1979, p.20). This proposal is important because it illustrates how closely the middle classes modelled their schemes on those operating within the working class.

The Friendly Societies, who remained fiercely independent of middle-class interference, provided an example of respectability and responsibility for some middle-class opponents of the Poor Law. How to 'civilize' the working classes appeared to some to be answered by encouraging existing good behaviour. As early as 1835, the *Manchester Guardian* was advocating the '. . . extreme desirableness of making the labouring classes the ministers to their own respectability and improvement' (quoted in Thomis, 1976, p.154). The Friendly Societies and savings clubs were desirable because they were both saving the rate-payer money and, just as importantly, character-building for the workers. Such societies were also cited as evidence, by their middle-class advocates, of the reliability of the working classes at a time when Chartism appeared to suggest otherwise. The crucial point is that middle-class observers who sought alternatives to the Poor Law, but who still wished to maintain the deserving/undeserving distinction, looked to the SDW that already existed within the working class.

Against those who proposed the adoption of Friendly Society and savings club styles of reform for the Poor Law stood the abolitionists. The influence of Malthus, Smith and Bentham was far greater than that of Pitt and the more liberal reformers. Nevertheless, the state acknowledged the part played by the organizations of the working class in providing relief. The debate was more concerned with how to encourage the whole of the labouring population to adopt such habits. In the view of the Poor Law Commissioners, a sustained attack on pauperism, the discipline of the workhouse clock and the principle of less eligibility were the means to encourage independence among the poor. As Crowther (1981, p.17) observes:

> If the able-bodied labourer feared the workhouse, he would provide for his old age; he would join savings banks and benefit clubs to provide for his family. In time, new provident habits amongst the

working class would save them from dependence on the parish, and private charity could cope with the residue whom thrift had not been able to protect.

This distinction between the independent labourer and the pauper was the cornerstone of the New Poor Law, and, arguably, has been the foundation upon which the SDW was built. Thus, the Act of 1834 did not create a divided working class, but it did successfully exploit and widen the divisions. For example, in the decade prior to the New Poor Law, 1825–1835, 455 new lodges were formed by the Manchester Unity of Oddfellows. In the decade after the Act, 1835–1845, 1470 new lodges were begun. In Sheffield, there was a similar reaction. In 1849, the filesmiths were prepared to pay £4000 to ensure that none of their members had to apply to the Poor Law. The edge-tool grinders, Britannia-metal smiths and file hardeners took care of their members by employing them on farms (Gosden, 1973, p.70; Smith, 1982, p.59).

Any account of how the working class responded to the discipline of 1834 has to recognize that, despite the riots in many northern towns, there was also a more pragmatic response. Commentators on the New Poor Law have suggested that one of the reasons that opposition to the Act dissipated was the fact that Chartism consumed the energies of the working class. Just as important is the fact that the best organized workers were able to avoid the Poor Law by joining a Friendly Society. Consequently, those workers most likely to pose a serious threat to the establishment of the Act were also those most able to escape its clutches. This course of action was to be more marked, and more keenly pursued, in the second half of the century.

A change of temper: 1850–1885

Between 1850 and 1880, the previously dangerous proletariat underwent a profound change. There is considerable argument, however, over whether the beast was domesticated, beaten into passivity, merely feigning sleep or whether it was simply a lamb in wolves' clothing all along. Without doubt, the defeat of Chartism, upon which so many working-class hopes had rested in the second quarter of the century, marks a watershed in labour history. Thus Anderson (1980, p.46) suggests that a sharp line can be drawn between the two halves of the nineteenth century: in the first half, the English working class '. . . was revolutionary in temper and ideology, but not socialist. After the mid-century metamorphosis, as sections of it became socialist, it ceased to be revolutionary.

Typical of this change in temper were the engineers and the carpenters unions, which are portrayed by the Webbs (1920) as 'Model Unionists', primarily concerned to establish trade union rights and accepting calls from employers for them to be 'responsible'. The formation of Institutes, Savings Clubs, Co-ops and Burial Societies, meant that the 'model' unionist was also a 'Society' man. By forming and joining so many welfare and benefit societies, these (mainly) skilled workers were quite quickly regarded by some sections of the Victorian middle classes as respectable and 'safe' (Crossick, 1978).

The extension of the franchise in 1867, and the recognition of trade union rights in the 1870s, served as a stamp of approval for this respectable stratum. The dependability of the working classes, particularly the English, was reinforced in middle-class eyes when they volunteered in their thousands to put down the Fenians in the 1860s (Richter, 1981). In contrast to the dizzy jig of Chartism, the middle classes saw the working class waltzing in a gentle embrace with Britannia – a Britannia bedecked in the jewels of the colonies and in her imperialist heyday.

For some Marxists, this shift in class consciousness is explained by reference to the development of a labour aristocracy within the working class. Arguably, this transformation provides both one of the most interesting examples of social divisions, and a guide to their development.

The labour aristocracy

In their discussion of the labour aristocracy, Marxist scholars have touched on many of the issues that would concern any study of social divisions and welfare. These can be summarized as follows:

1 The working class, it is acknowledged, is not a homogeneous whole but contains within it distinct fissures.
2 The degree of control workers were able to exert over the labour process is often used to define the labour aristocracy.
3 Various welfare benefits are frequently identified with the labour aristocracy.
4 It was the ability of certain workers either to limit entry to the trade and welfare society, or to achieve higher wages, which helped to distinguish them from the bulk of the working class.
5 Politically, the labour aristocracy was a force of conservatism. From its relatively secure position, it was able to dismiss radical and confrontational class politics in favour of economism and sectionalism.

In its early form, the labour aristocracy thesis proposed that a privileged stratum was created within the working class *by the capitalist class*. In effect, it was claimed, the employers 'bought off' the vanguard of the working class by using profits made from imperialist expansion. The supposed advantage to capital was the familiar one of 'divide and rule'. This was achieved by increasing wage differentials (Hobsbawm, 1968) and/or bestowing authority on the labour aristocrat (Foster, 1974). It was this authority which they came to exert over other less skilled workers. By separating the labour aristocracy from its class, the potential vanguard of the working class was detached from the rest of the proletariat. Interestingly, Foster uses the changes in the labour process that occurred around the middle of the nineteenth century as evidence of the employers' strategy to undermine class unity. Hobsbawm's account relies more heavily on wage differentials and Foster's hinges on the issue of authority. Both scholars propose that it was the location of the worker within the labour market that made it necessary for them to be 'bought off'. Hobsbawm (1968, p.332) suggests that 'Only certain types of workers were in a position to make or keep their labour scarce enough to strike a good bargain.'

There are two principal problems with this divide-and-rule version of the labour aristocracy thesis. First, the theory suggests bourgeois intent, but does not demonstrate this to be the case. As Musson (1976) argues, the claim that employers increased their labour costs, even if this was only in the short term, or until the effect of a divided workforce paid dividends, is difficult to support. On the contrary, it seems that in numerous cases, and particularly in the case of engineering in the early 1850s, employers sought to confront the very stratum that Hobsbawm and Foster suggest was bought off. It is debatable whether employers were capable of, let alone intent on, co-ordinating their activities in the fashion suggested. Given the competition between capitalists, it is stretching the bounds of credibility to claim that a whole class simultaneously decided to buy off the proletarian vanguard. Nor is the evidence of higher wages quite so clear as claimed (Pelling, 1968). In any event, there is little evidence that employers tried to divide the working class by paying higher wages to one stratum.

Secondly, it is implied that this was a development of the 1850s, whereas critics of the thesis claim that there is ample evidence that the labour aristocracy was not a new phenomenon. We saw earlier in this chapter that the privileges won by certain workers were jealously guarded well before 1850. If the vanguard existed before the 1850s, and already had a large measure of economic and social security, it is hard to understand why it was necessary to create one. What is more, the explanatory power of this version of the labour aristocracy thesis evaporates if it can be shown that it predates, by any considerable amount of time, the change in class consciousness associated with the 1850s. Thompson (1968, pp.259-96) claims that there was both an old and a new labour aristocracy in the 1830s! It seems unlikely that the early nineteenth-century capitalist class not only sought to create that which already existed, and were prepared to forego some of their profits in the process, but also to wait at least 20 years for their gamble to pay off in terms of a reduction in working-class unity and combativity.

In rejecting the orthodox theory of a labour aristocracy, it is necessary to exercise a little caution. Hobsbawm is surely correct when he points to certain groups of workers who were able to exercise a degree of control over the labour market. This would have given them a relatively privileged place within the working class. However, new technology or the introduction of unskilled or less skilled labour could undermine this position within a few years. Likewise, a prolonged period of illness or an accident at work could plunge even the best organized and well-placed worker into the depths of poverty. Membership of a savings club, Friendly Society, trade union or benefit club served as a safety net for short-term and foreseeable periods of dependence. As such, they did provide a measure of security for members, but the records of the Poor Law show that no section of the working class was immune from poverty (Crowther, 1978; Treble, 1979).

It is, once again, the contrast between those workers who had *some* form of welfare provision independent of the Poor Law and those who did not that is noteworthy. Crossick (1978, p.132) has put it well:

> The distinctiveness of this upper stratum of the working class is not that its members joined thrift and voluntary institutions, for so to an extent did lesser skilled and unskilled workers. The real point is that they joined so many that at one level it materially affected their life chances and experiences . . . while at another level . . . it helped determine their values and their culture.

Non-Marxist accounts of the third quarter of the nineteenth century have also acknowledged the shift in the form and direction that class struggle took. For example, Best (1972, p.82) argues that respectability was '. . . the sharpest of all lines of social division. A sharper line by far than that between rich and poor, employer and employee, or capitalist and proletarian.'

The supposed influence of Smiles' tracts on 'self-help', along with the impact of 'Victorian values' upon the working class, poses a number of questions. If, for instance, the predominantly pragmatic strategy of the trade unions was the result of their accepting middle-class values, it clearly challenges the claim here that the middle classes observed and adopted working-class practices when framing proposed changes in welfare. Fraser (1984, p.109) claims that for the middle classes, 'Trade unionism, adult education, Friendly Societies and the co-operatives were four facts of working class life which suggested a shared value system between the two classes.'

It seems that both Marxists, who have stressed the role of capital in promoting a labour aristocracy, and non-Marxists, who point to the filtering down of middle-class values, absolve or applaud the working class for the change in class consciousness that occurred in the middle of the nineteenth century. Either way, the working class are treated as if they are empty vessels into which the bourgeoisie pour their own values and culture. If the working class do make their own history, even if it is not under conditions of their own choosing, it hardly seems appropriate to regard them as empty vessels.

Pragmatic acceptance?

Rather than a shared value system, or the filtering down of dominant ideas, the concept of 'pragmatic acceptance', as used by Abercrombie *et al.* (1980), provides a more useful explanation of the part played by the labour aristocracy in the making of the working class in Victorian Britain. Abercrombie *et al.* (1980, p.122) suggest three reasons for the labourism and economism of the British working class, which do not rely on ideology to explain the change in class consciousness during the nineteenth century. Briefly these are as follows. First, as Anderson (1980) suggests, the series of defeats in the first half of the century had demoralized and exhausted the early labour movement. Confrontations with the army, deportations, the victimization of activists and imprisonment all took their toll. Faced with the prospect of personal injury, or the Duke of Wellington's canons – as Chartists were – it is hardly surprising that some began to consider whether there might not be an alternative strategy.

Secondly, by the middle of the nineteenth century, reformism had started to pay dividends. Trade unionism within the limitations laid down by Victorian capitalism was making some gains. Thus not only was the confrontational strategy fairly unsuccessful, but the alternative appeared to be more rewarding, especially in the short term.

Thirdly, and very importantly for this study, Abercrombie *et al.* point to the divisions within the working class which increasingly served to frustrate any broader-based class movement. The ability of the best organized and most articulate sections of the working class to improve their material position made it increasingly difficult to get them to align with the poorest, and weakest, members of their class. Pragmatic acceptance involved abandoning the language and tactics of a unitary class struggle. Instead, economistic and sectional struggles were pursued within particular industries, localities and even particular factories and workshops. Because the strategy relied on the location of workers within the labour market, and their ability to influence the labour process, it was a divisive approach. Of course, both pragmatism and conflict strategies occurred simultaneously. The earlier ideas of unity, socialism and utopian idealism were not entirely discarded, but they had to confront or rest alongside sectionalism, conservatism and the notion of 'respectability'.

Even in circumstances where it appears that middle-class ideas were widely accepted by sections of the working class, it is still necessary to consider how these might have been adapted. Gray (1976), for example, points out that ideological hegemony is never total and always ambiguous. Thus Co-ops, trade unions, savings clubs and Friendly Societies may well have been discussed in terms that were common currency in the middle classes. Thrift and self-help may have been mentioned on occasion, but at other times, when trying to recruit members or when criticized by economic individualists, the appeal would have been phrased in terms of collectivism and class solidarity. As Hinton (1983, p.9) succinctly explains:

Even . . . the most . . . accommodating slogan of mid-Victorian trade unionism . . . involved the operation of restrictive practices which orthodox political economy found deeply obnoxious. Behind the respectable face which trade union leaders liked to turn towards the established order, lay the day-to-day cultivation of an ethic of solidarity and the mutualism of the workshop community. . . . What the labour aristocracy sought was not escape from its class situation, but rather the establishment of an acknowledged status for itself within the existing social order.

As a consequence of this approach, other workers were effectively excluded. It is because class struggle took a pragmatic form, directed against the interests of the employer, but also excluding the weakest members of the working class, that Parkin (1979) is correct to regard it as 'dual closure' (see Chapter 6). It was not, however, a strategy that was available to the poorest sectors of the working class.

The residuum

Alongside the achievements of the best organized, we have to place the experience of 'the lowest sediment' (Marx, 1976, p.797). Stedman-Jones (1984) provides a fascinating insight into how this lowest stratum within the working class fared in the peculiar circumstances of Victorian London. Like the notion of an 'underclass' used in the last 10 years, the 'residuum', as it was called then, was the focus of considerable interest to social commentators of various persuasions. Charles Booth's work on the London poor is a standard reference point for undergraduates of social policy, but there had already been a host of surveys and journalistic pieces which sought to account for the plight of the very poor prior to the publication of Booth's work.

The publication of Darwin's theory of natural selection had encouraged some observers to believe that the residuum ought not to be assisted, for fear of disrupting nature's advantageous effect of eliminating the weakest of the species. The idea of natural selection was arguably as influential in promoting psuedo-scientific concepts of social inferiority as Booth's work was in challenging ideas about the pathology of the poor (Shaw, 1987). Indeed, the very poor were frequently physically deformed and, to the observer familiar with Darwin's theories, this might confirm the idea that the poor would 'infect' the race. That these deformities were due to overwork, accidents, a poor diet and illness was discussed, but seldom accepted.

The plight of the poor was particularly acute in London, with its enormous casual labour market. Many children developed physically and educationally in such a poor fashion that they were only suitable for unskilled and casual work. Moreover, they were required to enter the labour market at the earliest opportunity in order to supplement the household income (Stedman-Jones, 1984). Apprenticeships, one of the few ways for a working-class youngster to escape the casual labour market, were simply too expensive. Few parents, themselves in the casual labour market, could hope to sponsor their offspring through an apprenticeship, wages were too low in the early years and the period of training too long. Food was needed that day, and it was no satisfaction to know that in 5 years a considerably higher wage would be possible. The ranks of the casual labour market were thus restocked with each new generation of children born into poverty (Stedman-Jones, 1984, pp.96–7).

Even if parents were able to sponsor their children for an apprenticeship, there remained the difficulty of being accepted. Many trades recruited only workers from 'reliable' families, known either to the employer or the trade union via people already employed in the trade. In these circumstances, exclusion was indirect. Exclusion could take more direct forms as well. Trade unions, Friendly Societies and benefit clubs continued to exclude women, all Irish people, and men from the dishonourable section of the trade, i.e. those who had not served an apprenticeship, worked below the rate for the job or in 'sweated' branches of the trade (Gosden, 1973; Crossick, 1978; Boston, 1980; Mann, 1984; Seccombe, 1986).

There were also problems for the very poor in trying to form their own benefit and trade societies. Because they were in the types of work which were irregular, it was more difficult to be able to make regular contributions to the society. Where contributions were kept very low to ease this problem, the benefits had to be minimal if the society was not to exhaust its funds. If the society recruited too many workers who were likely to be ill or unemployed, the chances of effectively bankrupting the society were further increased. Frequently, societies had to decide to exclude certain types of worker simply because they were a 'bad risk'. The casual trades, sweated labour, labourers, women and immigrants were the worst risks. To add to these obstacles was the fact that, whenever the trade cycle took a downturn, the number of demands on the society's resources could be so great that it collapsed. By 1872, Friendly Societies are estimated to have had over 4 million members (Gosden, 1961, p.16). Only a minority of these were unskilled labourers and, for the poorest stratum of the working class, Friendly Society membership was not a realistic alternative to reliance on the poor law (Gosden, 1961, p.75; Stedman-Jones, 1984, pp.385–6).

It should be plain that exclusion was not necessarily vindictive nor designed to discriminate against the weaker sections of the working class. Frequently, there were good material and actuarial reasons for the differential access that workers had to welfare in the late nineteenth century. Nevertheless, and this point is crucial, the division of welfare in this period provided the middle classes with grounds for believing that the distinction between 'rough' and 'respectable' was one which could be empirically observed. Whether or not such a distinction was valid it was one they sought to maintain.

By the mid-1870s, the idea that the working class was homogeneous in any fashion was starkly contradicted by the gulf between the best organized and highest paid on the one hand, and the desperate position of the poor on the other. In between, of course, the vast bulk of the working class strove to join the former and to avoid the condition of the latter. In housing, health, education and income support there existed, by the third quarter of the nineteenth century, a division of welfare within the working class. This social division of welfare was built on the division of labour and the opportunities it afforded for organization of, and control over, the labour process and the labour market. The condition of the poor, the dependencies they experienced and the solutions some workers found by pursuing a more pragmatic and exclusive strategy, were set within the bounds of capitalism.

In so far as certain types of worker were excluded from the pragmatic strategy, it served the economistic interests of the best organized and most privileged workers at the expense of the weakest (Rose, 1981; Walby, 1986).

The distinctions that the middle classes were able to make within the working class encouraged them in the belief that the survival of the fittest held true for human society as well as the animal kingdom. Middle-class observers began to discuss the poor as though they were a race apart (Shaw, 1987). By the 1880s, 'Social Darwinism' had translated the theory of evolution into an ideology that explained the physical condition of the poor in terms of 'natural selection'. The poor could only survive because of the Poor Law and charity. In 'normal' circumstances, natural selection would have seen this stratum die out. The residuum were seen to be fit only for the most menial and undemanding work. They were part of 'Darkest England' as William Booth, founder of the Salvation Army, saw them. Booth's analogy with 'Darkest Africa' typified the view that the world that the poor inhabited was a different world to that of the middle classes. In many respects, of course, it was. The suggestion was also that, like the tribes of Africa, the poor were 'backward' and 'uncivilized'. The racist ideology of imperialism was, paradoxically, used to describe the very people who were called upon by the army to protect the empire.

Redrawing class boundaries – the labour process and the Liberals: 1880–1914

The period after 1886 deserves to be distinguished from that of 1850–1885 because of a number of significant changes which can be identified. At the same time, changes in the production and labour processes, and the growth of general unionism on a fairly rapid scale, have to be set in the context of continuities. Craftism, sectionalism and a desperate attempt to resist the new working practices must also be borne in mind. The privileged place that the old labour aristocrat had earlier maintained was henceforth constantly threatened by new technology and the breakdown of production into disparate tasks (Braverman, 1974; Burgess, 1980).

The growing multinational character of capitalism, combined with increased competition from Germany and the USA, placed tremendous pressure on British capital to restructure. In order to compete effectively, increased production and reduced production costs were seen to be necessary. The control that the labour aristocrat held was a major obstacle to this restructuring. The problem certain employers had to confront was how to dismantle the control of the most skilled workers. At the same time, the more astute observers felt there was a danger of driving the 'respectable' worker into the arms of socialism. Changing the labour process was facilitated in engineering by the introduction of modern lathes, milling and grinding machines combined with increased supervision of the semi-skilled operators. However, it required a political initiative to ensure that the 'respectable working class' was not estranged from parliamentary democracy. For the politicians, it was the 'respectable' workers who had to be handled most carefully. To confuse this stratum with the 'roughs' was to run the risk of either producing a unified working class, which looked to socialism, or to pauperize the respectable working class and thereby swell the ranks of the mob. As Hall and Schwarz (1985, p.14) have observed:

> Just as from the 1880s the dominant class underwent an important phase in recomposition, so too the working class was 'remade'. The drive of capital to break down the skills of those workers strategically placed in the production process had crucial implications in the re-structuring of the division of labour and in fracturing and disorganizing the cultural and political ties which had held skilled labourers to Liberalism.

Alongside the gradual decline of the old labour aristocrat came a growth in the numbers employed in industry. What is more, a number of service industries became more industrial in character. Transport workers, gas workers and dockers began to organize in the late 1880s and the 1890s. It was a slow and painful process that only really bore fruit after 1906. The most rapid phase of union development came between 1910 and 1914, when the number of trade unionists doubled from 2 million to 4 million, and it was to rise still further in the next 6 years.

In 1886, however, the labour movement was still dominated by the craft unions. The first major strike by a 'general union' was the Bryant & May women workers' strike of 1888. It was a successful strike and was to prove an inspiration to all those workers in sweated and casual trades. The dockers' strike in 1889, organized by two skilled ex-engineering workers, John Burns and Tom Mann – an indication of the shift in the attitudes of at least some skilled workers to their less fortunate fellows – also marks the beginning of an *organized unskilled* working class. It was, however, many years before the dockers had a truly viable union. Likewise, the riots of 1886, although stimulating the middle classes into a panic about 'the mob', also highlighted the latent political power of the poor themselves. Thus, on the one hand, there was a growth of general unionism among the unskilled and the semi-skilled (at a time when there were an increasing number of semi- and unskilled industrial jobs) and, on the other, there was the growing threat of social unrest by those who remained trapped in poverty.

Deserving and undeserving

By the late 1880s/early 1890s, intra-class divisions were seen by many as hopelessly entrenched. For those workers in secure employment, wages were, in real terms, rising. At the same time, for those workers in casual employment, or unemployment, poverty was as harsh as it had ever been. In 1887, Hyndman, the leading light of the Marxist Social Democratic Federation, wrote:

Everywhere no doubt there exists a certain percentage who are almost beyond hope of being reached at all. Crushed down into the gutter, physically and mentally by their social surroundings, they can but die out, leaving it is hoped, no progeny as a burden on a better state of things (quoted in Stedman-Jones, 1984, p.289).

Intra-class divisions were further emphasized by the response of the labour movement to immigration in the 1890s, when the TUC was committed to excluding all Jews from Britain. Anti-Semitism included the call to exclude Jews from Friendly Society and trade union membership. Often the call for immigration controls or the need to control 'the hook-nosed Rothschild' – as the journal *Labour Leader* put it in 1891 – linked unemployment directly to the activities of Jews (Cohen, 1985). Irish immigration was a similarly contentious issue, but so long as the Union with Ireland remained it was not possible to prevent entry to England (Swift and Gilley, 1985).

The place of the 'mugger' in the late twentieth century, frequently portrayed as young and black, was occupied by the Irish 'hooligan' and the cunning Jew 100 years ago (Pearson, 1983). Murray's (1990) suggestion that the 'the underclass' of the 1980s and the 'dangerous criminal class' are virtually one and the same thing, was quite commonly accepted 100 years ago. These ideas have also seen sections of the labour movement try to distinguish 'respectable' from 'the roughs', or the deserving from the undeserving. Thus, in 1908, Ramsay Macdonald could state that: 'The Labour Party [would] never willingly touch a slum population, or one that has shown no signs of intelligent initiative, like trade unionism and co-operation' (quoted in Jones, 1983, p.52).

Similarly, the London Trades Council argued in the 1880s that it was necessary to distinguish between different types of workmen. They wanted artisans to have the 'right to buy' their own homes, and suggested that the poor should be allowed to rent 'cheaper blocks' subsidized from the rates (Stedman-Jones, 1984, p.226). Marx (1976, p.797) too seems to have accepted that the 'lumpen-proletariat' was beyond the reaching hand of socialism. Marx's views will be examined in more detail in Chapter 7, but it is important to acknowledge how widespread were the concepts of deserving and undeserving. One of the more interesting aspects of these Victorian evaluations of the poor is in respect of the history of ideas. The similarity between Booth's class A, nineteenth-century notions of a 'residuum', ideas of a criminal class, Social Darwinism and Marx's portrayal of the lumpen proletariat deserve further examination.

The administration of labour

The combination of changes in production techniques, the vagaries of the labour market, and the apparent degeneracy of the race, evidenced by the behaviour of the poor, prompted some middle-class observers to consider alternatives to the Poor Law. If, as some feared, respectable workers were to be thrown onto the Poor Law, as a result of changes in the organization of work, the consequences might be a greater degree of unity and class consciousness (Gosden, 1973; Langan, 1985). It is crucial that the links between unemployment, casual labour and changes in the management and control of production are recognized. For many middle-class observers in the last 10–15 years of the nineteenth century, it seemed that there were essentially two problems, both of which derived from the operation of the labour market: (1) how to get rid of the residuum and (2) how to relocate the respectable, skilled worker as new working practices eroded his status and control.

The first problem saw a variety of proposals for labour colonies (Harris, 1972). Some of these, particularly those run by the Salvation Army, were essentially punitive. The poor and the unemployed were to be disciplined into work. Other proposals, notably the Poplar Poor Law Guardians, saw labour colonies as a form of public relief work. There was, however, always a tension between disciplining the casual worker and giving relief.

The second problem was how to protect the deserving and respectable working class, when semi-skilled workers threatened employment prospects, and the Poor Law threatened the workhouse. The proposed solution was to give the respectable worker a place in the administration of relief. Among those who supported such an approach were some of the 'founders' of Social Administration, among them Charles Booth, the Webbs, Beveridge, Marshall, Toynbee and C.S. Loch. Although by no means in agreement about the mechanism to be used, these observers represent a fairly weighty body of opinion. They argued, with varying degrees of enthusiasm, that if the respectable worker was confused with the residuum, particularly if the Poor Law was the agent of this confusion, not only might demoralization of the respectable occur, but there was also the threat of the residuum and the respectable combining. It had been the possibility of the 'respectable' being confused with the 'rough' which, following the riots of 1886, had concerned Chamberlain. He decided that to avoid the dangers of stigmatizing the 'deserving', the Poor Law had to moderate its activities. Accordingly for Chamberlain, outdoor relief, in the form of public works, should be offered.

For Alfred Marshall the *only* way to ensure that the 'roughs' and 'respectables', 'deserving and undeserving', were not thrown together was to give the respectable working man a part in the administration of welfare (Harris, 1972). After all, the respectable trade unionists had been administering their own schemes for many years, as of course had the Friendly Societies. What is more, both forms of relief had been careful to root out the malingerer. So, for Marshall, it was vital to have such respectable working men overseeing the relief of the residuum. Likewise, Beveridge's proposals for labour exchanges were intended to eradicate the 'residuum', and Barnett, like Marshall, argued the need for the respectable working class to administer them.

Numerous working-class activists accepted positions of responsibility, as Halevy (1961) first observed in 1932, and they often finished their days in the new bureaucracy the Liberal welfare measures created. It is this sort of influence, whereby policy recognizes and builds upon existing divisions, that is emphasized here, rather than the more obvious flexing of class muscle which so often accompanies discussions of class and social policy change (Pelling, 1968; Thane, 1984). The growth of strikes and political activity at the turn of the century up until the outbreak of the First World War is important. These activities reflect 'the challenge of labour' (Burgess, 1980) and they reinforce the view that social reform had to head off socialism, but they tell only part of the story. Against the radicals, syndicalists and those advocating extra-parliamentary change, we must compare the activities of the gradualists, Fabians, working-class Liberals and those who sought some accommodation between capital and labour.

It was by participating and having a say in the administration, that the gradualists hoped to have some influence. The minutes of the Parliamentary Committee of the TUC at the turn of the century provide evidence of a desire on their part to be consulted and to be included in debates over industrial and political questions. Following the Taff Vale decision, such consultation was seen to be even more important and was, they thought, a mark of their new and more respectable status. In 1908, the TUC's Parliamentary Committee undertook a visit to Germany to assess the schemes operating in Bismark's authoritarian and highly 'statist' regime. If they were opposed to the Liberals' proposals, it might be thought they would not have even undertaken such a trip. On their return, they reported favourably on the system of German labour exchanges – one of the more controversial aspects of the Liberals' measures. The unemployment and sickness schemes also gained their approval. The delegation said of the German unemployed that they:

> . . . seemed to lack that dejection and absolute misery that . . . is so frequently met within the streets of English towns. A spirit of sturdy self-reliance seemed to manifest itself, even in the demeanour of those out of work . . . (quoted in Harris, 1972, p.277).

Of course, the TUC's Parliamentary Committee hardly represents the full range of opinion within the organized labour movement. But Hay (1975) points out that state pensions had the support of most trade unions. When working-class opposition was voiced to the Liberal reforms, it frequently took the form of defending existing craft, Friendly Society or sectional privileges. Harris (1972, pp.276–329) notes that one of the objections the unions put was that they felt that the state benefits should only go to trade unionists, and that their objections focused on the need for trade unionists to be involved in the administration of the exchanges. Nor when opposition was expressed was it particularly strident, and the sceptic might suggest that there was a good deal of posturing.

More vocal opposition to state welfare was expressed by syndicalists and socialists. In some cases, their opposition had subsided by the time the Liberal reforms came before Parliament. On the other hand, their criticisms often centred on the cost of the schemes and the fact that workers would be compelled to provide the funds for the reforms. In this there are similarities with their Australian counterparts, who objected to high levels of taxation – albeit in this instance in the form of National Insurance – which they felt made one group of workers pay to support another. This line of argument suggested that it was capitalism that created poverty and, therefore, capital should bear the cost from its profits, not the workers from their wage packets (Yeo, 1979; Castles, 1985). It is probable that these sound socialist principles found favour with many workers, and as Ginsburg (1979) makes plain, there is nothing in the insurance principle that is especially socialist. Indeed, it is all too easy to forget that National Insurance served as a form of regressive taxation.

However, labour movement opposition to the Liberal reforms cannot be clothed in the mantle of the defenders of the poor. Most opposition to the reforms was either reactionary and backward looking, or based on sectional interests. Certainly there was little in the way of a radical socialist alternative advocated by the most powerful groups within the Labour movement. For example, the proposals that had been put forward to assist the unemployed at a special TUC conference in 1904, which involved many organizations besides the trade unions, were neither radical nor socialist. These tepid proposals were a mixture of banning overtime, which had been tried before and failed, due to lack of shop floor support, public works and the re-issuing of the Chamberlain circular. The last of these measures, as Chamberlain himself made plain, had been more concerned with protecting the 'respectable' workers from the taint of pauperism than with providing relief. If these proposals are taken as evidence of organized labour's alternative – and these measures were supported by most trade union activists – it is difficult not to conclude that there was no articulate alternative strategy for dealing with the poor and the unemployed (Harris, 1972; Novak, 1988, pp.99–101).

The Liberals were, of course, keen to stay in tune with their working-class constituents. Moreover, Beveridge and Churchill were fully aware that their plans required the cooperation of the skilled working class. Ironically, the government had anticipated that the various trade unions would want to retain their own schemes, which under the new scheme they could do, in order to attract workers, who were unorganized, into the unions. Instead, opposition from organized labour was specifically designed to exclude such workers. Thus the Parliamentary Committee of the TUC warned that the insurance scheme should be restricted to trade unionists:

> Otherwise you will have men to support who never had been and never will be self supporting. They are at present parasites on their more industrious fellows and will be the first to avail themselves of the funds the Bill provides (Harris, 1972, pp.317–18).

Buxton of the Board of Trade took a more generous attitude and argued that it was unreasonable to exclude non-unionists, but assured the TUC that they would have full representation on the advisory committees (Harris, 1972, pp.315–18).

Consequently, the claim that organized labour was hostile to the Liberals' proposed welfare legislation has some validity (Thane, 1975, 1984; Ginsburg, 1979; Yeo, 1979; Novak, 1988, pp.86–9). But the objections were not that the Liberals' proposals treated the poor less favourably, nor that they entrenched the concepts of deserving and undeserving within state legislation. Most opposition suggested that the legislation did not go far enough in distinguishing respectable workers from the roughs. While it is accepted that a suspicion of the Liberals' proposals and of state provision is a healthy sign of class consciousness, the organized labour movement never developed this beyond a concern with their own sectional interests. The Friendly Societies in particular took a reactionary view of how they could assert the interests of their members, looking back to the period when membership flourished and their funds were ample. The opposition may have stressed the overbearing role of 'the state', but this did not mean they advocated a more equitable system of relief. Many clearly felt that long-established inequalities within the working class were justified. The organized labour movement, including in this instance the Friendly Societies, was more concerned with its own survival as a welfare provider than with those people who most frequently had to survive on welfare. State welfare was a threat to the traditional trade unions, those representing craft- and trade-based workers, and a threat to the Friendly Societies, because it sought to perform their welfare functions. State welfare, under most of the Liberals' social policies, was to be reserved for those who deserved it. The Poor Law was to continue to provide for the rest of the working class.

Nevertheless, it is one thing to show that certain attitudes and organizations were important within the working class, but another to show that these had an effect upon legislators. Consequently, a measure of caution is appropriate when attempting to address the question of how far the SDW reflected the interests of organized labour. There is, however, prima facie evidence that organized labour influenced the Liberals, and that this influence took two forms.

First, there was a direct influence in that organized labour sought, and was granted, a voice within the policy-making procedure. Trade unionists were clearly consulted at length. Ministers discussed the ideas put to them by trade unionists and Churchill, for one, was keen to ensure their support for his legislation. Braithwaite, who had a great deal of responsibility for framing the insurance legislation, was at the centre of the struggle, in which he tended to sympathize with the Friendly Societies – his own father having been a stalwart Friendly Society member – and he clearly wanted the Friendly Societies to play a central role in the administration of the Liberals' insurance scheme. Both the Friendly Societies and the trade unions were given a part in the administration of the insurance scheme, which was one of their principal objectives. In addition, but perhaps coincidentally, the industries that were initially selected for the national insurance scheme were those with high levels of trade union membership, as the TUC had requested.

The Old Age Pensions Act (1908) also acknowledged the deserving/

undeserving distinction within the working class. Under this Act, there was a subsection which disqualified certain groups from getting a pension. Lloyd George proposed:

> . . . an amendment which will exclude from this subsection [disqualifying paupers, drunks and the indolent, K.M.] all those persons who have been members of friendly, provident, and other societies, or trade unions . . . for ten years before the age of sixty (*Hansard*, June 1908, Vol. 190, col. 580).

The membership of a provident society meant, it would seem, that the person, however lazy or intoxicated, was to be treated as hard-working and sober. Not that the pension received was of great material value, the sums paid were quite small. But the Act did recognize the efforts of those who had attempted to provide for themselves and as such took account of the points made by organized labour.

The second way that organized labour influenced Liberal legislation was more subtle than the first. In many respects, this second influence is more important and yet more insidious. Hay (1975, p.45) suggests that at least some of those who favoured reform did so in order to encourage working-class thrift. This would inevitably reproduce the distinction between those able to afford the contributions and those who were unable to do so. The introduction of National Insurance in 1911 saw 2.3 million members in the scheme, of which Thane (1982, p.95) states 63 percent were skilled workers. However, she points out that sick pay amounted to only 11 shillings for a man and 7 shillings and 6 pence for a woman (Thane, 1982, p.85). The Manchester Unity of Oddfellows had paid this amount to members claiming sick pay 70 years earlier (Gosden, 1961, p.76). Consequently, the more generous societies were permitted to opt out of the state scheme, or were not covered by the legislation if their existing benefits exceeded those provided under the Act. Thane also points out that for a household earning 18 shillings per week, their tax and national insurance contributions amounted to more than 10 percent of their total income, whereas 'the respectable artisan wage of thirty-five shillings per week was paying only 5.27% in taxes and contributions' (Thane, 1982, p.96). Understandably, there were few calls from these 'respectable' workers for a more equitable system of contributions and taxes.

Moreover, there was virtually unanimous support among middle-class observers for the Friendly Society and trade union welfare provisions. For over 20 years, a succession of middle-class commentators had applauded the principles that the Friendly Societies applied. The adoption by the state of many of the administrative and exclusionary practices operated by working-class organizations was, therefore, a testament to the earlier success of these practices. Stated boldly, it simply was not necessary for anyone to invent ways and means of dividing the working class – these already existed.

There were, of course, other powerful influences upon the Liberals besides the labour movement. Among these the insurance companies, employers and the examples provided by Germany, Australia and New Zealand were all significant, and in some cases, far more significant than the labour movement. However, none of these influences contradicted the view of a working class that was, and had to be, divided between the deserving and undeserving (see Harris, 1972; Hay, 1975, 1977; Burgess, 1980; Thane, 1982; Langan 1985).

Perhaps the strongest evidence to support the view that the legislation sought to maintain, rather than create, social divisions, comes from Lloyd-George's defence of the Old Age Pensions Act in the House of Commons. He said of the 'industry test':

> It is a test to exclude the loafer and the wastrel. This man, I think, ought to be excluded for two reasons. One reason is applicable to the pensioners themselves. I think it is highly important that the receiver of the pension should be regarded as quite honourable, that there should be nothing in the nature of pauperisation, that the pension should be regarded as the recognition of faithful services to the state: . . . if men who have never done an honest day's work in their lives, receive this pension in common with men who have really worked hard, I think that the receiver of the pension will be regarded in the same light as he who is actually known to be of that stamp which we wish to ruthlessly exclude. . . . My second reason is this. . . . It is very important that all classes of the community, not merely those who receive a pension, but those who contribute towards it, should feel that it is fair, just, and equitable in all its essentials (quoted in Pope *et al.*, 1986, pp.54–5).

The Old Age Pension Act was the focus of so much concern regarding the need to distinguish carefully the deserving from the undeserving, in part because it was one of the first major Acts to break with the Poor Law. The interests of the poor, women and the unemployed were not articulated. Burgess (1980, p.127) has put it well when he says of the Liberal reforms, 'what was actually achieved serves to emphasize the limited scope of reform in terms of working class needs and expectations'.

It would be misleading to suggest that the only strategies pursued by the working class in the period prior to the First World War were pragmatic and sectional. Late nineteenth- and early twentieth-century Britain witnessed an upsurge in a variety of radical, feminist, socialist and syndicalist politics. There is little dispute among scholars that the period 1911–1914 saw the growth of socialist and syndicalist ideas among the rank and file, in a number of areas and industries. Nor is there any dispute that this 3-year period contrasts with the earlier periods of industrial unrest in both its intensity and its scope. Nevertheless, these disparate movements failed to extend their successes to the poorest stratum of society (Pelling, 1968, pp.137–40; Middlemass, 1979, p.35; Burgess, 1980, pp.141–6; White, 1982; Hinton, 1983, p.93). Henceforth, the organized labour movement was no longer to represent only a skilled and respectable stratum but was to encompass more workers from more industries. The craftworker would continue to maintain a privileged place, but the exclusivity of mid-Victorian Britain was impossible to sustain. It was, in part, these changes in the constituency of the movement that were to make the distinction between 'deserving' and 'undeserving' so difficult in the 1920s.

Summary

Poverty was a ghost that could haunt any working-class home in the nineteenth century. Avoiding the workhouse and ensuring food was on the table were the major objectives of virtually all working-class households. For those in casual trades, for working-class women, for Irish, Jewish and rural migrants to the growing cities, and for the unskilled, these simple aims were harder to achieve than for other members of their class. Despite the growth in socialist organizations, and the increasing support they could rely on, at the turn of the century the poor were still treated by many as a race apart. Social Darwinism, which on the one hand justified state intervention, served also to define the weakest and poorest as congenitally unfit. The poor, especially in London, were a hopeless stratum of degenerates who, a number of middle-class observers believed, ought to be allowed to die out.

Throughout this chapter, divisions within the working class have been shown to have influenced policy makers. These divisions were not the consequence of industrialization, nor of capitalism *per se*, although both affected the expression of social divisions. For those workers able to gain a relatively privileged place in the labour market, a place which depended to a large degree on the ability to exercise control over the labour process, it was possible to escape the worst effects of poverty. The guilds, the Friendly Societies, trade union membership and other working-class institutions provided a measure of protection, but they also served to exclude some of the poorest members of that class. The success of these organizations depended on their ability to adapt pragmatically to the constraints imposed by capitalism. Nevertheless, the success of pragmatism undermined the possibility of unity. Thus, the working class has played an active part in promoting social divisions. Sometimes this has been direct discrimination based on xenophobia or patriarchy, at other times it has been a consequence of the form and direction that class struggle has taken. The middle classes and policy makers have observed divisions within the working class and have constructed an SDW which builds on the existing pattern of social divisions.

*four*_____

Playing a part in the administration and befooling themselves: 1914–45

In this chapter, our historical tour takes in two world wars and two intervening decades of mass unemployment. During the First World War, unions, particularly in engineering, had numerous changes in work practices forced upon them. Other changes were negotiated, but the ability of the old labour aristocrat to control the labour process and the organization of work was henceforth severely restricted. This does not mean that craft control and demarcation lines were a thing of the past, far from it. The 1918 Restoration of Pre-war Practices Act was to be used to re-establish the relatively privileged place of the skilled male worker, and to reinforce both social and sexual divisions. Despite the industrial militancy of 1918–1922, the dominant approach of the organized labour movement was to be pragmatic and sectional. The part organized labour played in various administrative tribunals and in trying to gain access to the corridors of power, through both the parliamentary door and slipping in via the back gate of corporatist networks, served to exclude the poor and the unemployed in the inter-war period. Changes in industrial relations practices, including the growth of occupational welfare, paternalism and scientific management techniques, enabled some sections of the working class by the 1930s to enjoy consumption patterns previously reserved for the middle classes. The concentration of unemployment in the depressed areas, along with changes in public welfare, most notably in council housing, witnessed a geographical/spatial aspect to the SDW. Finally, we shall consider the impact of the Second World War and see how, once again, social divisions were redefined and the seeds of future divisions sown.

War and the battle of the sexes

During the 1914–1918 war, the organized labour movement was shaken by the numbers of women who were recruited into industry. The sexual division of labour was quite suddenly thrown into question as hundreds of thousands of women were called upon to perform jobs which had previously been exclusively 'men's work'. The response of the trade unions was at best ambiguous, and at worst they persisted with patriarchal arguments to justify their relative privileges. As Braybon (1981) makes plain, the unions argued, by and large, that women should be excluded from certain jobs. Moreover, they were often opposed to female employment in their industry, even when employers offered to pay them the rate for the job. For example, dockers in Liverpool refused to work with women, although the employers were prepared to pay them the same rate as men. The unions were only rarely sensitive to these issues. Some women did get equal pay, which was a tremendous boost to their incomes, and some trade unions did fight to ensure that women got it. However, the reaction of men to equal pay was mixed since, on the one hand, it prevented undercutting of the union rate, which was to be applauded, but, on the other, it was taken as a further sign of the erosion of their privileges and of the exclusive character upon which many unions had been based. As Joan Williams, a munitions worker, rather sarcastically put it:

> I could quite see it was hard on the men to have women coming into all their pet jobs and in some cases doing them a good deal better and I sympathised with the way they were torn between not wanting women to undercut them, and yet hating them to earn as much (quoted in Braybon, 1981, p.79).

Williams was fortunate, for the wages of many women were still pitifully low. Women's wages were so low in some cases that the Poor Law Guardians were called upon to supplement earnings. Some unions acted as advocates for the newly recruited women, but others maintained their policy of exclusion. Not surprisingly, the 1915 Delegate Conference of the Amalgamated Society of Engineers decided to keep its doors shut to women, and not until the Second World War were women able to gain entry.

The fear that many male trade unionists expressed was that the control over the labour process and the labour market, which they had fought to establish in the previous century, would be lost. If they were going to admit women, they wanted some guarantee that things would return to 'normal' after the war. By 'normal' they meant a return to the pre-war sexual division of labour. The Restoration of Pre-War Practices Act, 1918, was finally introduced to pacify the most powerful unions. Thus, any gains women might have made – and they were few – were to be erased when the war ended.

National Insurance schemes and scheming

At first glance, it seems that the organized labour movement's approach to National Insurance contrasts with their attitude to 'female substitution'. Throughout the war, and immediately after it, the TUC pushed for the low paid of all industries to be covered by the state insurance scheme. In response to the Women's Employment Committee of the TUC, Hodge, a former union leader, tried to persuade the Treasury and the war cabinet to include women munitions workers in the scheme. For his troubles he was transferred to the Ministry of Pensions (Whiteside, 1980, pp.868–9). Nevertheless, the TUC's concept of national insurance would have reproduced the type of divisions associated with the Friendly Societies in the previous century.

The discussions of the revised insurance scheme focused on a range of previously excluded industries, and the clauses for withdrawal illustrate the labour movement's sectional and pragmatic approach. As Whiteside (1980) has made plain, the attitudes of the organized labour movement to the extension of unemployment insurance during the war, varied from union to union. In the main, the unions which already had schemes for the relief of their unemployed members – some in conjunction with their employers – were reluctant to enter schemes which would see their low-risk members subsidizing other high-risk industries. Each union was simply articulating the sectional interests of their members, as the membership expected them to do, of course. The TUC also put forward a scheme, but they and the government had a different idea of what insurance in a state scheme should mean. The Treasury saw it as a means whereby the state could provide a single system of relief for the whole of the working class. The 'high risks' in the labour force, who, as we saw in the last chapter, had little opportunity of joining a society, and were often unable to join the state scheme either, were to be subsidized by the 'low risks'. The TUC wanted a state system of insurance benefiting the badly organized, the low paid and the high-risk industries, but with the Treasury providing additional funds from general taxation to cover the cost of including the high-risk groups. The TUC was simply reiterating the view that the better paid, low-risk groups within the working class ought not to have to bear the cost of supporting the poorest, and those who were an actuarial liability. Nor is it surprising that certain trades should object to paying into the state scheme when they already had schemes which were more generous. However, the Treasury had no intention of subsidizing any insurance scheme which it saw as an attempt to remove the necessity of the Poor Law. The problem that remained for the Treasury was that of trying to prevent the low-risk trades from contracting out of the scheme, without provoking disgruntlement. The need to maintain war-time production required the cooperation of the trades associated with the low-risk industries (Whiteside, 1980).

Not until 1920, with the Unemployment Insurance Act, was a solution found, and that proved to be temporary. This Act allowed industries to contract out, but forced them to include all workers in the industry in their scheme. Thus it was not possible for sections of an industry which were low risk to exclude others in the same industry that were a high risk. By the time this Act was passed, however, the scheme had no time in which to build adequate funds before it was hit by mass unemployment. When the contracting out clause was abolished in 1927, the contributory basis of the insurance scheme had gone by the board anyway (Whiteside, 1980). The failure to resolve the question of unemployment insurance during the war was, in part, to blame for the constant and *ad hoc* changes made in the 1920s and 1930s.

The dispute between the TUC and individual unions with the government over the question of unemployment insurance is significant for three reasons. First, it illustrates in a very clear fashion how trade unions are drawn into negotiation and discussion with government. If the organized labour movement was going to represent the interests of members, at a time when the state was proposing changes which would affect them, it was vital to sit down and discuss these issues. Secondly, it reveals their sectional nature, although some opposition was based on the principled position that the working class ought not to have to subsidize capitalism by funding the 'reserve army of labour'. However, it is difficult not to conclude that much of the opposition to the Treasury was based on the desire of the better off worker who already had a good scheme, to remain in this and not to join a national scheme which might pay less benefits. Thirdly, the issue of unemployment insurance provides an interesting example of the degree of support that the leadership had from the rank and file. While in the industrial relations sphere there is much evidence of dissent from below, the leadership appear to have been in tune with their members on the question of unemployment insurance (Middlemass, 1979, p.104; Burgess, 1980, p.178).

It is important to remember that there is little in the insurance principle that is socialist or egalitarian. National insurance serves as a means of redistributing resources within the working class. For Marxists, it represents a way for the capitalist class to avoid paying the cost of reproducing its own labour costs. Nevertheless, the lack of any radical alternative, any scheme which might have worked towards resolving intra-class divisions, and the ready acceptance of the inevitability of a division of welfare within the working class by the TUC and its affiliated unions, can hardly be excused so easily. The scheme advocated by the TUC promoted a three-fold division. First, those in the low-risk industries which could contract out, would have received high insurance benefits. Secondly, those in the high-risk industries who had not contracted out would have lower, state-provided benefits. The third group – those outside of the organized labour movement and/or the labour market – would have been dependent upon Poor Law assistance.

For women and most of the unskilled, the organized labour movement failed to represent their interests, despite the extremely favourable conditions for doing so. The Webbs were incapable of hiding their distaste for the TUC's 'pusillanimity', and '. . . for pitching its claims so low, when it had such an advantageous ground for bargaining' (Webb and Webb, 1920, pp.637–46; in Middlemas, 1979, p.898). In contrast, organized labour was far more belligerent when it came to defending craft and sectional interests against 'dilutees'.

Restoring pre-war practices and controlling the labour process

It was the buoyant labour market during the First World War which was mainly responsible for the improvement in the household incomes of the poorest. In large measure, this improvement was due to the long hours and greater employment opportunities that the war presented. The improvement was not universal, and skilled workers resented the erosion of their wage differentials. It was this decline in the economic advantages of skilled workers, particularly engineers, which fuelled support for the shop stewards' movement at the end of the war.

Perhaps the most significant feature of intra-class divisions during the war was organized labour's demand for the Restoration of Pre-war Practices Act. There can be little doubt that this was an Act designed to placate skilled workers, who felt that 'female dilution of labour' was undermining their privileges. Even if no-one could say what the privileges were that had been surrendered, organized labour was determined to establish some. As Lloyd George feared, there was intense industrial conflict after 1918 when 'restoration of privileges' was used to support a host of different claims regarding working practices.

For some commentators, the period between 1918 and 1921 posed a real threat of revolution. With revolution in Russia and the threat of it in many parts of Europe, there was a genuine fear that Britain would confront similar problems. By 1919, there were in the region of 10 million trade unionists. The hold of Liberalism, which had slackened since the last quarter of the nineteenth century, was finally broken. Strikes by the police and riots by some within the armed services added to the sense of insecurity felt by the middle classes. Alarming reports of industrial unrest being organized by socialists and syndicalists were relayed to the Cabinet by the intelligence service. Many of the grievances which had been set aside for the duration of the war were revived, and in virtually every town and city radical socialist demands were put forward. In the vanguard of the movement were not the union leaders, who were known to the government, but shop stewards and local activists. This is not, however, the place to run through all the arguments concerning the likelihood of revolution (Saville, 1975; Hinton, 1983; Cronin, 1984; Nottingham, 1986).

What is clear is that the disparate struggles lacked any real national leadership and were frequently sectional in nature. Demands were often centred on specific issues, places of employment or the interests of a particular stratum. The skilled engineer was, once again, at the forefront of many of the industrial disputes and he, for they were invariably men, demanded a return to the working practices of the pre-war period. The protection of wartime privileges, the restoration of differentials and an attempt to expel the 'dilutees' were more likely to be the objectives than any class-based issue. Moreover, these sectional demands could often be addressed in isolation from one another. Nor was the government slow to use force when necessary. A divided working class, therefore, confronted a government with a massive parliamentary mandate and some wily characters in Cabinet. The response of the government was a mixture of 'concession and coercion' (Deacon, 1977). There was not, though, any coherent or planned attack on the working class. Indeed, each manoeuvre and decision could be keenly debated within the ruling class and the outcome was seldom predictable (Nottingham, 1986).

For Braverman (1974), these contests mark a highly significant change in the nature of work and class struggle. Braverman argues that during the period 1914–1939, the detailed division of labour was used to facilitate greater control over the worker. This was achieved by using the methods advocated by Frederick Taylor and scientific management. The change in the organization of work can be seen in the structure of male employment. Between 1914 and 1933, the proportion of the workforce describing themselves as skilled declined from 60 to 32 percent (Hinton, 1983, p.129). Furthermore, the twin features of Braverman's thesis – increased regulation of workers and the subdivision of labour – can be seen to have underpinned many of the wartime and post-war industrial disputes.

Certainly, new forms of production and organization accompanied the First World War and these have much in common with Taylor's scientific management school of thought (Burgess, 1980, pp.166–73). Trade union hostility to labour dilution and substitution was undoubtedly provoked by fears that changes introduced during the war would be maintained during peacetime. This in turn led to pressure for the Pre-War Practices Act from the trade union movement. The aim, for skilled trade unionists, was to return to the custom and practice, along with the strict demarcation lines, that had operated prior to the war. As Middlemas (1979, p.142) has observed:

> Trade unions ignored the wartime expectations of most female and many unskilled workers who had taken the places of dilutees, and their understandable but generous haste to restore male skilled employment on pre-war ratios set back for years the standards briefly achieved in low paid and casual industries to say nothing of the cause of equal pay, which Lloyd George and Churchill had shown some inclination to adopt.

It should not be thought that scientific management techniques were universally introduced. Nor were they the only strategy pursued by employers in the period 1914–1939. Braverman takes too narrow a view of the options open to management in any given period. Alongside scientific management techniques it is important to remember that employers also used paternalism. This in turn expanded the occupational welfare package of some and widened the division between those in work and those without, a point that will be illustrated in more detail shortly.

Nevertheless, the fierce industrial conflicts that erupted in the immediate post-war period suggest that employers were especially reluctant to hand back control of the labour process. Having broken down the labour process during the war, they did not want to to see craft control being re-established. They were aware that using 'line production' techniques, combined with increased shop floor supervision, was in their interests. Production during the war had been cheaper and faster and many employers were, therefore, reluctant to cede control despite local and national agreements with the trade unions. Firms who had introduced new working practices had often made very handsome profits during the war. It was only natural that other firms, in other industries, would adapt and adopt these methods.

The crucial point to note is that, as Braverman (1974) claims, many of the conflicts have to be seen in the context of changes in the labour process during, and immediately after, the war. Skilled workers were struggling to avoid the degradation of their work. In doing so, they used the arguments of syndicalism, socialism and craftism. Their strategy was directed at employers and was confrontational. At the same time they tried, with varying degrees of success, to mount a form of social closure. In many respects, this is an excellent example of the sort of dual closure discussed by Parkin (1979) and elaborated upon in Chapter 6. As understandable as it may be for workers to mount defensive and sectional struggles, it is important to acknowledge the effects these had on other members of their class. Less easy to understand is the part organized labour played in maintaining and reproducing the deserving/undeserving distinction in the 1920s and 1930s.

Workpeople's representatives or judges of the poor

When unemployment insurance had first been introduced, the 1911 Act had made provisions for Courts of Referees. Of the three members that made up these tribunals, one was to be a 'workpeople's' representative who was almost invariably nominated by the local Trades Council. Alongside the workpeople's representative sat a representative of local business and a Chairman nominated by the Board of Trade (Wraithe and Hutcheson, 1973, p.172). These Courts of Referees had the task of deciding if a worker qualified for benefit under the conditions of the 1911 and subsequent Acts. Thus they had to decide whether claimants were to be disqualified for refusing to take available work, or for having left their previous employment without good cause. At the end of the war, women were often sacked in order to make way for returning servicemen. When they subsequently applied for unemployment benefit, they were shocked to find that they were not 'genuinely seeking work'.

For married women, the Genuinely Seeking Work Test (GSWT) was a stick to drive them back into the home (Deacon, 1976; Thane, 1982). By 1919, *Labour Woman* was denouncing the fact that in Manchester alone, 1000 women had been refused benefit since the end of the war (Braybon, 1981, p.182). It should be remembered that these benefits had previously been understood to be free from any enquiry into the personal characteristics of the claimant. Before the war, much had been made of the principle that contributory benefits ought to be an entitlement and not subject to personal inquiry.

Women were thus effectively excluded in three ways. First, they were expelled from the labour market. Then they were refused benefits they had been led to believe they were entitled to. Thirdly, they were denied the opportunity of voicing their discontent as the unions who had recruited them during the war maintained a conspiratorial silence (Boston, 1980, pp.126–8; Braybon, 1981). These measures to refuse women covenanted benefit, which it must be remembered were carried out with a trade union representative on the tribunal, must surely represent one of the best (worst) examples of how sexual divisions have been maintained. Thousands of women were thrown out of jobs and then told that they could not have the benefits for which they had been paying while in work. It was a fraud on a massive scale, made possible by the labour movement which had insisted on their exclusion and local trade unionists who collaborated with the Courts of Referees.

The refusal to pay covenanted benefits was to be reproduced for women and men claiming uncovenanted benefit throughout the 1920s. The initial decision to extend the system of unemployment insurance in the 1920s, so that it was possible for unemployed workers to claim, even though they had exhausted their benefit, was made in response to the perceived threat of the unemployed (Deacon, 1977, pp.9–14). However, to simply pay a ransom was not to the liking of the Treasury and there was, therefore, a perpetual desire to reduce the cost. The way to do this, it was decided, was to have both a 'household means test' and a 'genuinely seeking work test'. Both involved trade unionists sitting in judgement on the unemployed, but while the household means test 'was bitterly opposed by all sections of the labour movement', the GSWT was not (Deacon, 1977, p.16). As in the case of Courts of Referees, a trade unionist sat as a workpeople's representative on the Local Employment Committees. It was to these committees that claimants had to submit evidence that they were genuinely seeking work. In practice, as Deacon (1977, p.20) says, 'the "seeking work", test was a futile and brutal ritual . . .'. And, as he goes on to show, the whole of the labour movement virtually ignored the seeking work test. What is more, trade unionists continued throughout the inter-war period to sit in judgement on the unemployed. On the Courts of Referees, on Local Employment Committees, on Boards of Guardians, as members of the Boards of Assessors and later on the Public Assistance Committees, local trade unionists, not the leadership, played a crucial role in 'the search for the scrounger'.

The views expressed by various middle-class observers in the previous century (see Chapter 3) – that the respectable working class were the most able administrators because they could apply the deserving/undeserving distinction with ease – appears to have be borne out in the 1920s. Thus Clynes, as leader of the Labour Party, assured the House:

Organised labour, I am certain, together with the employers, if both were called more in touch with the administration of benefits, could be of very great assistance in locating the shirkers and making it impossible to get money when work could have been got (*Hansard*, 1921, Vol.138, col.1199).

Eight years later it was still no idle boast to claim that organized labour would locate the shirker. In its evidence to the Morris Committee in 1929, the Trade Union submission included cases where union branch secretaries had reported suspected malingerers (Minutes of Evidence, 1929, para.763, p.58).

Why should organized labour have been so keen to play this role? In part, there was a genuine ignorance of the effects that the administration of benefits could have (Deacon, 1977, pp.21–2). But this is by no means the whole story since, even when the reality was made plain, sympathy did not always extend to the claimant. The letters sent to Ramsay Macdonald complaining about benefit abuse were not, we can assume, all from middle class critics. That at least some within the working class felt there was a serious problem with 'shirkers' seems probable and their effect on the leader of the Labour Party was to confirm in him his belief that abuse was a problem (Deacon, 1977, p.27). In the case of the seeking work test, it is clear from Deacon (1977, p.29) that 'The stigma of personal failing which became attached to those who failed the seeking work test isolated them from the rest of the unemployed and inhibited protest. It seems likely that not only did the stigma of personal failing attach to those who failed the GSWT, but it was also attached to those who sought to defend them, or criticize the test.

Another reason may have been the legacy of the Friendly Societies, savings clubs and independent workers too proud to seek relief. The idea that there exists a class of people who are undeserving has, as we have seen, deep roots within both the working class as a whole and the labour movement. Indeed, the issue of whether a person was genuinely seeking work or a scrounger to be rooted out and forced onto the Poor Law reflects the older concern with respectability, most usually identified with the Victorian period. Thus there was a manifest failure to confront what was seen as a delicate issue, and one which stigmatized those who challenged the concept of the undeserving.

Despite the evidence of social and industrial unrest between 1917 and 1921, organized labour, in general, had by 1922 changed its strategy. There was, once again, a desire to be consulted and to pursue working-class interests within the parameters of a capitalist democracy. Thus when the charge of Judas was made, the retort was that at least Judas had some gold. Indeed, throughout the 1920s and 1930s, some sections of the working class improved their living standards substantially. To persuade these workers that the economy was in a mess, or that they ought to express their solidarity with the unemployed, was always a difficult task. In this situation, some sections of the labour movement felt they ought to play their part in the administrative organs of the state.

There was some opposition to the GSWT, notably on Clydeside, but even here the scheme continued to operate. Arthur Hayday, one of the few vocal opponents of the GSWT from 1925, mounted a lone campaign against the test within the TUC. When he addressed the 1925 Trades Union Annual Congress, he summed up the position of the 'workpeople's representative':

> It is all very well to say that you have a share in the administration. Your share is to do as the regulations bid you do, and the time is coming when you will have to consider seriously whether it is worthwhile befooling yourselves and running the risk of hostile criticism on the part of men who cannot get extended benefit (quoted in Deacon, 1977, p.29).

It would seem that a great many local trade unionists were prepared to *befool themselves* that their part in the administration was to do more than the regulations bid them do. It is not, therefore, simply that the leaders were bought off by their incorporation into the machinery of an emergent corporatism, as Middlemas (1979, p.163) implies. At the local level, too, there was a parallel acceptance that organized labour had a part to play in the administration of state policy. It was against this type of trade unionist that the National Unemployed Workers Movement (NUWM) was to direct many of its vitriolic accusations of collaboration.

It must also be acknowledged that the geographical distribution of unemployment in the inter-war period was important. In the cities and industries of the industrial revolution, workers were far more vulnerable to long-term unemployment. These were not the casual workers of Victorian London, and yet the 'deserving/undeserving' distinction used similar language and criteria to the late Victorian period. And once again the middle-class observers identified an underclass who were demoralized and incapable of ever holding down a proper job (MacNicol, 1987). Despite the severe hardship experienced by workers in the depressed areas, other areas – notably the West Midlands and the South East – were quite prosperous. It is this contrast, between those who were in a relatively buoyant industry or locality and those who were not, that makes the SDW in the inter-war period so stark.

The social division of welfare in the 1930s

The major division within the working class in the inter-war period was between those in work and the unemployed. Between 1920 and 1939, unemployment among the insured population never fell below 10 percent and climbed as high as 25 percent in January 1933 (Hinton, 1983, p.119). Not only were significant sections of the working class unemployed, but they remained so for long periods. In 1936 in Crook, Co. Durham, 7 percent of the unemployed had not worked in the previous 5 years (Thane, 1982, p.183). Moreover, unemployment was more severely concentrated in particular areas and localities. In Jarrow, which had been heavily dependent on shipbuilding and engineering for employment, more than 67 percent of the insured population were unemployed in 1934 (Thane, 1982).

In contrast, for those in work wages rose by 15 percent between 1925 and

1934 and average household incomes rose by 30–40 percent in the 23 years after the outbreak of the First World War. In the same period, 1914–1934, the average standard of living rose by 70 percent (Cronin, 1984). Cronin (1984, pp.149–51) also points out that by 1938, 7.75 million workers were entitled to paid holidays out of a total workforce of 18.5 million. Indeed, it is the improvement in the living standards of many working-class households in the inter-war period which makes intra-class divisions in this period noteworthy. The fall in prices of consumer goods and the gains in real wages made by those in work, 'had the effect of reducing labour's sense of "relative deprivation" that had been extreme in the early 1920s' (Burgess, 1980, pp.244-5).

In housing, a massive programme of public sector building took place. This, along with increased expenditure on unemployment relief and education, saw roughly 6 percent of national income consumed by social expenditure (Hinton, 1983, pp.123-4) However, it was mainly the lower middle class and the skilled working class who benefited. Although council housing was subsidized by £6 per annum, rents, of between 13 and 20 shillings per week, still excluded the poorest. To put this in perspective, it needs to be borne in mind that the maximum state pension was still only 10 shillings per week. Thus the SDW was manifest in bricks and mortar as the unskilled, the unemployed and the poor were confined to the worst housing (Thane, 1982, p.207).

Fiscal welfare was enhanced during the inter-war years by a series of tax allowances. Titmuss (1958) pointed out in his essay on the SDW that the child allowances introduced in 1909, extended in 1919 and to all taxpayers in 1920, had a regressive effect. The low paid and the unemployed, exempt from tax, did not benefit at all. Allowances against tax were also provided for wives, for a child's education up to the age of 21, for savings towards old age, life insurance and occupational pensions (Titmuss, 1958, pp.46-8). Moreover, occupational welfare expanded considerably between the wars.

Occupational welfare and the labour process

The importance of the 1920s and 1930s for the growth of occupational welfare needs to be acknowledged and firmly emphasized. There are a number of reasons for the expansion of occupational welfare during this period, but two of the most important relate directly to the labour process and industrial relations. Changes in the industrial structure of Britain provide the backdrop to a picture in which paternalism and scientific management thinking are in the foreground. While the decline in heavy engineering and the industries of the nineteenth century was a feature of the inter-war period, so too was the growth of light engineering, electrical engineering and motor manufacture. It was in the South East of England, the outskirts of London and the West Midlands where these newer industries were established. Being new, the organization of work was not shackled by the custom and practice of older industries. It was easier, therefore, to introduce systems of production that made them more competitive with the USA and Germany. However, there were, even in these newer industries, particularly in the motor industry, those who sought to exclude the semi-skilled and resisted the 'dilution of labour' by women (Cronin, 1984, pp.101–10). In general, though, employers in these newer industries found it easier to organize working practices as they wanted.

Even in some of the older industries perceptive employers were able to expand, provided they were able radically to change the organization of work and production. For example, in textiles, many firms struggled to survive, but where production techniques had changed during the war, with the need to mass-produce uniforms, there were opportunities for growth. Firms like Burtons adapted their production and marketing processes to produce 'off the peg' suits for a mass market. The company used Taylor's ideas about scientific management and combined these with a paternalism that provided sports facilities (including a swimming pool), health services and welfare benefits (Redmayne, 1950). Moreover, Fitzgerald (1988) has demonstrated that the growth of occupational welfare throughout this period was extensive and widely accompanied by new working practices.

It is not always easy to distinguish between the ethos of scientific management and a genuinely paternalist philosophy and many employers may have used the latter to achieve the former. Sir Montagu Burton, whose Leeds-based firm flourished during the inter-war period, was one such employer who advocated paternalism on the grounds that it made it easier to achieve changes in the organization of work. The *Leeds Mercury* (10 October 1934) observed at the time that: 'The Welfare work is not a sort of luxury. It has become a necessity for creating esprit de corps among those who, without it, would live lives of deadly monotony and depression.' J.B. Priestley (1934, p.98) was well aware of the implications and took a less generous view:

> Very soon, when this atmosphere has been created, you begin to hear talk of 'loyalties' that soar high above the common and reasonable fidelity of a decent man trying to do the job for which he is paid. Business cant swells into business mysticism, as it did in the United States before the slump, when there was no end of rubbishy talk about 'service' and loyalty, the kind of talk we get here chiefly from advertising men in their windy conventions.

Since the perks and packages that were offered frequently accompanied mass production techniques that were mind-numbingly boring, Priestley's scepticism seems quite legitimate. As Fox points out, many forms of occupational welfare were provided in a cynical attempt to gain employee compliance. Fox (1985, pp.76–81) also suggests that the provision of these has to be seen in the context of changes in the organization of work.

The crucial point is that occupational welfare served to reinforce the differentiation of the workforce which the labour process initiated. Thus there were clear distinctions in the benefits provided for different grades and type of employee. Pensions, sick pay and holiday entitlement were not common for manual workers in the 1930s. Clerical and managerial staff were able, therefore, to regard themselves as relatively privileged. Staff canteens, a company pension and not having to 'clock on' were the distinctions which segregated manual and non-manual workers. By 1936, it is estimated that 13 percent of the working population, in both the private and public sectors, were members of an occupational pension scheme. This figure continued to rise throughout the 1930s and for the next three decades (Hannah, 1986, p.67). When it is remembered that sick pay schemes for those in work were becoming more widespread, council housing was increasingly available to 'suitable' members of the working class, the disposable income of some sections of the working class enabled them to purchase consumer durables, and increasing numbers of workers could take holidays with pay, the picture of social divisions during the the 1930s becomes clearer.

Although Titmuss outlined his thesis on the SDW in the 1950s, many of the developments he refers to have their roots in the inter-war period (Titmuss, 1958, pp.34–55). As Titmuss (1958, p.53) noted, such benefits were clearly designed to promote 'good industrial relations'. Likewise, Hannah (1986, p.27) points to the pressure exerted by public sector unions, particularly the National Association of Local Government Officers (NALGO), for occupational pensions. Thus the context within which occupational welfare developed was one of changes in, and contests over, the labour process and the rewards and status provided by the labour market. Of course, these rewards were not available to those who were excluded from the labour market, or those who were confined to the least rewarding niches of it.

The challenge of the poor and their marginalization

An aspect of the SDW that Sinfield (1978) was keen to emphasize was the political powerlessness of those who rely on public welfare. Although this point has been accepted in principle (see Chapter 2), this should not be taken to mean that the poor are passive. The poor have consistently challenged their location within the SDW despite the obstacles (for a discussion of political and organizational responses to welfare dependence, see Bagguley, 1991). In the inter-war period, this challenge took two forms: first, there was an attempt to influence the operation of the administrative machinery which provided public welfare; secondly, there was the traditional response of the poor, which involved social disorder, riot and marches.

Alongside the collaboration of trade unionists in the administration of various tribunals, and the prosperity that enabled many workers to turn a blind eye to the plight of the unemployed, it is necessary to remember that there were various forms of resistance. Some Local Employment Committees (LECs) and some Public Assistance Committees did rebel, even if the vast majority did not. It would be an entirely erroneous picture of the organized labour movement's attitudes to the poor and unemployed in the inter-war period if we only discussed complicity and acceptance.

Despite the fact that 'Poplarism' never became widespread, the approach that it involved, 'decent treatment and hang the rates', disturbed successive governments (Ryan, 1978, pp.70–84). It was the 1918 extension of the franchise which allowed the 'pauper vote' to have an impact on Boards of Guardians, although political pressure on the local Guardians had had an effect since the passing of the 1834 Act (Foster, 1974; Knott, 1986). Poplarism, in brief, saw local Boards of Guardians elected who were known by the electorate to be sympathetic to the poor. In Poplar, this sympathy meant that the Poor Law was levying much higher rates from businesses and wealthier individuals than in the much richer areas of London. The generosity of the Poplar Guardians led to them being sent, eventually, to prison. In South Wales during the 1921 coal strike, the Boards of Guardians virtually financed the strike out of the rates paid by local coal owners and there were other examples of the 'pauper vote' being used to provide 'decent treatment' irrespective of the cost to ratepayers (Briggs and Deacon, 1973, pp.42–50).

It was not only in the case of the Poor Law that the 'pauper vote' had an effect. The generosity of some Public Assistance Committees (PACs) also showed that those charged with administering benefits could have, at times, a very different perspective to that held by the Ministry. In some areas, the government replaced the PACs, notably in County Durham and Rotherham, but on a broader scale this was not a politically acceptable solution, since it would have attracted even more attention towards the unemployed. Instead, the answer lay in 'taking the politics out of relief' (Prosser, 1981). Briggs and Deacon (1973, pp.58–62) have suggested that the establishment of the Unemployment Assistance Board (UAB), with its independent status and its own tribunals, was designed to avoid pressure for more generous allowances. Prosser (1981, p.160) claims that the events of the mid-1930s were intended, in the case of the UAB, to reduce the 'visibility of government policy and that in this the Act was successful'. Furthermore, the result of the Act was to leave claimants with only 'the work people's representative' as an advocate within the administrative machine. As we have seen, this could not have inspired much optimism. The establishment of appeals tribunals became a means of silencing the constituency-conscious MP who had constantly tried to raise matters relating to relief with the Minister responsible (Lynes, 1976, p.30). The effect of the UAB, following some considerable rioting and consequent modifications to the scheme, was virtually to disenfranchise the poor again. They could no longer elect those who sat in judgement upon them, as they could for the PACs and the local Boards of Guardians; neither could they raise their case with the Minister or their MP, since the matter was now to be resolved by the appeals tribunals.

The other way that the unemployed challenged their position was by taking to the streets. In contrast to earlier periods, this was politically motivated and highly organized. From 1920, the unemployed raised among the middle classes and the Cabinet the fear of social unrest (see Murphy, 1972, pp.216–19; Hannington, 1973; Middlemas, 1979, pp.189, 238–41; Kingsford, 1982). Certainly, there was a great deal to worry the government, not least the fact that many of the unemployed were ex-soldiers who were believed to have retained their weapons (Hannington, 1973, p.13). What is more, the Communist Party was largely in the vanguard attempting to direct the struggle through the National Unemployed Workers Movement (NUWM). With unemployment throughout the 1920s and 1930s over 1 million and at times well over the 2 million mark, the NUWM could legitimately claim to represent a significant section of the working class. Middle-class fears were understandable even if they were unlikely to be realized because, once again, there were profound divisions within the working class over how to conduct class struggle.

Political sectarianism, essentially between the Communist Party and the Labour Party, ensured that the unemployed were something of a political football in the inter-war period. This political sectarianism, which was most intense within the trade union movement, spilled over into attitudes to the NUWM (Pelling, 1958). The NUWM was able to organize thousands of the unemployed on demonstrations and marches, even though the TUC frequently attempted to frustrate them by instructing local Trades Councils not to cooperate. However the TUC tried not to disassociate itself completely from the unemployed, and was forced by the NUWM's size alone to voice at least some support (Cole and Postgate, 1961, pp.560–6; Middlemas, 1979, p.189). There can be little doubt that the NUWM, whether it was despite or because of its politics, was *the* organization of the unemployed. It was the driving force for nearly all of the marches and demonstrations that are today associated with the 1930s and unemployment. It occupied the offices of Boards of Guardians, it attempted to represent claimants at the LECs and PACs and did so for appellants to the UAB. It certainly played a part in the delaying of the introduction of the UAB scale rates in 1934 and, if Orwell (1970, pp.199-206) is to be trusted, had substantial local support. It organized a variety of services for the unemployed and was the principal source of political agitation on the question of unemployment throughout the inter-war period (Orwell, 1970, pp.199–202; Hannington, 1973; Kingsford, 1982). Indeed, it could be argued that the NUWM was successful in organizing the unemployed despite the Communist Party. The changes of 'line' that the Comintern insisted upon could easily have split the organization irrevocably but for the fact that Hannington appears to have had a greater commitment to the unemployed than to the directives of his own party (Pelling, 1958, pp.63–4; Pimlott, 1977, p.81).

Whatever the effect of the Communist Party's leading part in the NUWM, it is important to note that the Labour Party was slow to address the question of unemployment. So slow in fact that the TUC and the Labour Party were outflanked by the Communist Party. This led to a strategy on the part of the leadership virtually to exclude the NUWM and the Communist Party from the labour movement. At a local level, especially in the 'depressed areas', the strategy was an abysmal failure. However, nationally, and in the more prosperous West Midlands and the South East, it had a measure of success (Hannington, 1973; Kingsford, 1982).

The inter-war period illustrates how difficult it can be for the poor and the unemployed to organize if they are not supported by the most powerful sections of the labour movement. Political power was effectively denied to the poor and the unemployed. The net effect of the strategy and attitudes held by the TUC, and the Labour Party's more widespread suspicion of the unemployed and the poor, was to marginalize the unemployed and their organizations. The Hunger March, despite its place in the popular historical consciousness, was not a successful political strategy. It represented an attempt to get the issues of poverty and unemployment onto the political agenda and, as such, was more a sign of frustration and exclusion than of anything more dangerous.

Middlemas (1979, p.215) has summarized the inter-war period thus:

> . . . for those in work the 1930s turned out to be a period of steady, even complacent prosperity, and the unions only reflected their members' preoccupations when they gave priority to the defence of existing jobs and wages, rather than to the creation of new jobs or betterment of the conditions of the unemployed.

The impact of war

For Titmuss (1958, pp.75–87), the Second World War marked a profound shift in attitudes to welfare provision. Evacuation, centralized state planning, a reduction in stigma, an acceptance of state provision and a sense of social cohesion, combined to ensure the development of welfare. As the person who took on the responsibility of writing the Social Policy History of the Second World War, Titmuss started from a position that was likely to emphasize change rather than continuity. Relying heavily on Andrzejewski's (1954) work, Titmuss (1958, p.86) argued that: 'The aims and content of social policy, both in peace and in war, are thus determined – at least to a substantial extent – by how far the co-operation of the masses is essential to the successful prosecution of war.' Subsequently, a number of scholars have queried this assertion (Addison, 1975; Fraser, 1984). Thane (1982), in particular, has provided a convincing argument that there were a number of important continuities and that the Second World War did not, of itself, herald a period of radical change.

Nevertheless, the war saw a shift from conservatism, in terms of both governments and outlook, to 'not plain "Labourism", but a leftish volatility' (Thompson, 1984). The Labour Party election victory of 1945 is, quite simply, inexplicable without referring to a change in popular consciousness. For the organized labour movement, the war clearly marked a change in fortune. Between 1938 and 1945, the percentage of workers in unions rose from 30.5 to 38.6 percent. This can be put into even starker contrast when we consider that, in 1933, only 22.6 percent of the workforce were union members (Price and Bain, 1983, p.5). Without the cooperation of the unions, the prosecution of the war would at best have been difficult, and at worst impossible.

During the war, social divisions were markedly reduced, partly as a consequence of full employment, considerable overtime, and the massive induction of women into paid employment. It was also partly due to wartime social policies. Rationing, the increased numbers in receipt of school meals and free school milk, nursery provision which enabled women to work, the part played by the Assistance Board in supplementing pensioners' incomes, a more redistributive tax system, tax controls on war profits and a more co-ordinated health service, all combined to improve the condition of the working class as a whole. Much of the legislation was arguably a rationaliz-ation of social policy that was long overdue, but the SDW seems to have been modified in favour of the weakest and poorest members of society. The backdrop to these changes has often been seen as the consensus which existed during the war, a view that has to be questioned (Titmuss, 1958).

The constructed consensus

A closer examination of the war suggests that: (a) if there was a consensus, it was short-lived, and carefully constructed; (b) that while some social divisions were reduced, the seeds of future divisions were sown and that some of the older divisions were deeply rooted; and (c) class conflict was muted through incorporation and collaboration rather than being resolved.

In 1944, Orwell wrote that: '. . . cynicism about after the war is widespread, and the "we're all in it together" feeling of 1940 has faded away'. And he went on:

> . . . the great political topic of the last few weeks has been the Beveridge Report on Social Security. People seem to feel that this very moderate measure of reform is almost too good to be true. Except for the tiny interested minority, everyone is pro-Beveridge – including left-wing papers which a few years ago would have denounced such a scheme as semi-Fascist – and at the same time no-one believes Beveridge's plan will actually be adopted (Orwell, 1970, p.318).

Orwell's scepticism was well founded. Powerful interests and individuals were concerned that Beveridge may have raised false hopes. Among those concerned were the Treasury, the Chancellor of the Exchequer and the Prime Minister – fairly weighty opponents it might be thought – who all expressed grave doubts about the implementation of the various proposals. In the post-war economy, they felt it would be difficult to direct scarce resources to social policy.

Incorporation

The war ensured the need for organized labour's cooperation in the production of goods and armaments. The quid pro quo was that the coalition government would ensure that the burden of the war was borne by all classes. If the government had not appeared to be willing to introduce social policies that promised a better future – with the Beveridge Report and the 1944 White Paper on employment apparently promising a very real break with the pre-war period – it is doubtful if organized labour could have retained control of grass roots activists in the last 2 years of the war. The welfare state was part of the price that had to be paid for 'consensus' – it did not arise from it. This 'bribe', as Orwell had called it, was the necessary cost of cooperation.

During the war, thousands of rank-and-file trade unionists had been involved in tripartite committees and bodies. In June 1944, there were 4500 Joint Production Committees alone. On these committees, employers and trade unionists discussed how to resolve production difficulties, industrial relations problems, attain production targets and generally assist in the war effort (Cronin, 1984, pp.118–19). It was not only in these factory-based committees that organized labour was accorded a voice. Throughout the whole range of social, political and economic issues, the labour movement was accorded credibility. By the end of the war, organized labour had a central role within the machinery of the state. As Crouch (1982, pp.21–2) has observed of the 1940s:

> A major motive of the government in extending participation was to reduce the area of conflict between the unions and capital by taking union leaders into a structure in which they could be persuaded to cooperate and adopt the views of government and industry on economic priorities.

And writing from a Marxist perspective, Gough (1979, p.70) has observed that:

> A post-war political "settlement" between representatives of capital and organized labour was essential to lay the basis for (what later transpired to be) the unprecedented boom of the next two decades. As part of this strategy, welfare reforms and the welfare state played an important role.

This neo-corporatist strategy was not one that was foisted upon organized labour and big business by the state. Organized labour had built up its industrial strength during the war but feared a return to the conditions of the 1930s. It sought to cooperate with government to ensure there was no return to the pre-war conditions. Likewise, many employers were nervous in case a Labour government was elected. They hoped to influence the policies of any Labour government by discussion, as they had during the war. In the event, the election of Labour in 1945 with a massive Parliamentary majority, and a trade union movement which was as strong and well organized as it had ever been, made the employers' strategy appear most prudent. The basis of the post-war settlement, in which organized labour, big business and the corporatist welfare state each played their part in ensuring social harmony, was set during the war. Thus, it is not that the leadership suddenly began to collaborate with capital that marks the shift, for many had been trying to do so since the 1920s. Moreover, by 1945, the vast bulk of the population, including the Communist Party, expected the leadership of organized labour to cooperate with big business and the state (Marwick, 1968, pp.288–95; Addison, 1975, pp.234–5; Gough, 1979, pp.69–71).

Munitions, motor manufacture and aircraft manufacture all underwent radical transformation during the war. The processes of production had to be expanded and speeded up. The assembly line had to operate faster and had to be applied to new items. The detailed division of labour was further subdivided to enable the unskilled draftees to perform their tasks as rapidly as was humanly possible. The decline in the number of unskilled workers between 1939 and 1949 can partially be explained in terms of displaced agricultural and domestic workers, but there was simultaneously an increase in the numbers engaged in 'semi-skilled' work (Cronin, 1984, pp.134–6). These changes encouraged shop floor representation, as did the emphasis during the war on production targets and a cooperative effort to meet these, along with bonus and incentive schemes, piece-work and a large amount of overtime. The shop stewards movement gained a new lease of life following the defeats of the 1920s. As we shall see in the next chapter, these changes would return to haunt governments throughout the 1950s and into the 1970s.

And exclusion

It should not be thought that the TUC, Labour ministers, shop stewards and local labour movement activists, spent a great deal of energy pressing for welfare reforms – in the main they did not. Rather, welfare policies were politically crucial in the eyes of the government and, in the wake of the Mass Observation reports, if wartime morale was to be maintained (Deacon, 1984). The TUC was given a 'place at the top table' (Newman, 1981) because it was functionally necessary to wartime production, and because it was seen as a representative of 'working people'. MacGregor's (1981, p.13) assessment of the evidence presented to the Beveridge Committee suggests, however, that the TUC only represented the interests of particular working people:

> The trade union's representatives to the Beveridge Committee had expressed the traditional values of the labour aristocracy: they were in favour of contributory insurance; contemptuous of 'dodgers', the 'very poor', and of 'the type of person who will not join a Friendly Society'; and, perhaps surprisingly, the leaders of the delegation favoured the withdrawal of public assistance from the wives and children of workers who went on strike.

And, as Harris (1977, pp.150–5, 400–2, 415) points out, Beveridge was far more concerned to note any objections from the unions during the Second World War than he had been in the past.

Whether or not it was due to the TUC's evidence, the Beveridge Report removed any proposal to assist single parents, through the insurance scheme, prior to publication. Few voices were raised in opposition, despite the fact that the report was laying the basis for millions of women to be dependent on a male 'breadwinner' (the old family wage) or on means-tested public welfare. It is remarkable that women, who were asked to make such tremendous sacrifices during the war, were so poorly rewarded for their efforts (Lewenhak, 1977, pp.234–70; Braybon and Summerfield, 1987). Beveridge's 'promised land' held some hope for women but very little that would endure in the post-war world. Beveridge, despite considering the particular needs of women, largely excluded them from his report. Like so many others, he concluded that once the country returned to 'normality', women would return to the family home (Harris, 1977; Wilson, 1977, pp.150–6; Thane, 1982, pp.243-67).

In effect, the needs of women could be ignored because of their political marginalization. Women were not considered part of the necessary consensus. Although equal pay gained support and played some part in income redistribution during the war, this too has to be accepted only with some qualifications The Amalgamated Engineering Union (AEU), for example, finally relaxed its exclusion of women workers and sought equal pay for them. But they were confined to a special 'women's section', with lower subscription rates and benefits than even the lowest grade male worker. Cronin (1984, p.116) suggests that if it had not been for the pressure that Bevin applied, even this small advance would not have been realized. Nor did the engineering union pursue equal pay out of consideration for its women members. Rather, they were looking to the post-war period when they anticipated – correctly in the main – that employers would dismiss women workers in favour of men where 'a rate for the job' applied (Lewenhak, 1977). Women gained most in those trades and sectors of employment which had previously been very difficult to organize. Bevin used the Essential Works Order Act of 1941 to direct labour and prevent workers changing jobs, but in return he expected employers to recognize the relevant trade unions. Employers who failed to conform were not protected by the Essential Works Order and often thereby lost their workers to the better paying war industries (Hinton, 1983, p.163).

Nor did the supposed 'universalism' and 'consensus' of the 1940s extend to black people. During the war, with US servicemen in Britain, the importation of black labour, and the arrival of many black Commonwealth subjects keen to defend the 'mother country', it might be thought that racism would have been out of the question. It seems, however, that institutional racism did not evaporate in the warm glow of 'universalism' (Sherman, 1985). Although the British Government urged the USA to come to the aid of a friendly state, it was nervous of ordinary citizens who might extend their friendship to black American troops. The colour bar was extensively used to segregate black servicemen, and workers recruited from the West Indies, Belize and elsewhere were often confined to labour camps (Fryer, 1984;

Sherman, 1985; Smith, 1987). Cohen (1985, p.88) suggests that even the Beveridge Report, and Beveridge himself, exhibited 'the most narrow kind of racial and sexual chauvinism'. It is certainly a strange 'universalism' that reproduces racist arguments for the need to propagate the 'British peoples'.

For white workers, whether they were skilled or not, social divisions were reduced during the war. Certainly the post-war prospects for even the poorest white male were considerably better than could have been expected in the mid-1930s. The war radically reduced unemployment and once again the idea of a hopeless class of unemployables, which had gained ground in the 1930s, could be dismissed. The massive increase in the employment of married women, combined with the millions of men drafted into the forces, ensured that the household incomes of the poor rose substantially. Simultaneously, the ground was prepared for the seeds of social divisions in the post-war period.

Summary

During the First World War, the 'residuum' – that hopeless class of idlers of late Victorian Britain – were recruited into the army and a buoyant labour market. The implication was obvious: they had always been prepared to work if it was available. Women were brought into industries from which they had previously been excluded and, as a consequence, the sexual division of labour was radically redrawn for the duration of the First World War. At the end of the war, however, divisions were restored as a more dynamic working class struggled to assert itself. Following the defeats of 1918–1922, culminating with the ill-fated General Strike of 1926, the strategy reverted to economism and sectionalism. Throughout the period 1914–1945, the labour process underwent rapid changes and the trend towards breaking down the craft control of the skilled and well-organized workers, apparent for at least 20 years before the war, increased. The transformation of the labour process was bolstered by the ideas of scientific management and paternalism. The former divided workers according to the tasks they performed, whereas the latter increasingly used occupational welfare as a reward system which simultaneously reinforced these divisions. Both had the effect of widening differentials within the SDW.

The SDW was also redefined in this period by the use of administrative techniques in which organized labour played a major part. The unemployed were stigmatized by the GSWT and impoverished by the household means test. Public welfare, in the form of local authority housing, segregated sections of the working class and, with improvements in the consumption patterns of some workers, these factors effectively divided the working class according to location. The political marginalization of the poor and the unemployed was facilitated in part by their place in society both geographically and in relation to the labour process. However, the activities of the poor themselves should not be forgotten; after all, the hunger march is an enduring image of the inter-war period. Nevertheless, this too was profoundly influenced by the form and direction of class struggle. By their desire to gain access to the corridors of power, seen by some as a 'corporatist bias', the leadership of the labour movement abandoned the poor and the unemployed, led by the NUWM, to their own devices. As a Communist Party organ, the NUWM was often isolated from those in work due to the sectarianism and suspicion between themselves, the TUC and the Labour Party.

Finally, the Second World War, although reproducing many of the mistakes of the Great War, did regenerate a more unified and homogeneous view of the future. In this it sought to develop a welfare package which, despite the improvements, did nothing to overturn the pattern of privilege inherent in the SDW before the war. Rather, it reasserted the insurance principle in a manner which ensured that social divisions in the future would not, by and large, affect white, male, skilled workers.

Corporatism, exclusion and a new 'underclass'?: 1945–1990

Well I'm a union man,
Amazed at what I am
  I say what I think,
Coz the company stinks
Yes, I'm a union man.
When we meet in the local hall,
I'll be voting with em all,
and with a helluva shout
  it's 'Out brothers out'!
and the rise of the factory's fall.
Oooohwwwwwwwwwwhhhh . . . .
You don't get me I'm part of the union.

(The Strawbs reached number 2 in the charts with this song and it was a 'hit' for 11 weeks in 1973)

In this chapter, our historical trip reaches its end. The reader is transported back to the present and asked to consider the implications of current changes in the SDW. The chapter initially looks at the post-war scene, which is often associated with 'universalism' and consensus. As we get nearer to the 1990s, it will be observed that social divisions are once again a major concern of the middle classes. One of the key factors in the revival of interest is the observable gap between the well-placed worker in the SDW and the poor.

A new Jerusalem

Full employment was the cornerstone of post-war reconstruction. It underpinned both political and economic strategy. Arguably, every government until the 1970s was committed to maintaining full employment, but the price was wage restraint. This in turn gave organized labour a major role in post-war Britain. However, it is necessary to clarify what 'full employment' meant. Not until the 1950s did politicians and economists begin to believe that unemployment could be kept below 3 percent, even though it had been close to 2 percent for most of the post-war years. The figure most commonly accepted as the minimum level to which it might be reduced was 8.5 percent. Indeed, in 1944, when Beveridge had suggested unemployment might be kept down to 3 percent, this was 'greeted with some scorn in Whitehall' (Deacon, 1981, pp.64–7). The point is that, even at the higher levels of unemployment, it was firmly believed that wage restraint was a necessary precondition of success. As Deacon (1981, p.65) makes clear:

> The need for moderation in wage claims was stressed in the White Paper (p.18) and in virtually every discussion of the subject. There seemed no alternative, however, but to rely on the common sense of the trade union leaders and the patriotism and responsibility of the individual worker.

Wartime experience and the close relationship that had been established between the state, employers and the trade union leadership suggested that everyone understood the ground rules that were to govern the post-war period. In brief, these consisted of a commitment on the part of the state to a form of Keynesian economics and Beveridge's social policies. State intervention through planning controls, grants and nationalization restricted industrial capital's flexibility, and it was expected that capital would continue, as it had during the war, to cooperate with the state. Incomes policies, both statutory and voluntary, were intended to prevent organized labour from exploiting the favourable labour market conditions produced by full employment-policies. Through a host of committees, quasi-autonomous government organizations (Quangos) and regular consultation, big business, organized labour and the state were bound together. The wartime model of cooperation towards a common goal was adopted for peacetime as well.

The corporatist pact was meant to ensure restraint, cooperation and an acceptance that it was not possible to pursue sectional interests too vigorously. In return, organized labour expected the state to deliver economic prosperity, welfare legislation and labour market buoyancy. In part, all sides honoured their commitment during the late 1940s and early 1950s. However, even in the 1940s, some employers sought to gain an edge over their competitors by hoarding skilled labour (Gamble, 1985). Rank-and-file trade unionists were also quick to exploit their labour market strength. Closed-shop agreements began to flourish, and the shop steward's movement grew in strength, partly as a result of changes in production and bonus systems, and partly because the leadership were not exploiting the favourable labour market. As a consequence, wages in the late 1940s and 1950s, when reconstruction was *the* objective, outstripped production and Britain's share of the world market steadily fell. The progressive taxation policies of the early post-war years were quickly abandoned (Dow, 1964, p.47). Profit levels were maintained by tax concessions on corporate income and nationalized industries soon became heavily subsidized services (Hinton, 1983). In addition, there were grants, direct investment allowances and subsidies to private sector companies. By 1971, Hinton claims, the combined value of these subsidies amounted to more than the total expenditure on housing. Hinton estimates that nearly 40 percent of research and development costs in the private sector were paid by the government (Hinton, 1983, p.180). The welfare state, it appears, consists – as Titmuss observed in the 1950s – of more than the visible benefits paid to the poor.

The incorporation of organized labour is significant for two reasons. First, it represents 'the logic of collective action' within the parameters laid down by capitalist social relations. Like the artisans of the early nineteenth century and the 'labour aristocrats' of the second half of the nineteenth century, it enabled sectional interests to be articulated without changing the overall balance of power within capitalist society. By the 1970s, trade union leaders were so tightly enmeshed in the web of corporatism they had little time for anything else (Coates and Topham, 1986). Secondly, corporatism in Britain has a certain 'close fitting relationship' with social democratic politics. In this sense, Jessop's (1979) view that corporatism provides the shell within which social democracy operates describes well the events of the post-war period.

Simultaneously, it is important to recognize that corporatism was not the only strategy that was open to organized labour. Panitch's (1981) claim, that industrial relations in Britain has produced both the corporatist tendency and its contradictions, has to be borne in mind. Thus, despite the involvement of the leadership in a variety of tripartite arrangements, the rank and file developed their own strategies designed to exploit the favourable labour market. Many of these strategies hinged on the ability to maintain demarcation lines, protect existing working practices and restrict entry to the trade, industry or workshop. In other words, the labour process was at the heart of many of the industrial conflicts of the post-war period.

Labour market and labour process

It is impossible to discuss changes in the labour process in the 1940s and 1950s without setting these in the context of full employment. The post-war commitment to full employment, embodied in the 1944 White Paper, represented a major concession to organized labour. The reservations many Ministers and civil servants had about the viability of keeping unemployment levels below 8 percent were shared by some trade union leaders. Nevertheless, the assertions of commitment to this objective were both presented as a major break with the pre-war period, and perceived as such by workers and their representatives. It remains to be shown how this dovetails with the changes in the labour process made during and after the war. It is equally important to acknowledge the ability of particular trades and industries to resist change. The image of responsible, cooperative and progressive trade unionism, which many people had in the early 1940s, was to be transformed in the 1950s and 1960s. Whether the subsequent image, of bloody-minded and selfish workers, is one that the media ought to be blamed for is debatable. Certainly, the two images can be contrasted and 20 years after the war 'restrictive practices' were being identified as one, if not the major, brake on productivity and Britain's ability to compete internationally. However, what the employer sees as 'restrictive practices', the worker may regard as defending craft skills.

During the war, shop floor workers – many of whom were inexperienced in the arena of industrial relations – relied heavily on direct and immediate representation to management. The lessons of this period were to be applied by both management and unions in the 1950s. In the car industry in particular, management tried to introduce new production processes while workers used their shop floor power to disrupt production (Willman, 1986, pp.149-63). In most other industries after the war, there was a return to the pre-war traditions. The language of 'modernization', newer management techniques and line production – all of which involved breaking the hold of certain well-organized workers over demarcation lines, working practices and skills – was not heard in mining, textiles, heavy engineering, shipbuilding and chemicals (Cronin, 1984, pp.134–7; Barnett, 1986).

As early as 1943, Stafford Cripps foresaw the problems of low productivity and conflict over production processes that would be likely to arise. In 1948, he was Chancellor of the Exchequer, fighting a lone battle to persuade Cabinet colleagues, union leaders and the wider public of the need to change. He appreciated that longer working hours, pay restraint and cooperation would not alter the productivity of British industry without changes in the organization of work. In order to compete with the USA, Germany and, increasingly, Japan, investment would have to be directed towards the modernization of machinery and, arguably more important, the organization of production itself. Employers, management and investors were partly at fault for failing to take even a medium-term view of their prospects, let alone investing for the longer term. However, the trade unions were also blamed for their 'I'm all right Jack' attitudes. Thus the much vaunted 'power of the unions' lay not with the leadership and bureaucrats, who so often were the butt of Fleet Street's wrath, but the shop floor. Shop stewards who resisted change in the labour process because it would undermine their ability to negotiate directly with management – as indeed it has since 1979 – were pressing the leadership and rarely vice versa (Middlemas, 1986, pp.159–64, 176–8).

While the TUC jealously protected its privileged position on various tripartite bodies, the rank-and-file activists sought to improve pay and conditions through unofficial disputes and the less obvious control of working practices. The shop floor organizer, and 'custom and practice', stood in the way of the trade union leadership and 'modernization'. Resistance to technological change has a long history when it threatens well-organized sections of the working class. Not that resistance is any guarantee of success, and it may be a better tactical move to negotiate changes. The failure of the Luddites is deeply ingrained in the popular consciousness, and consequently there are numerous examples of negotiation between employers and trade unions over new technology. Indeed, Willman (1986) suggests that between 1945 and 1970, organized labour as a whole was in favour of technological innovation. Certainly, the TUC wanted to encourage investment in new technology and the Wilson government of the 1960s made this a central plank in their electoral appeals. On the other hand, Willman admits that changes in the production process, rather than in products and product development, were more likely to face opposition. Thus the relationship between organized labour and technological change is not straightforward, but there has been a consistent attempt to resist changes in the labour process which might undermine the position of well-organized workers.

Despite the reservations above, it remains the case that class struggle and the labour process have been closely related since the war. On the one hand, the labour process is contested and is therefore the site of class struggle; on the other, it also serves to enhance or reduce the combativity of workers. To a certain extent, success breeds success. A weak or non-existent grip on the labour process not only makes it more difficult to mount any solidaristic struggles with workers in a similar location, but it also makes it harder to resist any further weakening of that hold.

This point is emphasized by Therborn's (1983) discussion of the labour process in relation to class struggle. Therborn identifies two important aspects of class struggle that play a crucial part in explaining success or failure. (A third feature is the source of wealth making, which we can leave to one side since it is not directly relevant to our discussion at this point.) The two claims that are most interesting are:

1. The more homogeneous the workforce, the more easily collectivity may develop out of it.
2. The greater the degree of autonomy available to workers as a collectivity in the labour process, the more successful they will be.

Since the Second World War encouraged homogeneity, we should not be surprised that the working class exercised their collective muscle. They may have used it for economistic and sectional purposes but we must acknowledge the part played by economistic trade union struggles within the broader pattern of class struggle.

The second of Therborn's criteria concerns workers' 'skill' in relation to management's control of the labour process. However, 'skill' does not necessarily refer to dexterity and training. He points out that dockers are rarely regarded as skilled workers but they have, since the Second World War, exerted considerable collective control over their work process and this has only been threatened by the container depot. Indeed, the managerial capacity for control was severely restricted until the mid-1970s and Ther-born claims that the growth of container cargo can be seen as the first initiative in the employers' counter-offensive. Therborn also points out that the ability of organized labour to assert control and to attain homogeneity is circumscribed by the local labour market. In the 1950s and 1960s, with virtually full employment, and trade union control of apprenticeships and – in some unskilled industries – admission to the industry, Therborn's analysis is persuasive.

The advantage of such an analysis is that it locates arguments over 're-strictive practices' in the context of class struggle. But, as Therborn also acknowledges, class struggle involves adversaries and, by the 1960s, 'the managerial revolution' and the increasing use of immigrant and female labour were to see a counter-offensive by the employer class (Therborn, 1983, pp.37–56).

Controlling the unions

The long boom of the 1950s and 1960s was accompanied by two strategies, both designed to counteract the effects of 'full' employment. There was an attempt to import cheap labour and at the same time a desire to control the unions. Taking the second point first, the state sought greater control of the trade unions and a more flexible response from them towards 'restrictive practices'. This strategy, however, was a response to the control that labour had asserted. In the 1960s, the state entered the fray because the trade union leadership either would not, or could not, regulate the rank and file. Thus in 1966, Harold Wilson, then Prime Minister, made a deliberately well pub-licized speech to the Party Conference in Blackpool in which he attacked restrictive practices. He said:

> The biggest challenge facing the trade union movement in the produc-tivity drive is the elimination of every avoidable restrictive practice. . . . In the conditions we face today, so far from being a protection against unemployment they are the surest road to it. . . . One false careless step could push the world into conditions not unlike those of the early thirties (Wilson, 1974, p.355).

In using the spectre of the 1930s, Wilson was, in effect, threatening the union rank and file with a paper tiger. It was thought to be political suicide at this time for any government to preside over a return to mass unemployment.

There can be little doubt that most shop floor activists were unimpressed by such threats. Nor, despite their frequent attempts at doing so, could the trade union leadership and the government find a means by which the rank and file could be restrained. The 'British Disease', as it was called, involved unofficial disputes, 'restrictive practices' and trade union pettiness. Al-though every attempt was made to identify shop floor representatives as the culprits, since in the main these were matters over which the leadership had little control, the policy backfired. By the late 1960s and early 1970s, the leadership of many unions was looking to what its membership demanded and resisting government attempts at restraint. Jack Jones and Hugh Scanlon, of the Transport and General Workers Union (TGWU) and the Amalgamated Union of Engineering Workers (AUEW) respectively, came to epitomize a more aggressive leadership. The media was not slow to characterize such leaders as the scourge of the nation. In reality, the leadership was never too far behind, nor too far ahead, of the membership. During the 1960s and 1970s, the rank and file were frequently in combative mood, and certainly not ready to relinquish control over working practices. As Panitch (1981, p.35) has observed of the late 1960s and early 1970s: 'The effect on the union leadership was readily visible, as they ran after the members, not merely in a cynical attempt to retain organizational control, but often as a genuine response to their base.'

Throughout the 1970s, however, successive governments made vain attempts to resurrect the corporatist pact of the 1940s. Despite the Industrial Relations Acts and an incomes policy, the Heath government of the early 1970s still maintained the appearance, and usually the practice, of the corporatist pact. Although unemployment rose in the early 1970s it was too low to deter the rank and file. In the end, Edward Heath's administration was defeated by the best organized sections of the working class who, for the moment anyway, were prepared to support local and unofficial leaders. The shop stewards' movement was able to retain a large measure of autonomy from the official union leadership and continued to be the first line of defence for many workers.

The period 1974–1979 when Labour was in office is sometimes seen as the definitive period, and climactic eclipse, of corporatism. If so, it bears out the claim above that exclusion is the other side of the corporatist coin. The rhetoric of the 'Social Contract' was never matched by action. Indeed, as will be shown when we consider the changes that occurred in the SDW at this time, welfare divisions within the working class appear to have widened. At a time of wage restraint occupational welfare – sick pay and pensions especially – was often improved for the best organized workers. These benefits were frequently tied to a spurious productivity package (Green et al., 1984), although it is necessary to qualify this by noting that few trade unionists now say that they tried to circumvent incomes policies at this time (Mann and Anstee, 1989).

By late 1978 the Labour government appeared to be impotent in the face of 'union power' during 'the winter of discontent'. Many workers openly flouted the incomes policy and this was a major reason for Labour's electoral failure. With the election of the Conservatives in 1979, the gloves were taken off. The corporatist deal was dropped and with mass unemployment a reality, employers had the go ahead to 'rationalize' production and hold down wages. The effect was to encourage those social divisions that had been developing since the 1940s.

Creating an underclass?

The second feature of post-war Britain that has to be emphasized is the importation of workers from former colonies. As we saw in Chapter 4, racism had been apparent during the war and the 'colour bar' was carried over into the post-war era in a manner which segregated black settlers. Similarly, as early as 1949, Bevan was proudly telling Parliament that immigration officers were turning away aliens who sought to abuse the health service (Cohen, 1985, p.89). Racism did not, therefore, suddenly become a problem in the 1950s when immigration began on a grander scale. Racism had been a problem for anyone who was not white for many years.

What mass immigration did was to make racism a problem for whites when those who were recruited to do the most menial and dirty jobs began to question their second-class status. With very little unemployment in the 1950s, employers began to look to the poorest countries of the Commonwealth for workers. It was also hoped that labour from the former colonies would be more 'manageable' than the existing labour force. Enoch Powell, as Minister of Health, successfully recruited nurses and ancillary staff from the Caribbean islands, India, Mauritius and other former outposts of the Empire. London Transport also desperately needed workers and sought them from the same countries. Simultaneously, thousands of West Indians, Pakistanis and Indians were attracted to 'the Mother Country', as they were led to regard Britain, by the prospect of work, an absence of absolute poverty and natural disasters, and the hope of something better (Fryer, 1984, pp.372–86, Layton-Henry and Rich, 1986, pp.18–21).

Immigrant labour was actively recruited in order to fill the jobs previously done by poor whites. The workers who were recruited in the 1950s and 1960s, however, were easier to identify than those who had formerly filled the lowest ranks of the labour market because of their colour. The effect was to provide a stratum of workers who were drafted to Britain to perform the lowest paid and most menial jobs. Neither employers nor trade unions anticipated that these workers would be a permanent addition to the working class. Thus the failure to confront racism during the war, when it should be remembered we were ostensibly fighting Fascism, signalled what was to occur in the 1950s and after. One of the legacies of the Second World War was that the immigrants were confronted by landlords/ladies who refused to let rooms to 'coloureds'. Local authorities and building societies also discriminated against black and Asian applicants by setting certain 'zones' or estates aside. By the late 1960s, the situation led some academic observers to suggest that discrimination was creating a number of social divisions based on housing tenure. The idea of 'housing classes' was used by a number of social scientists to emphasize the effects racism had upon the ability of specific social groups to gain access to some of the more desirable types of tenure. Others, notably Giddens (1973), saw the prospect of intergenerational disadvantage, due to racism, and the possibility of a permanent underclass. The problems with these conceptions of social divisions is discussed in the next chapter, but it should be noted that this research did serve to emphasize the spatial segregation of black people (Rex and Moore, 1967; Pahl, 1970; Rex, 1971; Rex and Tomlinson, 1979).

Moreover, at a time when Marxists were clinging to 'the primacy of class' to dismiss racism within the working class, Weberian sociology was acknowledging, however inadequately, the specific feature of discrimination, i.e. racism based on colour. Although successive studies found that discrimination was widespread in housing, employment and virtually every other area of social life, this need not have disturbed many within government and Whitehall. Far more worrying for government was the prospect of US style 'racial disturbances'. Unprovoked attacks by white, mainly working-class youth – initially Teddy boys and later skinheads – saw black people respond. Riots in 1958 were the first sign that, as had happened with Jewish and Irish immigrants, black communities would defend themselves. Not only did the police rarely identify and arrest whites for attacks on blacks but they were increasingly accused of being racist themselves. By the 1970s, the police were seen by many blacks, as the front-line troops for the protection of a racist society. But it is misleading to point the finger at white working-class youth and the police and suggest that between them they were responsible for the situation that confronted blacks in the 1960s (Sivanandan, 1982; Fryer, 1984).

At every level of society there was a consistent failure to confront racism. As Fryer (1984, p.381) states:

> Between 1958 and 1968 black settlers in Britian watched as the racist tail wagged the parliamentary dog. It was a sustained triumph of expediency over principle. Fearful of being outflanked by fascists and each other, fearful of losing votes and seats, Tories and Labour politicians progressively accommodated themselves to racism.

Politicians of all parties tended to discuss 'the immigrant problem' and the 'race relations problems' posed by the new arrivals. The emphasis was subtly, and sometimes not so subtly, shifted away from the problems settlers confronted to the problems they posed for whites. Politicians, in the main, pandered to the white voter. It was electorally safer to blame the victims than to confront racism. Despite commitments to former colonies, entry to Britain was made increasingly difficult for people of colour in order to placate white electoral opinion.

Once again, however, it is important to note that the state was, in the main, responding to divisions within the working class and not intent on creating them. The stance taken by the labour movement at this time, 1958–1972, was crucially important, since it was to provide government and politicians with an indication of working-class opinion. Consequently, when dockers and Smithfield meat market porters downed tools and marched to the House of Commons in support of Enoch Powell's inflammatory racism, the message was unequivocal. The white working class, by and large, wanted restrictions on black immigration.

However, if exclusion from the country failed, then they would be excluded from the defence organizations of the working class. Thus, when black workers took industrial action in the 1960s, they were rarely supported by white trade unionists, and on occasions shop stewards and full-time officials undermined their efforts. Simultaneously, some trade unionists complained that West Indian and Asian workers were reluctant to join unions, a claim that was not sustained by the evidence. Where black workers had not joined trade unions it was likely that discrimination was rife within the shop stewards' committee or the local union branch. Where black workers felt they could present their views, they were more likely than their white counterparts to be union members (Smith, 1977; Sivanandan, 1982; Fryer, 1984, p.385). For skilled and semi-skilled white workers in particular, who had enjoyed the greater rewards that a buoyant labour market bestowed upon them, black workers were seen as a threat. How much of this perceived threat was based on xenophobic racism and how far a genuine belief that the strategy based on 'dual closure' (Parkin, 1979) was threatened, is debatable. Certainly racists appealed to both lines of argument in shop floor discussions.

Of course, racism was not confined to discrimination in housing, in attacks on blacks in the streets, police harassment and exclusion at work. Abuse at school, shit pushed through letter boxes, petrol bomb attacks on homes and businesses, and the daubing of homes, were all intended to push the 'settlers' into a second-class status. Even going out for a quiet drink could run into a wall of exclusion. Pubs and working men's clubs frequently banned 'coloureds'. The organized labour movement's response in the 1950s and 1960s was in line with that witnessed during previous periods of immigration. At best it consisted of pious resolutions at national conferences; at worst it involved discreet collaboration with employers and trade union activists operating blatantly racist policies. Of course, there was also institutional racism and the practices of employers, schools, universities, the professions and the media, among others, were arguably as significant. Overall, the effect was to assign the black population a kind of second-class citizenship. The point is that organized labour, from the shop floor up to the parliamentary Labour Party, failed to confront racism. In not doing so, organized labour assisted, as Ramdin (1987) puts it, in 'the making of the black working class in Britain'.

All the subsequent anti-racist policies have to be set in this context. Labour governments, the Labour Party, local authorities, the TUC, national and local trade union officials, right down to shop stewards, they all either retreated from confronting racism within the movement or were frustrated by their peers who were pursuing racist policies. Nor did such policies evaporate as the trade unions began, belatedly and cautiously, to take racism as a more serious issue. For example, in the 1980s, 'ring fencing' policies by trade unions in the public sector sought to protect the jobs of their members during local government reorganization and the privatization of public utilities. The policy, in brief, sought to draw a line around existing employees and to ensure that no outsiders were given the opportunity of competing for jobs within the 'ring fence'. Unfortunately, the vast majority of the membership was recruited in the 1960s and 1970s and was over-whelmingly white. Thus the sectionalism and defensive nature of British trade unionism has served to reinforce social divisions, even when national trade union policy has emphasized equal opportunities. Not that this should be surprising given the evidence presented in previous chapters. As has been shown, intra-class divisions have often focused on race and gender and have been articulated through defensive class struggles.

A new sexual division of labour?

The other group of workers asked to accept a secondary status in the 1950s and 1960s were women, when the sexual division of labour was redefined once more. By the late 1960s, married women in particular were being recruited into the labour market at an increasingly rapid pace. There have been two major features of female employment since the 1960s: first, there has been a massive influx of women into service industries and clerical work; secondly, there has been a growth in the numbers of workers who are employed on a part-time basis. In tandem, these features of the sexual division of labour mean that women are confined, in the main, to the lowest grades of work in the clerical and service sectors. Moreover, the oppor-tunities for most women to escape low-status, poorly paid, part-time work have been, and continue to be, restricted by training schemes, employers' expectations and women's principal responsibility for domestic labour and child care (Buswell, 1987).

Although changes occurred in the sexual division of labour, there is ample evidence of continuity, particularly in respect of wages. There have been improvements, but in the last 100 years women's wages have only risen from roughly 50 percent of the male wage to 65 percent. If the same rate of change were sustained in the future, equal pay would not be achieved until the year 2218, or thereabouts. The sexual division of labour also prevents women from gaining promotion even in those sectors in which they con-stitute the bulk of the workforce. Thus, although women comprise more than 70 percent of all clerks, they are only rarely promoted (Crompton and Jones, 1984, p.3). Despite trade union and TUC conference resolutions supporting equal pay and opportunities, leading to the adoption in the 1970s of the Working Women's Charter, the sexual division of labour has remained intact.

Women's employment and opportunity patterns have been profoundly influenced by changes in the labour process. The introduction of new tech-nology, and the application of older scientific management techniques to the organization of clerical work, have had the effect of dividing non-manual occupations into two categories. The bulk of the work is routine and for-mal, in line with the classically Weberian concept of bureaucratic admin-istration. Distinct from these tasks are a range of decision-making and administrative tasks which involve the use of discretion. In general, women are confined to the former types of work, whereas men are promoted into the latter (Crompton and Jones, 1984). The combination of employment within specific industries and sectors, low pay, part-time employment and lack of promotion to managerial positions has encouraged the idea that the labour market can be divided into two sectors. For some commentators, there exists a dual labour market (Barron and Norris, 1976), and more recently others have identified 'core and peripheral' workers (Atkinson and Gregory, 1986). Both accounts point to a measure of segregation in the labour market based in part on promotion, internal labour markets and occupational welfare. For those who are permanently employed, there is a range of welfare benefits. For peripheral workers, on the other hand, it is possible that they will be excluded from any welfare benefits. These ideas will be examined in more detail in the next chapter, but it is important to note the implications for the SDW. Core workers will be in a relatively more privileged position than peripheral workers. For women, this has ensured the perpetuation of a sexual division of welfare within the SDW. Similarly, access to the more advantageous positions in the labour market is denied to the bulk of the black population. However, for the rather woolly claim that there exists a new underclass (Field, 1989) to be justified, evidence of these divisions being maintained over decades and generations is required. Fortunately, as in the past, the creation of social divisions generates *resistance and challenge* which, in turn, *makes the idea of a static underclass redundant.*

A movement of poor people

The various and diverse groups who have been excluded from the corporatist arrangement have not passively accepted being pushed aside. For example, one response to exclusion was the strike by women at Ford's Dagenham plant in 1968 when demanding equal pay. Subsequently, Barbara Castle took the issue to the Cabinet and the end result was the Equal Pay Act which, despite its flaws, did see some improvement in pay for some women. Of course, the process was not as simple as the above outline suggests. There had been pressure for a considerable period of time and Castle was independently committed to some type of equal pay legislation. However, the women at Ford's played a key part in promoting the issue to the top of the political agenda.

Even those who were supposed to be cowed into silence by the stigma of the means test refused to accept quietly their marginal status. By the early 1970s, Claimants Unions had been formed throughout the country. Social security offices were occupied by single parents demanding discretionary payments and the social security system was manipulated by various groups to try and improve their lot. Social workers and welfare rights organizations were increasingly prepared to be very vocal advocates for the poor. Mass claims and, for the administrators of the supplementary benefits system, the nightmare of mass appeals encouraged the idea of reforming the system (Donnison, 1982). Although the cost to the Treasury of making additional payments was small, the value to the claimant, and the percentage increase between 1968 and 1979, was remarkable. With a net increase of only 100 000 claimants the amount paid rose from £2 million to £38 million in this 11-year period. By 1979, nearly five times as many claimants were getting weekly additions as in 1968 (Novak, 1988, pp.188–9). Claimant's Unions and pressure groups were not solely responsible for this change, but they certainly played an important part (Walker and Lawton, 1989).

The homeless also took direct action to both highlight their plight and to provide relief from it. Squatters' groups demanded 'people before property' and painted this slogan on office block developers' hoardings. Labour-controlled local authorities were the target as often as the Conservatives. Trades Councils were pressed to give recognition and voting, or speaking, rights to Claimants Unions. We saw in the last chapter that the trade unionists who sat on LECs in the 1920s were seen as 'befooling themselves' according to Arthur Hayday. In the 1970s, the Trades Councils were asked to explain the policy which guided their representatives on Supplementary Benefit Appeals Tribunals. This was often embarrassing because they frequently did not know they had these representatives, or did not have a policy. Likewise, when local councillors were asked about their policy towards the local Police Committee, they frequently had to admit that they simply went along to 'keep an eye on things'. This hardly satisfied people who had been assaulted by the police or who felt that the 'Sus' law was being used to harass young blacks.

Similarly, women passed resolutions in their union branches, and pushed for their adoption at conferences, which challenged the idea of 'proper' industrial relations. For example, there were calls for child care facilities, maternity leave, abortion rights, non-sexist language, an end to sexual harassment at work and, perhaps the cruelest demand, union meetings that were *not* held in the local pub at about the time when women were putting the kids to bed. These were not issues with which full-time union officials felt at ease.

In short, the early 1970s witnessed a challenge to the comfortable existence of the establishment of the labour movement. The challenge came from those groups and interests excluded from the corporatist arrangement. Frequently, it should be admitted, the tactics used antagonized potential supporters and there was an anarchic, occasionally nihilistic, tendency which made broader alliances difficult to establish. For example, the smashing up of DHSS offices did nothing to forge alliances with the over-worked and lowly paid staff, even if it did force the manager to think twice before refusing a discretionary allowance. Nor were many of the organizations of the excluded always representative of those they claimed as their constituents, but that is true of most organizations. The poorest groups have, however, always had the problem that they are excluded from expressing their interests within the confines defined as legitimate. Like the burning of the workhouses by the poor in the 1830s, the riots of 1886 and the occupation of workhouses in the 1920s, the movement of the poor in the 1970s forced their interests onto the political agenda. To be rid of sexism, racism and poverty are not insubstantial demands and the subsequent failure to achieve change owes more to the ambitious nature of the objective than the tactics employed. It is doubtful whether a more conciliatory approach to organized labour, Labour politicians and the welfare bureaucracy would have been any more successful. What is clear is that the corporatist arrangement was incapable of absorbing the radical demands raised by the various excluded groups.

One of the problems for the corporatist arrangement in the 1970s was that it was called upon to represent the interests of an increasingly wide constituency. In the face of calls from, among others, women's groups, black groups, the low paid, the poorest members of society, the homeless and the unemployed for their grievances to be resolved, the most articulate and powerful sections of the labour movement retreated (Donnison, 1982, pp.73, 81–6). The leadership of the labour movement persisted with the strategy which they knew best, felt most comfortable with, and which had paid the best dividends for their natural constituency (Novak, 1988, pp.172 3). These constituents were not concerned with the racism of the police, the difficulties of being a single parent on supplementary benefit, the dire housing shortages, or the operation of the 'poverty trap'. Unless they were directly affected, most of these constituents were content to see themselves as 'respectable' members of the working class and, however mistakenly, they looked down on 'scroungers', 'blacks', 'women's libbers' and 'dossers'.

For the vast majority of the population in Britain, living standards have risen in the last three decades. In 1979, when Mrs Thatcher was first elected into office, the majority of households already had their own car, more than half were either buying their own home or had done so, consumer durables such as colour TVs, washing machines, refrigerators and vacuum cleaners were commonplace in working-class households, and wages were higher, in relation to prices, than ever before (Cronin, 1984, pp.198–9). Simultaneously, inflation reached a record high of 24 percent in 1975, unemployment was also rising and by 1979 stood at the alarmingly (for the post-war period and a Labour government) high figure of 1.25 million. Moreover, the tax threshold had fallen to include even the lowest paid workers. This in turn resulted in the ludicrous situation whereby a wage increase resulted in a lower total net income, because the wage had risen above the level at which benefits were paid – the poverty trap (Sandford et al., 1980). The overlap between public welfare and fiscal policy is, perhaps, most painfully illustrated by the late 1970s and the failure of the Labour government to appreciate the affects of low tax thresholds and high levels of income tax on popular support. For example, a single person on an average wage would have paid more than twice as much, in percentage terms, in income tax in 1975 as in 1955. For a married couple with two children, again assuming they were manual workers on the average industrial wage, they would have paid seven times as much (Pond *et al.*, 1976, p.1).

By 1979, there was little political mileage in claiming the welfare state giveth, when many people simply retorted that the welfare state also taketh away. It was in this context that Sinfield reasserted the significance of the SDW. The task of the rest of this chapter will be to try and unpick some of the most recent and important elements of the SDW.

Welfare divisions

In Chapter 1, it was seen that the link between fiscal policy and public welfare was central to Titmuss's analysis of the SDW. The implication of having different systems of welfare – occupational, fiscal and public – for social divisions was also apparent to Titmuss. In the period since Titmuss wrote his seminal essay, the situation has become even more complex. For example, it is not easy to disentangle fiscal and occupational welfare. Accountants expend a great deal of time and energy trying to ensure that any occupational welfare an employer provides can be set against the organization's tax liabilities. Consequently, although the following discussion segregates fiscal, occupational and public welfare, the overlap between the different elements of the SDW means that some forms of welfare are not confined to any one element. Nor can the following be regarded as a comprehensive picture of the SDW. Rather it is illustrative and summarizes from the existing literature.

Transport

It may seem strange to consider transport as welfare, but Le Grand (1987, pp.91–107) claims that rail subsidies are one of the most significant ways in which resources are distributed indirectly to the middle classes. (Although whether we can define all commuters as middle class is debatable.) Certainly, however, the regular commuters from Kent, Essex and the Home Counties are unlikely to appreciate their hidden welfare benefit and are vocal in their calls for more subsidies. Likewise, the distribution of subsidies to car owners is skewed in favour of the better off. Company cars, which are both a fiscal and an occupational welfare benefit, tend to be confined to sales/service staff and middle management or above. A number of self-employed people will also purchase their car through the business in order to claim tax relief. The tax system ensures that the advantage to recipients amounts collectively to at least £1.1 billion in lost revenue (Ashworth and Dilnot, 1987, p.24). A more accurate audit of the subsidy to car owners would have to include the hidden costs of providing the infrastructure and services involved in road transport. From road signs, street-lighting, policing, court time on traffic offences, accident and emergency hospital services, the cost of the DVLC, to the impact on the environment and global warming, it is plain that any balance sheet would be difficult to construct. Since car ownership and usage is biased against the poor, these hidden incalculable costs have to be seen as regressive.

Housing

One of the forms of fiscal welfare most often cited is the tax relief given to mortgage payers on the interest of their loans. Moreover, like the pension funds, building societies are in a privileged tax position in respect of any investments that they might make. It should also be remembered that mortgages can be a part of the occupational system of welfare. Banks, building Societies and other, mainly financial institutions provide mortgages for their employees at considerably lower interest rates than the norm. In housing, the SDW has, perhaps, been most noticeable in recent years. The regional variations in house prices, and the variations within regions, provide one of the clearest examples of how fiscal welfare can reinforce inequality. For many young people trying to find somewhere to live, the high cost of property is prohibitive. Even for those lucky enough to have started on the road to owner-occupation, the cost of mortgage repayments can mean a very low disposable income overall. Nevertheless, the exchequer indirectly provides a massive subsidy to owner-occupiers in general. By 1990, the Inland Revenue estimated that the cost to the exchequer of subsidizing mortgages was in the region of £7000 million per annum, a 27 percent increase on the previous year (Inland Revenue, 1990, p.107). In addition, council tenants have been given cash discounts on their purchases worth on average 43 percent of the purchase price. With 528 000 houses sold by 1984, under the Right to Buy legislation, it is clear that the state is providing massive subsidies to encourage the form of housing tenure it favours (Social Trends, 1986, p.140).

The money lost through these subsidies must also be compared with the expenditure on housing in general. Gross capital expenditure on housing in 1987–1988 is estimated by the government to have been £3661 million (Social Trends, 1987). Although it was expected to rise to £3.8 billion for 1988–1989, this amount is considerably less than that provided to purchasers. For Sinfield, the fact that public welfare is the focus of criticism and cuts, whereas fiscal welfare is increased and protected, is a central feature of the SDW.

Not surprisingly, owner-occupation is becoming the dominant form of housing tenure, both in terms of expenditure and in the proportion of the population who are buying their own homes. Between 1951 and 1985, owner-occupation rose from 30 percent to approximately 62 percent of all tenancies. Because of the age structure of the population, the percentage will almost definitely increase for at least the next 20 years. If the under 30-year-olds are able to join the housing market in the same numbers as the 30–44-year-olds, the figure could reach 70 percent before the end of the century (Social Trends, 1987, p.137).

In so far as the 'respectable' working class has embraced owner-occupation, this is not a new development. Mrs Thatcher did not initiate the trend towards owner-occupation within the working class. Dissatisfaction with council housing, petty restrictions by local authority housing depart-ments and the material advantages of owner-occupation over the past 30 years have largely been responsible for the change in tenure patterns. However, the contrast with those who remain in local authority accommod-ation appears to support the view that a process of 'residualization' is taking place.

Pensions

The pattern of pension provision provides another indicator of how social divisions, occupation and the SDW interact. Some types of occupational welfare – pensions are an obvious case – are well known to be tax-exempt up to a certain point. Thus 'exempt approved pension schemes' – those that produce a target level of benefits of no more than two-thirds final salary with as much as a quarter of this payable as a lump sum on retirement – can be regarded as both occupational welfare and fiscal welfare. The favourable treatment of pensions is enhanced by the tax system because any exempt approved scheme is free from income or capital gains tax. The total value of the employer's contribution can also be set against their income for tax purposes. The employer and the fund are the main beneficiaries of the favourable fiscal treatment of pensions. The pension itself will probably be liable to income tax, but this will depend on the value of the pension and the circumstances of the recipient (Fry *et al.*, 1985, pp.5–8). Thus pensions are both a fiscal and an occupational welfare benefit.

Between 1953 and 1983, the proportion of employees belonging to pen-sion schemes rose from 28 to 52 percent. However, the high point was 1967, when 53 percent of those in employment belonged to an occupational pension scheme. Since then, the percentage has remained fairly stable, but it has risen again from 49 percent in 1971. This, however, is slightly mislead-ing, since there were approximately 1.25 million more women working part-time in 1983–1984 than in 1967. It would be reasonable to assume that with the general increase in the numbers of part-time and temporary workers, that they ought not to be included in the figures, since they are far less likely to be members of a company pension scheme (*Social Trends*, 1987, pp.63–84). When the numbers of self-employed, who often subscribe to personal pensions – roughly 58 percent – are also removed from the total labour force, the proportion who are covered by occupational pension schemes appears even larger. Indeed, the proportion of full-time perma-nently employed persons in an occupational pension scheme may be closer to 60 percent than 50 percent once the necessary adjustments are made. If a larger proportion of the population are covered by occupational pension schemes, there are obvious implications for the state scheme, not least that the political constituency of support for the state scheme is reduced.

Moreover, the political power of the pension funds has recently attracted a great deal of political attention. They are a massive source of investment and can have a profound influence on the finance markets. Not surprisingly, a measure of political power is derived from their influential market position, a fact which reinforces Sinfield's claim that power is an important element in the SDW. Likewise, their success has meant that it has been possible for many to have a freeze on contributions for a year without adversely affecting the scheme's actuarial standing. At a time when government is emphasizing the cost of state provision, contribution freezes for occupational pensions may enhance the reputation of the market. The effect may be to reinforce ideas which suggest that the market is better able to provide welfare than the state. Once again the power of the poorest, those who will have to rely on the state scheme, is undermined by the ability of the best placed workers to gain access to a relatively more privileged form of welfare.

Another important aspect of occupational pension schemes is the fact that specific groups are excluded. Thus in 1983, 1 million workers were excluded from their employer's pension scheme because they were too young or had not been with their employer long enough to qualify. A further 3 million were excluded for other reasons, e.g. because the scheme did not cover part-time or manual employees (Government Actuary Report, 1983, p.29). The Equal Opportunities Commission (EOC) has expressed concern that some pension schemes may indirectly, but importantly, discriminate against women. Although only a small minority of part-time workers are in pension schemes, the number doubled between 1979 and 1983. Nevertheless, in the region of 70 percent of all those in occupational pension schemes are men (Actuary Report, 1983; McGoldrick, 1984; EOC, 1985, p.23).

The SDW for pensioners in the 1990s will be an increasingly significant feature of social divisions more generally. With recent changes to pension rights, and the subsidies to people taking out personal pensions, the government is clearly trying to encourage the private insurance sector. It may also encourage a three-fold division in pension provision. High-income groups, particularly people who change jobs frequently, are likely to receive a personal pension from an insurance company. For others, in secure employment over a long period of time with one employer, the likelihood is that they will obtain a company pension. Thirdly, the poorest people in society and groups confined to the 'flexible workforce' are likely to be dependent upon the state pension. As with mortgages, the state has effectively promoted and subsidized these trends by providing tax relief worth, it has been estimated, £5 billion in 1985 (Ward, 1985). The present Conservative government clearly feels that its housing policies have been very successful and it may well feel that this success can be repeated in respect of pensions. If, as has happened with council housing, state pensions are provided for 'a mere residuum' (Hanson, 1972), it may be possible for the state to further reduce support for public welfare.

Occupational welfare

Income from paid labour is not an occupational welfare benefit, but since welfare benefits are, as a rule, proportionate to income, they do provide a rough guide to change (Green *et al.*, 1984). Incomes will also, of course, provide the basis for 'consumption cleavages' (Dunleavy, 1986). Earnings have risen markedly and constantly since the 1950s. From 1956 to 1966, earnings rose by 10 percent. By 1973, they had risen a further 28 percent and between 1973 and 1979 they increased by a further 10 percent (Cronin, 1984, pp.198–9). After 1979, and up until 1985, wages rose yet again by between 22 and 28 percent, depending on who we believe (Winyard, 1987; Halsey, 1989). However, the rises since 1979 have benefited the top 60 percent of the population far more than the rest. Indeed, the top 10 percent were 80 percent better off in 1985 than in 1979, whereas the bottom 10 percent of wage earners were 3–5 percent worse off (Novak, 1988, p.183; Leadbeater, 1989, p.47). As with the statistics on unemployment, there are massive regional variations in the average earnings of workers. The best guide to variations in pay within the working class in the late 1980s remained a person's location within the labour market. Skilled and clerical workers earn 40–50 percent more than the semi-skilled and unskilled. Women still only earn roughly 60 percent of average male earnings and black workers are generally 20–40 percent poorer than their white counterparts (Lewis and Piachaud, 1987, pp.28–52; Novak, 1988, p.181; Leadbeater, 1989, p.47; Miles, 1989, pp.93–107).

Nor can any discussion of occupational welfare ignore the host of 'unequal fringes' (Green *et al.*, 1984) available to those in secure employment. The provision of company cars has been shown to be a substantial benefit to many managers and company directors (Ashworth and Dilnot, 1987). However, it is unlikely that company cars will be provided for staff below middle management in the next 10–20 years. Although some trade unionists have claimed that they are trying to persuade employers to provide company cars, it seems unlikely that this practice will be widespread in the near future (Mann and Anstee, 1989). Many firms do, however, already provide transport subsidies for their employees. In the London area especially, subsidized bus and rail travel is widely available and quite common for many types of work. With the increasing difficulty employers claim to face in attracting staff to London, it may be that this will become an increasingly significant occupational benefit in the future.

Perhaps the most interesting aspect of the distribution of occupational welfare, excluding the inequalities it reinforces between classes, is the variation between industrial groups (Green *et al.*, 1984). In the public sector and the privatized industries of gas, electricity and communications, pension schemes, sick pay, paid holidays, benefits in kind and subsidized services are all more generous than elsewhere. This may simply be a function of size, but the suspicion remains that their formerly powerful unions have negotiated some good deals. The other industrial groups that show a high benefits-to-wages ratio are vehicles, chemicals and allied industries, coal and petroleum products, and engineering. While the provision of occupational welfare within these industries may be skewed towards management and high-status staff, there is little evidence that this bias is any greater than in, for example, textiles, leather and fur products, or clothing and footwear. These last industries are notable because they all have a low benefits-to-wages ratio. Thus these secondary sector industries are doubly disadvantaged: they pay low wages and provide few benefits (Green *et al.*, 1984, p.16). Although Green *et al.*, whose study is one of the few in-depth pieces of statistical research on fringe benefits, stated that unionization rates had little or no effect on the provision of benefits, there are grounds for querying their conclusions (Green *et al.*, 1984, pp.43–6, 85–6).

Mann and Anstee (1989) suggest that not only do trade unionists press for improvements in their benefits 'package', but management often ac-knowledge this pressure. In addition, the industries that provide the most occupational benefits tend to be those with a recent history of aggressive trade unionism. Leather goods and textiles, for example, are noted for their weak unions, whereas mining is noted for its more militant trade unionism. While British trade unions are, in general, more interested in improving pay, trade unionists are quite prepared to claim responsibility for improvements in occupational welfare. Indeed, every trade union respondent in Mann and Anstee's (1989) study wanted to improve their occupational welfare pack-age in the near future.

A further factor in the promotion of occupational welfare has to be the industrial relations strategies of many employers. Two of the most common terms to be used in British industrial relations in the 1980s have been 'flexibility' and 'harmonization'. Both terms involve management and the unions renegotiating the organization of work and 'custom and practice' within their enterprise. The link with changes in the labour process is vitally important. In short, 'flexibility' will normally involve changes in the tasks that particular workers are asked to perform. For example, in an engineer-ing firm even skilled workers might be asked to perform semi-skilled – or in some circumstances unskilled – work. The objective for management is to ensure the smoothest and most flexible response to the production of the commodity. In return, it is common for the union to ask for increased pay, holidays and benefits. Sometimes this will involve the whole of the work-force gaining 'staff status'. The pension scheme may be extended to cover everyone, the clocking-in system changed and benefits, associated in the past with white-collar staff, extended to all full-time employees (Mann and Anstee, 1989).

Harmonization is a narrower proposal and usually involves staff status being used to break down a 'them and us' attitude between management and workers. A variety of benefits can be harmonized, including share parti-cipation schemes, profit sharing, the eradication of the distinction between staff canteens and management canteens, and company pensions. Many of these benefits have additional advantages to employers, but the principal aim is often to retain skilled manual labour. The objective, therefore, is often to promote a paternalistic relationship between worker and employer (Fox, 1985). Both flexibility and harmonization tend to be traded off against occupational benefits. These benefits are themselves intricately linked to the tax system, which effectively provides a subsidy to employers. Occupational welfare can, for the employee, have certain negative effects. For example, share participation schemes and, to a lesser extent, profit-sharing schemes, can be viewed as tying the employee to the enterprise. Simultaneously, however, they act as a type of bonus scheme.

Other forms of occupational welfare are widely recognized to be the focus of intense discussion between management and unions. Sick pay schemes, holidays with pay and benefits in kind are often a thorn in the side of the personnel manager but an important perk for employees. Workers recognize the importance of having a job where you get a few 'perks'. The brewery that provides a gallon of free beer per week, the supermarket chain which offers a free hamper at Xmas and discounts on goods, the free 'protective boots' which are also suitable for wear on the allotment, the airport which provides parkas, are seen by workers as 'good firms to work for' (Mann and Anstee, 1989). Compared with the director's Mercedes, the sales manager's Ford Sierra and the perks offered by firms in the City, such 'fringes' are not significant. Set against the situation which confronts claimants, where any and every addition to income must be declared, even the smallest perk may assume the status of a windfall.

Public welfare

Table 1   Housing stock by tenure in Britain, 1951–1985 (percent)

Year	Owner-occupied	Rented from local authority or new town	Rented privately and miscellaneous
1951	30	18	52
1961	44	26	30
1971	50	31	19
1981	57	31	12
1985	62	27	11
1989	66	24	10

Adapted from Heath and McDonald (1989, p.31) and *Social Trends* (1991, p.135).

As can be seen from Table 1, the most significant feature of changes in the housing stock, as far as public welfare is concerned, is the massive increase in council housing between 1951 and 1961. Although the percentage of council houses continued to rise until 1981, it has since begun to fall slightly. Subsidies to council tenants have at the same time fallen, with rents being raised to bring them more in line with those in the market. For example, the average weekly rent in 1978–1979 was £5.90p per week; in 1985–1986 it was £15.66p, a rise from 6.6 to 8.3 percent of average weekly earnings (Forrest and Murie, 1989, pp.236–7). What is more, average wage levels are an inadequate guide to the effect of these increases on the poorest groups. Their incomes have not risen as rapidly as the bulk of the population in the 1980s as the discussion earlier has shown.

Between 1978–9 and 1986–7, it should also be noted that the government reduced spending on public housing by as much as 55 percent (Hills, 1987, p.89). Simultaneously, however, the cost of housing benefit increased three-fold to £3.056 million. The two reasons for this massive increase are economic recession with the related problem of high unemployment, and a change in the social composition of public sector tenants (Forrest and Murie, 1983).

Forrest and Murie (1983) point out that the sale of council houses, with usually the best 10 percent having been removed from the stock, and the growth of 'dump' estates, where the poorest and newest tenants are concentrated, has led to the 'residualization' of council housing. Between 1981 and 1985, the proportion of households renting from local authorities fell by 3–5 percent. This followed the 'Right to Buy' legislation. As sections of the working class who are able to do so flee the council estates, social divisions become more apparent and firmer. As Flynn (1988, p.300) has observed:

> In terms of social composition, those remaining in council housing are generally very poor, young with young children, unemployed, elderly, retired or single person households. These groups are in effect doubly disadvantaged, because the sale of better quality and more desirable dwellings takes units permanently out of the local public rented stock and thereby removes choice and opportunities for 'upward' mobility for existing tenants and potential tenants, who are already vulnerable because of class, income, age and life cycle stage.

The housing that some of the poorest people in Britain are confined to is rapidly deteriorating. For example, in 1986, the Audit Commission estimated that outstanding repairs to existing local authority housing would cost £10 billion to put right. Many of the worst housing estates are reserved by the local authority for 'problem cases', which marks both the tenants and the estate out in the wider locality. These estates deteriorate still further due to poor social amenities: chemists move out because of break-ins; new health clinics can rarely find suitable space; shops and cheaper supermarkets, along with leisure and sports centres, are rarely built on council estates, catering instead for those who can drive to them; and the police are more likely to treat residents as potential criminals rather than as the potential victims. Even the briefest visit to any of the council estates known locally to be 'a bit rough' is likely to confirm this picture of social and spatial segregation (Flynn, 1988).

For some commentators the most significant feature of housing in the past 10–20 years has been the 'residualization' of council housing (Forrest and Murie, 1983; Williams *et al.*, 1986; Flynn, 1988). The impact on intra-class relations has also been the subject of debate along with the idea that these trends are part of the changes in class formation. Thus, approximately two-thirds of skilled manual workers were owner-occupiers in 1985, whereas 58 percent of unskilled manual workers were renting from the local authority (*Social Trends*, 1988, p.143). Of those remaining in council houses in 1989, 40 percent expressed a preference for owner-occupation and 22 percent intended to purchase their own home (Building Societies Association, 1989).

Some commentators have gone so far as to suggest that patterns of consumption, and especially housing, have served to make older concepts of class structure based on production redundant (Dunleavy, 1986; Saunders, 1986). Whether the type of housing or the location of it can be used to explain changes in intra-class relations is considered in the next chapter. Certainly, however, there is a prima facie case for concluding that social divisions have been reinforced by changes in patterns of housing tenure.

Health

Even in the area of health, the persistence of social divisions has been noteworthy. The poorest groups in society use the services less and service providers are less sensitive to their needs (Le Grand, 1982). The Black Report (1980) detailed at length how health care varied between areas and social classes, with the poorest 10 percent of the population faring worst of all. More recently, Whitehead (1987) claims that the health divide has actually widened since the late 1970s. Even mortality figures for the poorest are markedly worse than for the rest of the population (Field, 1989, p.63).

Unemployment

Since 1946 and until 1976, the annual unemployment rate had rarely risen above 4 percent. However, in 1976, the rate rose to 5.5 percent and continued to rise to over 12 percent and 3 million persons in 1984. In 1986, the numbers unemployed would undoubtedly have exceeded 4 million if the means by which the statistics were gathered had remained the same as in 1976 (Lonsdale, 1985, pp.29–42; Novak, 1988, pp.180–3). In addition, the distribution of unemployment has been extremely uneven. By 1987, nearly a third of the unemployed had been on the register for over a year and in the North, the North West, and West Midlands, roughly half of those unemployed had been unable to find work within a year. The unemployment rate also varied widely, with a rate of 8.5 percent in the South East, but 16.9 percent in the North, 14.3 percent in the North West and 13.8 percent in Yorkshire and Humberside. Even within these areas, however, unemployment was concentrated in particular localities and communities. Thus Sunderland had a rate of 21.4 percent whereas Kendal had only 8.3 percent unemployment, despite the fact that both are classified as the North. Even within Sunderland, unemployment was concentrated in particular areas (Byrne and Parson, 1983; Winyard, 1987, pp.40–3).

Particular groups are also more likely to find they are excluded from the world of paid work. For black men, the rate of unemployment was double that for white men in 1985. In the same year, young blacks aged 16–24 had an unemployment rate twice that for young whites and three times the national average (Arnott, 1987, p.62).

When it is borne in mind that the value of social security has fallen in relation to earnings and the retail price index, it is clear that the poor were worse off in the 1980s than they were in the 1970s. Not only were they poorer, but they have been poorer for longer periods of time (Piachaud, 1987a, pp.22–5). Not surprisingly, in these circumstances, the Social Fund provided grants and loans to over 1 million claimants in its first year of operation. All but 153 000 of these loans will have to be repaid by claimants who might previously have been given grants (Campling, 1990, p.93).

The contrast between the different elements within the SDW is quite stark. It is not, however, a new development as previous chapters have shown. Vulnerability to poverty, i.e. dependence on public welfare, continues to be a mark of working-class life in general. For some working-class households, owner-occupation has been a traumatic experience rather than a privilege. In 1988, 37 000 people were more than 6 months in arrears with their mortgage, which is four times as many as in 1979. Moreover, 16 150 properties were repossessed compared with 2500 in 1979 (Booth, 1989). With the rapid rise in interest rates since 1988, these figures are likely to be greater for 1989–1990 and higher still if property prices pick up in 1991, when it will make more economic sense for building societies and banks to repossess.

Nevertheless, it should be clear that for significant sections of the working class, particularly those well placed in the social division of labour, access to fiscal and occupational welfare is vitally important. The degree to which their relatively more privileged place in the SDW amounts to a cleavage within the working class will be discussed in subsequent chapters.

Summary

Since the 1950s, when Titmuss wrote his essay on the SDW, the evidence of social divisions is overwhelming. Despite all the rhetoric from the Conservative governments of the 1980s, they have continued to provide generous benefits to some people while ignoring the needs of the poorest. Tax and occupationally related welfare benefits are difficult to calculate, but these elements of the SDW have not been the focus of Tory attention. For some sections of the working class, living standards have improved in a way that was unimaginable before the war. A buoyant labour market and strong trade unions between 1950 and 1980 were powerful pistons driving working-class incomes upward. Owner-occupation, changes in consumption patterns, occupational welfare, pensions and geographical location, have combined for some workers to place them in a more privileged place in the SDW. By exerting a measure of control over the labour market and the

labour process, many have been able to escape the clutches of public welfare, or to exploit its less stigmatizing elements, the NHS and education for
example.

In contrast, those who have been excluded from the labour market, who
have found it difficult to resist new working practices or negotiate new ones,
who live in areas of high unemployment and industrial decline, who are
forced to rely on public welfare and have little chance of escaping from it,
who have not been able or allowed to gain skills, or who are trapped in the
trench of dependency, are effectively excluded from the benefits of the so-
called 'post-modern' society. They are, in terms of their day-to-day experience, in the same social position as the paupers of the 1840s, the 'residuum'
of the 1880s and the 'unemployables' of the 1930s.

It is against this background that a number of observers have suggested
that social divisions in Britain are hardening. A number of these accounts
have been mentioned in passing in this chapter and it is to these attempts at
explaining social divisions that we shall now turn.

six

Life chances, labour markets and closure

Do you want to swing on a star,
carry moon beams home in a jar
and be better off than you are,
or do you want to be a pig?

(*Swinging on a Star*, a 'hit' for Big Dee Irwin that reached number 7
and remained in the charts for 17 weeks in 1963)

Here we all live in a state of ambitious poverty (Juvenal, Roman satirist,
c. A.D.100)

In this chapter, we turn to a number of theoretical models which have been used to explain intra-class divisions. Although Titmuss originally argued that the role of the division of labour and the link with industrial relations was extremely important, he did not relate the SDW to the stratification system. This is unfortunate, since it is very difficult to see how the unequal distribution of welfare can be explained without referring to the class structure of society. For the observers discussed in this chapter, it is especially important to avoid forcing social divisions into broader class categories. Class and intra-class relations are discussed but, in part, because all the accounts in this chapter are non-Marxist, they point to social processes and structures which are not simply aspects of a class society. With the exception of the idea of an underclass, the accounts considered here can be regarded as Weberian, although the extent to which any particular approach is indebted to Max Weber is debatable.

In this chapter, the idea of an underclass, housing classes, social security classes, consumption, the labour market and social closure will be addressed. Interest representation and the effects of the production process will be touched on, but these will be considered in more depth in Chapter 7. Nor does this chapter cover each and every account of social divisions from a non-Marxist perspective. That would be a massive task beyond the scope of this book. Rather, the intention is to identify some of the most interesting and influential explanations. Picking and choosing in this fashion is a necessarily evaluative exercise. Hopefully, the advocates selected provide an adequate cross-section of the diverse views expressed in the social sciences.

Underclasses

Previously in this book, the term 'underclasses' has been mentioned. Since the 1970s, it has been used by a number of observers, including journalists, TV and radio commentators, fiction writers and politicians (Giddens, 1973; Mann, 1984; MacNicol, 1987; Field, 1989; Murray, 1990). The concept was imported from the USA and one of its most vocal advocates has been Murray (1990). In discussing Murray's view of the underclass in this chapter, I do not intend to imply that he is a Weberian. Few Weberian scholars in Britain, or other writers who use the term, would want to be associated with his ideas (Wilson, 1987, 1989; Field, 1989, 1990). Murray's account would not warrant serious consideration if it were not for the fact that he has had access to a wider audience than most academics, through the pages of the *Sunday Times* (26 November 1989), and his argument is therefore likely to gain saloon bar support.

Murray's version of the underclass, which he suggests is emerging but may not have become established in Britain yet, takes the marital status of a child's mother, violent crime and voluntary unemployment as the definitive indicators. It is tempting to suggest that he sees the underclass as criminally violent bastards who refuse to work. In the USA, but not in Britain, the underclass is overwhelmingly black. His argument relies heavily on anecdotal illustrations and an imaginative use of statistics. One of the attractive features of his account is that, like many right-wing Libertarians, he credits the individual with rational choice. The underclass are not passive victims in his view, but active agents logically pursuing their own best interests. They do so in a void without moral regulation or social restraints, and the values of the underclass are 'now contaminating the life of entire neighbourhoods' (Murray, 1990, p.4). He considers it quite natural for young men and women to want to procreate and to seek public welfare benefits if they are available. At the same time, if they take these benefits, they are failing to exercise the moral righteousness Murray feels distinguishes the underclass from the deserving poor. Thus he makes no bones about blaming the underclass for their condition. At the same time, the culprit who undermined the ethics of self-help is seen to be the state. By making excuses for the poor, and for providing a host of welfare benefits to ease the pain of failure, the state has provided not a safety net, but a feather bed. In these circumstances, we should not be surprised that able-bodied young men refuse to get out of it or that irresponsible young women conceive on it.

Murray provides the best example of the worst kind of writing on social divisions. The problems that derive from his type of polemic relate not so much to what he says, although there are problems enough with this, but more with what he refuses to say. Murray (1990, p.79) says of his own lack of policy proposals, 'Hence the quandary: for me to expand on my policy prescriptions is to give large numbers of readers too easy an excuse for ignoring my analysis of the problem on grounds that I am obviously a nut'. Although the presentation of a theory need not contain any policy proposals, it ought to have a number of other elements. It ought to be informed by history for example. Murray correctly points out that historically there have been numerous attempts at identifying an underclass. What he fails to mention is that while each generation has seen a sub-stratum within the working class, each period has also witnessed the rehabilitation of that stratum. The Victorian residuum appears to have evaporated in the heat of the First World War. Likewise, the class of unemployables of the inter-war period failed to survive the Second World War. Why, we must ask, have these disappeared if the values of the underclass are transmitted across generations?

Similarly, if, as Murray claims, generous welfare provisions are a principal reason for the growth of an underclass, why is it that this class was thought to be so large in Victorian England? Was poor relief so generous in the 1870s and 1880s that it undermined family values, thrift and individual effort? Murray fails to explain the historical transformation of the underclass and simply asserts that it has existed in earlier times. It was shown previously that it is not welfare which creates an underclass but a person's location in the division of labour that assigns them a place in the SDW.

In contrast to his focus on the poor, Murray is not very vocal about the welfare provided for the middle classes and the 'respectable' working class. There is no consideration, unfortunately, of how fiscal welfare or occupational welfare promote dependency and mendacity among the middle classes. Given the greater value of the benefits paid to the middle classes, we should expect to see their moral standards slipping. The drivers of company cars, owner-occupiers, members of occupational pension schemes and those who get tax subsidies on their unit trusts are rarely berated for their sexual immorality, violent nature or illegitimacy rates.

Murray only considers public welfare, and in so doing fails to appreciate the scope of the welfare state in the late twentieth century. Such a blinkered view of welfare makes it difficult to take his account seriously. The political implications of Murray's polemic (cuts in public welfare and authoritarian measures to 'remoralize' the poor) have led others to suggest that the term 'underclass' should be dropped from the academic vocabulary. I sympathize with this view and feel it is vitally important that the term, when used, be carefully qualified and/or defined (hopefully I have done so here). However, and whether academics approve or not, Murray has been given a platform from which he has promoted the term. Unless an equally 'catchy' label can be invented, journalists, politicians, publishers and academics will probably continue to use the ill-defined and misleading concept of an 'underclass'.

Social security classes and housing classes

As we saw in Chapter 2, Sinfield was implicitly critical of Titmuss for not locating the SDW within the context of class. In revising Titmuss's concept of an SDW, Sinfield was keen to stress the link between the class structure and the distribution of resources. At one point, Sinfield (1978, p.137) admits that 'there is a strong temptation to introduce the idea of social security classes to make evident the ways in which particular benefits may effect the resources and social status of recipients'. Nevertheless, Sinfield resists the temptation, but he clearly found the idea attractive. Like his use of the term 'underclass,' he uses the notion of separate stratum for polemical purposes only. He does not, for example, go on to promote the idea of separate identifiable classes. What is more, it is worth noting that there are important differences in the concept of social security classes and underclasses.

Social security classes are, by definition, linked to a particular system of income distribution. Presumably, other classes would be defined in relation to other distributive networks. In contrast, the concept of an underclass is less specific but implies a relationship to other social classes, beneath which the underclass is located. It is possible, therefore, to use a definition of class which is based on the relationship to the means of production (assuming this was felt to be the best way of defining classes), and still identify an underclass. Classes defined in terms of distributive networks avoid the problem of reducing social divisions to functions of a capitalist economy, but they have their own drawbacks.

It is worth exploring, albeit briefly, the way that the idea of 'housing classes' developed, because these were seen as attractive by Sinfield, and they illustrate some of the problems that can arise when distributive networks are taken as the basis for a system of stratification. In the late 1960s and throughout the 1970s, a number of urban sociologists used the idea of 'housing classes' (Rex and Moore, 1967; Rex, 1971; Pahl, 1975; Rex and Tomlinson, 1979). The researchers were usually trying to explain how discrimination occurred in the allocation of housing. Simultaneously, these studies were questioning concepts of class, which were principally tied to the structure of the occupation and production systems.

Housing is a scarce resource, the argument runs, over which groups and stratum compete. The researchers asserted that if it was valid to regard conflicts over wages as an aspect of class struggle, it was equally valid to consider how conflicts over housing effect the stratification system. The ability of some groups to obtain 'better' housing than others was seen to be a function of their greater power. Moreover, when examining housing, it was clear that different types of housing and forms of tenure were, more or less, stigmatized. Status and housing coincided they argued, to produce distinctive class boundaries depending on the type of tenure held. The approach used by Rex and his colleagues is clearly derived from Weberian sociology. Class, status and power are inextricably linked and these are used by the researchers to assess the 'life chances' offered to individuals and groups. The notion of housing classes relies, therefore, not simply on housing, but combines this with other factors related to life chances. Education obviously provides 'life chances', or is supposed to do so, but if the schools in a particular area are disadvantaged opportunities will be restricted. Likewise, employment opportunities vary from one area to another. The person who lives in an area of high unemployment has less opportunity than the person in an area with very low unemployment rates. If it could be shown that there is a direct relationship between housing tenure and 'life chances', the concept of housing classes would clearly provide an interesting approach to social divisions. Moreover, it did seem that there was at least a prima facie case for accepting the idea of housing classes.

In the 1960s and 1970s, there was increasing evidence of discrimination, mainly on the basis of race, and this led to a measure of geographical segregation. People unable to move out of a 'deprived' area, where the schools were unable to provide an adequate escape route and unemployment rates were higher than elsewhere, could reasonably be seen to have restricted life chances. Indeed, the combined effect of these restrictions on life chances might ensure social division. Nor is it too difficult to see why Sinfield found the concept of social security classes tempting in this context. The powerlessness of social security claimants, their reliance on the most visible and most stigmatized elements of the SDW and their inability to engage in many of the 'normal' elements of social life (e.g. holidays, going out, etc.), combine to encourage the view that they are segregated from other social groups. However, the similarities between the ideas of social security classes and housing classes means they suffer from similar problems.

The concept of housing classes has been the focus of considerable criticism. Indeed, any definition of classes which takes a particular allocative, distributive or consumption network as its starting point is likely to confront the same criticisms. One of the most coherent critics of the housing class model has been Saunders (1981, pp.136–48). He points out that Rex and Moore initially identified five different housing classes: owner-occupiers, council tenants, tenants of private landlords, owners of lodging houses and lodging house tenants. Later, they added a sixth and then a seventh class:

> . . . and in his latest study Rex has elaborated on this schema to identify four more classes or sub-classes, thereby bringing the grand total to eleven (Rex and Tomlinson, 1979, p.132). Yet there is no reason why taxonomic invention should end there; for Moore (1977, p.106) has suggested that two more classes could have been analysed in the Sparkbrook study, Rex (1977, p.21) has argued that any group (such as one parent families) that is discriminated against in housing may constitute a housing class, and Pahl (1975, pp.242–3) has pointed out that the framework fails to take account of large landowners or of local authorities (who are, after all, more significant providers of

housing than lodging house owners), both of which could, given the logic of Rex and Moore's approach, be included. There are, it seems, dozens of potential housing classes (Saunders, 1981, p.139).

What the concept of housing classes does is to illustrate the danger of confusing status divisions, networks of allocation and distribution, with class divisions. If status is taken as *the* determinant of class, it is impossible to distinguish classes because status is simply a reflection of socially held views. Any model of class which takes status as its definitive feature will, therefore, simply reflect popular attitudes. If it can be accepted that many popularly held views are misplaced, then discussion and research must turn to the production and maintenance of beliefs, and away from housing and class.

Moreover, what would be the case if there isn't a unitary value system from which we can derive status distinctions? What if there are a variety of competing values held by different groups? Are we to construct different models of class depending on who is asked about the desirability of different forms of housing? Is the terraced house in the inner city universally less attractive than a semi in the suburbs? Since the 1960s, there can be few 'experts' who have not learnt that what is desirable from one perspective, e.g. that of the architect of a high-rise block of flats, may not be so attractive from another, e.g. that of the the person asked to vacate their small terrace to go and live on the tenth floor. Similar difficulties would arise with the idea of social security classes. Stigma may be attached by some people to single parents, the unemployed or even to all claimants; but, for others, there may be no disgrace in being poor and they might regard the stock-broker, the estate agent or the merchant banker with disdain.

Nor are housing and social security the only scarce resources which can provide the basis for differentiating classes. Access to health care, education or a pension could each claim to be the primary determinant of a class system based on distributional networks. The fact that urban sociology developed the use of classes based on allocative networks ought not to confine them to housing. Unfortunately, the potential for class fragmentation and division seems boundless. Ultimately, any explanatory power the concept of class might have evaporates in the heat generated by competing academics each claiming that 'their' distributive network has primacy.

Residualization and consumption cleavages

Before addressing consumption approaches directly, I want briefly to discuss an approach which falls between the consumption-based school and the older housing classes approach. Residualization is a term that has gained some currency within social policy. The claim is that as local authority housing has been vacated by the more affluent sections of the working class, it has also had to accommodate more problem cases. Single parents, the elderly, the long-term unemployed and others who are unable to get a mortgage are segregated, in effect, on particular estates (Forrest and Murie, 1983; Flynn, 1988). As some estates are seen as desirable, the tenants living there will buy their homes and the stock of 'good' housing available to the local authority will thus dwindle, thereby further isolating those particular estates defined as 'rough'.

Descriptively, there is much to admire in this account. The key problem is that the service (housing) and those who use it are confusingly linked. That is not to say that there are not a large number of 'dump' estates where local authorities shunt their problem cases and which have been stigmatized by the process. Rather, the problem is that 'residualization' uses the features of both the housing and the inhabitants to prove its point. This was illustrated for me when an undergraduate referred throughout an essay to 'the resid-uum' who lived in council housing. Now this might have been an example of a confused student who had been taught badly, except that the same confusion exists in accounts of 'residualization'. If the concept refers to the service, it cannot then point to the inhabitants to support its argument. If, on the other hand, the problems that the inhabitants have define the area as residualized, it matters little what the buildings are like. In other words, we are unable to say whether it is the service which is residualized or the people who rely on it.

Although many start with housing, consumption-based approaches tend to take a bundle, or package, of services and consider how these relate to social divisions. These collective consumption packages are seen to include, among other things, education, income support, health, fringe benefits, transport and recreation as well as housing (See Dunleavy, 1980, 1986; Saunders, 1986; Warde, 1990). One of the tremendously attractive features of analyses which rely on consumption is the vulgarity of the alternatives. Rather than explain change in terms of the state reacting to a crisis within capitalism, a view associated with some Marxists (e.g. O'Connor, 1973), i.e. collective consumption, emphasizes the impact of change in its own right. In many respects, the concerns of the collective consumption school(s) are remarkably similar to those in Titmuss's and Sinfield's discussion of the SDW.

In brief, the argument runs as follows. In the past 20 years or so, there have developed a number of social divisions which, while related to social class in most accounts (but not in Saunders' case), can only be properly understood through an analysis of consumption. It is pointed out that in a very material sense the lives of those able to gain access to the 'better' services are remarkably improved. The 'better' services tend to be those which are in the private sector. Public sector services, such as council hous-ing, the NHS, state schools and public transport, are less attractive and less responsive to consumers. Dunleavy (1986) suggests that the causal link between crisis in the state welfare sector and reduced state commitment to welfare on the one hand, and the behaviour of the electorate on the other, tends to be assumed. Simply because, as radical political economists see it, capitalism is in crisis and has to restructure, does not, in itself, lead millions of people to vote for political parties committed to this end. Too often functionalist and deterministic assumptions are central to the analysis in which the electorate are either ideologically manipulated or, alternatively, politicians are responding to the economic requirements and interests of capital. It is not necessary to agree with Dunleavy's simplified model of radical theorists to accept his basic point that there is a tendency for them to neglect questions of agency (Mandel, 1978; Gough, 1979; Glyn and Harrison, 1980; Piven and Cloward, 1982; Offe, 1984). Similar criticisms have been made throughout this study and elsewhere (Mann, 1986).

For Dunleavy (1986, p.131) it is necessary to explain the response of the electorate, political parties, political leaders, policy advisors and the mass media and show how they respond to the changing priorities of capital. Dunleavy points to the growth of socialized consumption (public welfare) and how, over time, social inequalities are restructured to produce new social divisions. These developments, he argues, have to be explained and not reduced to a mere function of capital. One of the examples he gives is the provision of council housing and the manner in which particular interests have been able to influence (Labour-controlled) local authorities' allocation policies. The ability of 'respectable' white working-class people to get council housing in the 1960s, when poor whites and blacks were effectively excluded, might be an example which supported Dunleavy's case. More recently, the increase in individualized transport through increasing car ownership has witnessed a shift in resources away from mass transit systems (Dunleavy, 1986, p.138). The shift from one mode of consumption to another occurs because 'people enter the exchange to prevent their welfare being reduced' (Dunleavy, 1986, p.138). Consequently, the growth in, for example, home ownership, is a defensive action taken by those who realize that if they remain in rented accommodation they will suffer in the longer term. This pragmatic response is one which has been mentioned in previous chapters and can be endorsed without accepting the consumption cleavages approach *in toto*.

The political implications arise when people, who feel they are no longer relying on public welfare, believe it is unfair that they should still be taxed to pay for services they do not use. Furthermore, the social cleavages formed by consumption provide politicians of the Right with a constituency for further reductions in state intervention in social consumption. Consumption is still organized by the state and the costs may be borne by the exchequer. However, it now appears that individuals make choices, which in fact they do, but these are being encouraged in one direction and discouraged in another. There is an incentive for individuals who are able to do so to join private schemes and to oppose more spending on public services. As Dunleavy (1986, p.142) observes:

> The most important consequence of the partial realignment of political parties and conflicts around sectoral issues is to crosscut social class divisions, and to undermine unity of the class-based electoral

coalition which initially constituted the political driving force behind welfare state growth.

In short, the working class has been split by the ability of its most privileged members to gain access to forms of welfare which protect them better than other identifiable groups. The state is not portrayed, therefore, as an executive of the capitalist class, as Marxists might argue, but as a structure which responds to social forces that may cut across classes.

However, the waters are muddied by a number of different interpretations, and some serious shortcomings, in the collective consumption approach. There are, not surprisingly, differences of opinion among scholars who take consumption as the benchmark of social divisions. One of the key issues on which agreement is difficult to find is the degree to which consumption cleavages provide the basis for new political and social movements. Castells (1978) took the view in the 1970s that new political and social movements would arise which cut across class boundaries and linked consumer and political interests. Preteceille (1986), however, feels that any new movements are likely to overlap with older class boundaries. New social divisions, he points out, show a degree of fit with class. Preteceille is not, as Saunders (1986, p.157) appears to think, arguing that class is the prime motivator of consumption cleavages but that it is a significant determinant in many instances. What is more, Preteceille is reluctant to consider consumption cleavages, without also considering the impact of the production process upon these. The crux of the argument is, however, not whether production or consumption spheres are the sole determinant of social divisions, but how much weight to give the different spheres. Preteceille differs from Saunders in placing more weight on production relations and less on consumption while still regarding consumption as significant. Saunders (1986, p.155) addresses the central concern in a typically forthright manner when he says:

> The basic point at issue . . . is . . . the significance of social class in influencing or even determining people's life chances, ways of life, and political alignments in Western capitalist societies in the contemporary period. This is an issue, of course, which has long divided Marxist and Weberian sociology.

Saunders rejects the claim that there is any link between social class and consumption cleavages.

The strengths of the consumption-based approach can be stated quite simply. First, it avoids economic reductionism, i.e. there is no attempt to reduce each and every manifestation of inequality back to the production process or, necessarily, to the interests of capital. If the working class has played a major role in 'the making of a claiming class' (Mann, 1986), it is vital that any account of social divisions should not be tied down by structural and reductionist argument. The point is that collective consumption cannot simply be 'read off' from a list of requirements that the state establishes in the interests of capital. Thus the working class has played a major part in promoting social divisions by opting, quite rationally, for the most attractive elements of the SDW. The fact that this has left the weakest sections of the class to rely on the least attractive and least rewarding elements is an unfortunate consequence.

Secondly, the approach acknowledges the divisive effects of welfare and other forms of consumption. Whatever criteria we might want to apply there can be no dispute over the fact that the world looks very different from the respective positions of, for example, the lone parent isolated on a peripheral council estate in Liverpool and the computer systems analyst who purchased his or her own home 10 years ago in, say, Essex. They may both share a common relationship to the means of production – although this too could be a bone of contention – but it would be sociological folly to argue that their material life chances had much in common. Of course, the dogmatist can find examples which illustrate the common interests of people in such situations, but there seems to be little point in refusing to acknowledge the relative privileges the latter has over the former. Thus the consumption-based approach emphasizes life chances and is, therefore, in the Weberian tradition. It may, indeed, mark a decisive break with Weberian sociology in other respects, but the focus on differential access to consumption spheres highlights one of Weberian sociology's traditional strengths, namely an acknowledgement of social cleavages based on the opportunities individuals have for improving their position within the stratification system.

Thirdly, the consumption-based approach attempts to explain the political impact of culture, life chances and material interests on recent political developments. The rise of 'Thatcherism', for example, clearly found an echo among, at least some, working-class people. Whether the aim of Conservative administrations in the 1980s was really to create a 'property-owning democracy' or not, significant numbers of working-class people felt it provided them with more security than the neo-corporatist policies of previous governments. By considering who benefits and who loses out in the consumption sphere, changes in political allegiance may be clarified. What is more, such changes can be explained without recourse to the patronizing theories of 'false consciousness' or ideological hegemony. Rather, it is possible to regard such changes as pragmatic.

Fourthly, the consumption sphere emphasizes changes in culture and lifestyle. This is not to suggest that working-class traditions and culture are defunct or that life-style and culture are principal determinants of class allegiance. Nevertheless, significant changes have occurred and the embarrassing attempts of some on the Left to come to terms with these have been noteworthy. For example, the Labour Party re-launch in 1989 included the party leader disco dancing to a gospel/pop song which had all the cultural credibility of the Eurovision Song Contest. Likewise, in the 1980s, the Communist Party sought to project an image of cultural awareness in tune with the 'post-Fordist' era. Whether brightly coloured T-shirts, arty coffee mugs and designer condoms were fully engaging with the cultural and political ideals of the day is, however, questionable. Nevertheless, a failure to recognize consumption changes can effectively marginalize the Left, leaving it with an audience composed of idealistic students and those who are excluded from the new patterns of consumption. Of course, the extent and depth of change, and quite how to engage with it, are matters of intense and continuing debate. It is perhaps a testament to collective consumption that such issues have been forced onto the political agenda.

Finally, the consumption-based approach has managed to develop theoretical models and analytic categories which, at the very least, attempt to escape from the restraints of nineteenth-century social theory. It is quite remarkable that social theory should still be dominated by the writings of men (for they are male) who were not even familiar with the automobile, airports, televisions, computers or nuclear power and weapons.

Against these successes, it is necessary to consider the shortcomings of the consumption-based approach. The first and most obvious difficulty arises in selecting which sphere of consumption or distribution is *the* most important. Are we to insist that housing is a more significant feature of collective consumption than, say, income? To simply retort that none of the different elements in the consumption package has primacy, ignores the fact that life chances for some will be more readily influenced by transport facilities or health care services than housing or social security. How are we to decide whether access to education, health care, the personal social services or transport are more suitable measures of collective consumption?

If it can be accepted that collective consumption refers to life chances, in its broadest sense, then the taxonomic problems encountered by Rex and his colleagues have a corollary in the sphere of consumption. How are we to locate consumers, both individually and collectively, within different spheres? If the answer is that this is not an aspect of collective consumption that deserves attention, then the ability to explain differential and unequal access is considerably weakened. Going further, it would also be virtually impossible to relate collective consumption with any concept of class location, since there are no guidelines on which aspect of consumption is most significant, or even more significant, than others. Furthermore, class location would be likely to change so frequently, as services changed and as people became more or less dependent on different services, that the stratification system would soon lose any explanatory power it might have had. Nor is there any guarantee that any new, or different, consumption classes would correspond with the previous ones. Unless the variables are kept to a minimum, it becomes pointless to talk of any relationship at all between consumption and class. Even if it were possible to weight each and every consumption and distribution network, the resultant scale would, in effect, be closer to a deprivation index than to a definition of class. Leaving aside the advantages of using deprivation indices, there is little argument that they are, by definition, relativist (Townsend, 1979; Piachaud, 1987b). Thus, while consumption cleavages may provide an alternative explanation to economic reductionism, they can all too easily lead to relativism. That is, the analysis invariably hinges upon the relative weight given to different consumption spheres and processes.

In Saunders' case (it should be noted that this does not necessarily apply to all those who use the notion of consumption cleavages), the slide into relativism is such that he rejects any idea that consumption cleavages relate, in any manner whatsoever, with '. . . forms or expressions of deeper class divisions, but nor are they examples of Weberian status groups or parties' (Saunders, 1986, p.156). Consumption is treated as a new and powerful determinant of social divisions in its own right. Consequently, either consumption sectors (or cleavages) suffer from the problem of weighting or, as in Saunders' case, they mark a completely new form of social division. It should be noted that Saunders' claim is not limited to pointing to new social divisions, but implies a paradigmatic shift in sociological theory also. For Saunders implies that the analysis he advocates is a departure from the two principal theorists of contemporary sociology.

Saunders' claim to be providing a paradigmatically new approach to social divisions has to be queried. Goldthorpe and Lockwood (1968) appear to have made a number of similar points about consumption and class allegiance 20 years ago. Galbraith (1967) might claim some credit for developing the new paradigm in the 1950s. Samuel Smiles might also feel that the move from socialized consumption to private consumption was something he had commented upon in the middle of the nineteenth century. Moreover, both Marx (e.g. 1976) and Weber (e.g. 1968) deserve some credit for their respective analyses of consumption patterns. Perhaps Titmuss's work was not familiar to Saunders, but the concerns of the SDW essay certainly touch on a number of similar points.

The 'newness' of consumption sectors/cleavages poses the third problem that this school of thought has to address, namely the ahistorical nature of the discussion to date. In their 1986 papers, Dunleavy and Saunders either use historical examples to support their case or to repudiate the argument of the other. In citing historical examples Saunders and Dunleavy appear to be acknowledging that any 'new' development has to be located in its historical setting. When the process began and when it marked a break with 'older' forms of social division would be questions that they might usefully address. Dunleavy assumes that the first link in his causal chain was working-class pressure for reform in the period prior to the First World War. Saunders, in criticizing Dunleavy, draws a simplistic picture of the power and influence that the Friendly Societies were able to exercise over the medical profession in the nineteenth century. Moreover, both Dunleavy and Saunders mistakenly assume that consumption cleavages/sectors are a recent development. As we have seen previously, intra-class divisions on the basis of access to welfare can be traced back to at least the New Poor Law and arguably even earlier. Certainly, in the 1860s, the 'labour aristocrat' and the pauper were in very different consumption locations: the 'self-help' of the former contrasting starkly with the public dependence of the latter. In the 1930s, there was considerable variation between regions in the standard of life and consumption patterns they might expect. Quite when such patterns produced cleavages is, therefore, an important question which neither scholar adequately addresses.

Once Saunders' grandiose claims are rejected, it becomes apparent that what is actually under discussion is consumption cleavages *within* classes not instead of classes. The credit boom of 1987 saw many working-class people indulge in spheres and patterns of consumption previously only available to the middle classes. However, the greater economic vulnerability of the working classes makes their access to credit fraught with danger. Repossession by building societies, credit company bailiffs and the frantic pursuit of new forms of credit in order to keep these wolves from the door, have been the nightmares of working-class life since 1989. Static or falling house prices and a rise in interest rates, followed by oil price rises, have peeled off the veneer of consumption that some observers took to be the substance and reality of working-class life in the 1980s. With fewer people able to afford overseas holidays, forecasts of a recession in 1991 and debt counselling one of the fastest growing tasks for the Citizen's Advice Bureau, support for the Conservatives has waned. This is not to deny the fact that consumption patterns have changed or that many working-class households have been less vulnerable than others. However, it is vitally important to acknowledge the basis upon which changes in consumption have often been built.

Many working- class households might promote an image of prosperity, but it is not an image that can be unequivocally accepted. Their access to, and location within, a particular consumption sphere may be extremely tenuous and the possibility of falling into the trench of dependency remains. It is this vulnerability which is one of the characteristics of working-class life. The fact that certain types of provision – the Friendly Societies in the nineteenth century and home ownership in the 1980s – have made the fall less likely or the climb out easier does not alter, of itself, their class location. Thus, class retains an important place within sociological theory and, rather than seeing consumption replacing class, it might be more useful to regard it as complementing, or heavily qualifying, class theory. Preteceille (1986) is surely correct to express the need for consumption and class to be linked.

A further difficulty with consumption-based approaches has been emphasized by Warde (1990), who points out that there is some confusion between consumption and service provision. Too often, services such as health and education are discussed as if they are consumer goods, like cars or TVs. The implication that might be drawn is that public welfare services can be provided by the market, or that market principles ought to be introduced into public welfare agencies. The market for services, however, is very different to that for consumer durables. For example, if I do not like my house, I can sell it and move. If I am unhappy with the way my broken leg has been reset, I have no such choice. To confuse services with consumer goods runs the risk, therefore, of promoting the principles of the market and the privatization of public welfare. Such a focus neglects occupational and fiscal welfare and, once again, increases the 'visibility' of public welfare.

Finally, it is necessary to consider how factors other than consumption relate to social divisions. This is not a criticism of consumption-based approaches; as was noted earlier, there is a need for accounts which break with production. It only becomes a problem if consumption is taken as the sole determinant of social divisions. Previous chapters have shown quite clearly that the division of labour has provided the basis for intra-class divisions. Titmuss acknowledged this point in his original essay, and there is nothing in the collective consumption school of thought to contradict the view that it is still a significant feature in the promotion of social divisions. It is to the demands and operation of the labour market, and how these have promoted social divisions, that the discussion will now turn.

Labour markets

The idea that the labour market could be characterized as a duality, which restrained certain groups, was developed in the USA in the 1960s. The dual labour market model set out to challenge the orthodox theory of a free and functional labour market. In orthodox labour market theory, it is suggested that individuals pursue rational labour market careers. The labour market is portrayed as 'open' to all and, depending upon qualifications, skill and competence, individuals will climb the labour market ladder in order to maximize their personal rewards. Simultaneously, employers – so the argument runs – will seek the most able workers to fill the most demanding jobs in order that the firm can maximize its resources.

In contrast, the dual labour market model highlighted the limitations placed upon mobility, both within particular enterprises and within the broader labour market. The civil rights movement in the USA, and later the women's movement, provided the impetus for research into discrimination in the labour market in the late 1960s and early 1970s. Research was not confined to explaining discrimination; low pay, for example, has also been related to the dual labour market model. Moreover, while some of the restrictions imposed by dual labour markets corresponded with the ability of the worker, there also appeared to be a correlation with the type of industry, the technology required within certain industries and, most importantly of all, the characteristics workers possessed. Race was shown to be an especially significant feature of labour market location in various studies carried out in the USA. Initial interest was, therefore, focused upon the restrictions placed on certain workers in particular industries.

The term dual labour market derived from the two distinct sectors initially identified. On the one hand, a primary sector was seen to exist in which wages were high, professional bodies and trade unions usually represented employees, and an internal labour market usually existed that allowed employees to progress from the more poorly paid, low-status jobs to the much better paid, high-status jobs. Certain types of industry were regarded as being more likely than others to operate within the primary sector. Thus high-skill, 'hi-tech' industries were thought to be typical of the primary sector (Doeringer and Piore, 1971; Barron and Norris, 1976). On the other hand, the secondary labour market was notable because it appeared to be much more restrictive. The secondary sector was characterized by, low rates of union membership, low status, few 'fringe benefits', the absence of internal labour markets to provide an escape, and work that required few skills. The primary sector worker has a fairly bright and secure future, whereas the secondary sector worker faces an insecure and bleak one.

By the mid-1970s, the dual labour market model was widely used to explain both racial and sexual discrimination in employment. Barron and Norris (1976) did much to encourage the application of the theory to women's employment patterns in Britain. The idea of different labour market segments, which utilize the sexual division of labour and are built upon the expectations employers have about their female employees, was an attractive idea. Nor is it too difficult to find evidence to support the notion of sexual divisions within the labour market. Nor does it require too much imagination to see how the theory can be applied to the SDW. Fiscal and occupational welfare depends upon access to particular forms of employment and these are only available to those in the primary sector. Likewise, consumption patterns largely depend upon income and again the secondary sector employee will be excluded from certain consumption spheres.

More recently, it has been argued that the labour market is segregated between a core and periphery. Before returning to the dual labour market model and its flaws, the similarities with the idea of core/periphery need to be made clear.

Post-Fordism?

The most recent changes in the labour process have prompted a number of scholars to talk of 'post-Fordism', although for some commentators the motor of change comes from consumers (Piore and Sabel, 1984). Post-Fordism suggests that contemporary capitalist countries have gone beyond the situation where mass production relies upon a strict hierarchy of work, and whereby the consumer can have any colour Ford so long as it is black. Today, Ford produce a range of cars – models within each range, 'specials' and modified versions of particular cars – which would make Henry Ford quite dizzy. The choice offered to the consumer depends, though, on relatively short runs, on highly automated production lines with workers prepared to be flexible in their response to change. There are a number of different versions of the post-Fordism theory, but they tend to point to similar issues: the move to flexible working, autonomous work groups, work group regulation and quality control by the group itself, the subcontracting of services (e.g. catering, cleaning, maintainence), and the idea of a multi-skilled flexible core of workers on full-time contracts complemented by part-time and/or temporary workers (Atkinson, 1984; Piore and

Sabel, 1984; Aglietta, 1987). It is the contrast between those in the peripheral sector and the core which is most stark.

Aglietta (1987), for example, argues that post-Fordism has much in common with the older forms of production. Thus he considers the newer production techniques and technology to be further deskilling and subdividing the workforce. Aglietta regards changes in both consumption and production to be the latest phase of capitalism. He focuses his work on the private manufacturing sector and, as Bagguley (1989) shows, tends to neglect the numerically larger public sector. This has the effect of concealing the importance of the service sector for the transformation of the private sector. More importantly for this study, is the fact that Aglietta neglects the use of women's labour in bolstering both sectors. It is not simply a coincidence that the manufacturing firms which have adopted post-Fordist production methods tend to rely on white male labour for the 'multi-skilled' tasks, but use women for the remaining servicing work. But Aglietta is not alone in neglecting the central significance of gender and race in the move to post-Fordism.

Piore and Sabel (1984) identify the market as the motor of change in the production process. Consumer demand for choice promotes specialization as both small firms and, following reorganization, larger corporations compete over particular niches within the market. Once again the specific impact of race and gender in supporting the changes are ignored. Thus the fact that many of the smaller firms have relied heavily on women workers, at extremely low rates of pay, even in the most dynamic sector of microtechnology, tends to be obscured. Instead, as Bagguley (1989) demonstrates, the emphasis is on the multi-skilled white male worker. The legacy of patriarchy which has continued to ensure a sexual division of labour is not addressed. Similarly, Atkinson (1984) is taken to task by Bagguley (1989) for failing to distinguish the core and the peripheral workers that are supposed to characterize the move to post-Fordism. As with the critique of the dual labour market model which follows, Atkinson's claims rest on demonstrating segregation between the secure core workers and the insecure periphery. This may be easier to show in some firms than others. The difficulty is that Atkinson, like other post-Fordist theorists, suggests that change was a general feature of the 1980s. Certainly, there were some important changes in the organization of work in some firms and, as was argued in Chapter 5, these changes may have had an impact on aspects of the SDW. Nevertheless, there are important continuities which have to be acknowledged.

Like the dual labour market theorists, supporters of post-Fordism identify a split between the full-time core workers, with stable employment prospects, company pension scheme and high wages, and the periphery. Consequently, post-Fordism suffers from very similar theoretical problems as those associated with the dual labour market model. It is to these problems that I shall now turn.

The critique of dualist models

The first obstacle the account faces if it is to assist in the explanation of stratification and inequality concerns the degree of segregation. As Blackburn and Mann (1981, p.79) have pointed out:

The dualist argument depends on demonstrating that there is actual SEGREGATION in the labour market. Yet the only supporting evidence produced concerns AVERAGE DIFFERENCES between say, blacks and whites, men and women and workers in manufacturing and service industry.

It is necessary to show that there is segregation, since if there is a measure of overlap, any explanatory power the thesis possessed evaporates. A dual labour market which is not a duality is simply a nonsense. Blackburn and Mann concluded that while women and some migrant workers might conform to the dualists model, there was little empirical evidence to sustain the theory. Only at the very top of the primary sector and the very bottom of the secondary sector was it possible to witness the type of segregation that supported the idea of a dichotomous labour market. This criticism led to a number of revisions of the dualist argument in which it was proposed that there was, instead of a simple dichotomy, a number of segments. It is not entirely clear, however, that by simply increasing the number of segments that the criticism is removed. Supporters of segmented labour market theory would, perhaps, experience a similar difficulty in identifying the respective segments and demonstrating separation. Moreover, once we go beyond two labour markets, we encounter the same problems seen earlier with housing classes, namely a tendency towards taxonomic invention. Is it permissible to create a new labour market segment every time a particular type of employee, employer, industry or type of employment fails to fit the existing classification system?

Nor, despite this first criticism, is it necessary to accept the dual or segmented labour market theory even if there is segregation within the labour market. For example, it is possible to accept that women's employment patterns do indeed impose a measure of segregation. Yet there is no need to resort to a dual or segmented labour market theory in order to explain this, since the concept of a sexual division of labour seems perfectly appropriate. If the various segments within the labour market are used to account for discrimination against specific social groups, it may be more worthwhile to emphasize the specificity of these groups.

Indeed, the long history of the sexual division of labour highlights a further problem with the dual labour market theory – it is ahistorical. Leaving aside the failure to explain the persistence of women's location within the labour market, a position it will be recalled that in some respects predates capitalism (see Chapter 3), the portrayal of internal labour markets raises further historical and empirical issues. One of the key elements used in the dualist argument is the notion of internal labour markets. These are central to the primary sector because they permit change and adaptation within the more dynamic industries. Thus, it is claimed, dual labour markets develop under pressure from two distinct sources. First, and despite their ability to exert control over their markets, primary sector employers have more difficulty controlling labour. In order to ensure a relatively stable and loyal workforce, employers in the primary sector have to offer more occupational welfare benefits and higher wages. Secondly, primary sector employers try to encourage labour loyalty because of the move towards more capital-intensive technology which, in turn, means they are loathe to lose expensively trained labour.

The difficulty with this causal account is that it is the employers in the primary sector who are portrayed as improving the position of primary sector employees. The relatively privileged primary sector workers are being bought off by employers. While it may be the case that some employees in the primary sector are offered greater rewards, this argument fails to explain the success of others in forcing concessions from employers. The miners in the mid-1970s were able to gain large wage increases and considerable improvements in their pension and other occupational welfare packages, but these were not offered by the National Coal Board (NCB). On the contrary, they were fought for and squeezed from the NCB at a time when the NCB was trying to shed labour. Likewise, during the 1960s, British car manufacturers complained constantly of 'overmanning' and work practices which restricted productivity in an industry which is highly capital-intensive, but were forced to concede improved wages and conditions. The medical profession has managed to maintain its relatively privileged position by controlling admission to the medical schools and not through the generosity of employers. Moreover, some small firms which are labour-intensive and appear to be typical secondary sector employers, pay very high wages and provide extensive welfare benefits for their employees.

The point is that the development, i.e. the history, of the dual labour market needs to be set in the context of industrial relations. Wages and conditions are not simply a function of employer strategies but depend also upon the strength of the labour movement. Viewed in this light, it seems that there have always been contests and conflicts over the price of labour, and that the labour market is no less and no more dichotomous today than it was 150 years ago.

A third aspect of the dual labour market model which poses some difficulty is the way it is identified and used. The primary sector, for example, is defined in terms of a number of characteristics: high wages, fringe benefits, career opportunities, etc. Because, as Blackburn and Mann point out, it is not possible to distinguish clearly between the primary and secondary sectors, some overlap or blurring of the boundaries is inevitable. (This is the problem of segregation identified earlier.) To use subsequently the dual labour market theory to explain the development of high wages, good career opportunities or fringe benefits is, at best, confusing. Thus, for example, Green et al. (1984) explain the growth of 'fringe benefits' (what

Titmuss called occupational welfare) by pointing to the dual labour market. Since dual labour market theory takes the existence of 'fringe benefits' as one of its definitive characteristics, it is clear that nothing has been explained. The existence of occupational welfare is 'explained' by reference to the dual labour market which, in turn, is identified by the very thing it purports to explain. Likewise, low pay, high pay, career opportunities and other characteristics of dual labour market theory have been 'explained' in a similarly circular fashion.

Following on from the above point, it is necessary to ask whether dual labour market theory simply confuses cause and effect. The labour market may, therefore, simply be a minor result of events and not the principal motor. From a Marxist perspective, it appears that the operation of the labour market is distorted by the requirements of capitalist social relations. As we have seen, the purchase and control of labour is a contentious and contested arena. Within this arena, labour organizes to ensure a better price and better conditions of sale. In short, the labour market is both the focus of class struggle (e.g. the closed shop) and the result of it. It is, therefore, as much *an effect of a CAPITALIST* system of production – which, as the Adam Smith Institute would be quick to point out, requires inequality – as *the cause of structural disadvantage.* In most respects, the benefits available within the labour market are the outcome of class struggle. Structured advantages – education, wealth, etc. – serve to give some an *a priori* advantage. Simultaneously, however, the labour market is the site of conflict and class struggle. The contests over the labour process and the form class struggle has frequently taken (e.g. the exclusion of women and ethnic groups) has distorted the capitalist labour market. Thus discrimination is one of the obstacles certain types of labour confront. Not only does the dual labour market theory fail to acknowledge the former – the idea that the labour market reflects the structural inequalities inherent in a class system – but neither does it adequately explain the latter, i.e. discrimination (Beechey, 1978, pp.172–80).

The failure to explain why women and ethnic groups are over-represented in the secondary sector is perhaps the theory's biggest fault. For a theory specifically designed to address the question of discrimination, to be unable to say why one group, rather than another, is consistently discriminated against is a serious omission. The only attempt at explaining this has been to suggest that because immigrant labour arrives on the scene later than indigenous labour, it does so at a disadvantage. This is tantamount to saying 'the early bird gets the worm'. In the USA, such a claim has a somewhat hollow ring, since numerous waves of white immigrant labour have been able to join the more privileged sectors of the labour market. Black labour was not late on the scene, nor were women – both have been actively discriminated against. Moreover, the racist and sexist ideologies which are used to legitimate exclusion are not the preserve of employers. Organized labour has consistently promoted the interests of only some of the working class.

The problems with the dual labour market model, which it should be remembered are often repeated in accounts of post-Fordism, are, arguably, irresolvable. The labour market is too often treated as both the cause and effect of social divisions. To an extent this is true, but it cannot be looked at in isolation from the way groups organize and attempt to contest their particular location in the labour market. For the last non-Marxist perspective to be discussed in this chapter, it is vitally important to consider how groups combine to contest the status quo.

Social closure

For Parkin, the essential problem confronted by any theory of class is what he calls 'the boundary problem'. Where to draw the line between one category and another is, as we have seen, something which can lead to tremendous intellectual contortions as scholars wrestle with their typologies and taxonomies. Parkin makes it quite clear that his model of class and intraclass divisions is in opposition to Marxist concepts. Instead, he takes the Weberian concept of 'life chances' and examines how these are enhanced or restrained. Eschewing the idea that classes can be defined in terms of their relationship to the means of production, Parkin identifies 'the mode of closure' as the definitive feature of class. The two principal forms are exclusionary closure and usurpatory closure. Parkin (1979, p.46) claims that:

> . . . the familiar distinction between bourgeoisie and proletariat, in its classic as well as in its modern guise, may be conceived of as an expression of conflict between classes defined not specifically in relation to their place in the productive process but in relation to their prevalent modes of closure, exclusion and usurpation respectively.

Exclusionary social closure serves the interests of dominant groups and helps to maintain their privileges. This in turn can be based on a number of different forms of control. Parkin argues that property rights are one way in which dominant groups are given control over resources which serve to exclude subordinates. Parkin is quick to distinguish between personal property and property which amounts to a form of social exclusion. Thus he regards the ownership of the means of production as one of a number of forms that exclusion can take. Another form of exclusionary closure which he stresses is 'credentialism'. He argues that the professions are given a privileged legal status by the state, which enables them to maintain exclusionary practices. Alongside the professions, he identifies the education system as an important method of perpetuating credentialism and thereby promoting exclusion. The social exclusion of subordinate groups/classes thus depends on the monopolization of life chances by the privileged at the expence of the rest.

Thus far, Parkin is reiterating Weber's model of class, but he adds to it by developing the idea of usurpatory closure: 'Usurpation is that type of social closure mounted by a group in response to its outsider status and the collective experiences of exclusion' (Parkin, 1979, p.74). Exclusionary social closure serves to keep others out and is operated downwards, against subordinate classes, and usurpation is used to push upwards as a challenge to the dominant groups. As examples of usurpatory closure Parkin (1979, p.74) cites 'strikes, sit ins, marches, picketing, symbolic vigils and the like'. It is important for his analysis to show that the legal status of usurpationary closure is highly ambiguous. Frequently, he argues, usurpationary closure will be unlawful, illegal or unclear as to its legal status. The precise role of the state and the law will be considered in more detail shortly, but it is necessary to highlight the centrality of the state in Parkin's analysis.

Usurpationary closure, it is recognized, rarely goes so far as actually to displace the dominant group, since a variety of tactics are employed to protect their privileged place. One important strategy, Parkin argues, is the integration of labour and trade union leaders. These leaders may act against the interests of those they represent by '. . . spread[ing] the doctrine of self denial amongst those whose active goodwill capitalism . . . requires in abundance' (Parkin, 1979, p.82). Similarities with Marxist accounts which point to incorporation, 'sell outs' and betrayals by the leadership of the working class are easily drawn. Whether it is a valid explanation of class conflict resolution is debatable; previous chapters have shown that the leadership is rarely completely out of step with its constituents. Moreover, Parkin himself provides a more convincing explanation of why subordinate groups fail to form a cohesive and coherent challenge to the dominant group, in his account of dual closure.

The most attractive and distinctive feature of Parkin's self-confessed 'bourgeois critique' of Marxism is the emphasis he places on intra-class divisions generated by dual closure. Dual closure occurs when a subordinate group/class simultaneously exercises closure against the dominant class and members of its own class. Thus:

> . . . exclusionary closure is an aspect of conflict and cleavage within social classes as well as between them. . . . This is also a way of saying that exploitation occurs within the subordinate class as well as against it, since the forms of collective action involved entail the use of power in such a way as to create a stratum of socially excluded inferiors (Parkin, 1979, p.89).

The claim is, and it is made in opposition to Marxist accounts which rest on a definition of exploitation based on the extraction of surplus value in the production process, that in exerting usurpatory closure, a subordinate group can also exert exclusionary closure. The aim, therefore, may be to challenge the dominant group, but in doing so opportunities for other sectors of the subordinate class may be restricted. For example, women, ethnic minorities and religious groups may be excluded from an organization which, nevertheless, challenges the dominant class. In mounting a challenge, the organization may be able to gain extra resources or privileges and this will encourage members to restrict entry. Therefore, exclusion is a consequence of usurpationary closure, and not usually an aim in itself. As an example, Parkin cites the nineteenth-century labour aristocracy. Parkin does not, as some Marxists have been shown to, suggest that the labour aristocrats were bought off, but rather that they monopolized certain market skills and thereby increased their bargaining strength. Success depended on restricting entry to the trade and the cohesion of the organizations of the labour aristocracy when confronting employers. The excluded groups tended to be 'socially visible target groups' (Parkin, 1979, p.92). (This question of visibility reminds us that Sinfield also felt that one of the key features of the SDW is the greater visibility of the poorest and weakest sections of the working class who are compelled to rely on public welfare.)

However, the identification of excluded groups raises the question of how they become 'socially visible'. Why, for example, do specific ethnic groups and women feature so frequently as the socially excluded? This question is often neglected by scholars, but Parkin does not shy away from providing a bold, if somewhat contentious, response. In so doing, it should be noted that Parkin rejects Weber's explanation that any criteria will be seized upon and used in the fight to control and monopolize opportunities. If this were the case, he claims, the pattern of exclusion would be more random and varied. Instead, specific groups are consistently identified and excluded following their visible status as inferiors. Parkin (1979, p.96) suggests that the key actor in the identification of excluded groups is the state:

> Proletarian exclusion against definable social groups thus only appears to occur in the wake of a similar policy conducted via the state by the dominant class itself. Indeed, *it is only through the action of the state that cultural groups become hierarchically ranked in a manner that enables one to effect closure against another*. If it were merely one group "seizing upon" some attribute or other, as suggested by Weber, it would not be possible to explain why Catholics in Northern Ireland failed to bring about closure against Protestant workers, instead of the reverse; or why blacks in the Deep South did not seize upon white skin colour as a criterion of exclusion, or why female workers did not monopolize employment opportunities at the expense of men. None of these possibilities could be realized because the dominant class and the state had not already paved the way by creating the appropriate legally and politically vulnerable category. There is thus nothing in the least arbitrary in the selection of exclusionary criteria (emphasis added).

It is worth quoting this passage at length because it illustrates quite clearly the central role Parkin assigns the state. Additionally, it emphasizes the part he sees power playing in the formation of classes. The state is used by dominant classes and it in turn enacts measures which subdivide the subordinate class. Thus immigration laws, the Poor Law of 1834, the creation of a privileged Protestant statelet in the six counties in Ireland, the inferior legal status of women throughout the nineteenth century, and slavery in the USA, might be given as evidence by Parkin of the importance of the state in creating intra-class divisions.

Unfortunately, by identifying state legislation as the precondition for defining particular groups as inferior, and thereby laying the foundations for social divisions, Parkin poses some problems which are not easily resolved.

Making a divided class

There have been numerous critiques of Parkin's social closure theory and there is little point in covering all of these (Giddens, 1980; Barbalet, 1982; Murphy, 1988). Much of the debate is concerned with the general framework used by Parkin and the validity of closure as the key determinant of class location. Simultaneously, and as Murphy (1988, pp.45–6) makes plain, even Parkin's critics find the concept of social closure attractive and assert that it can be incorporated within their preferred stratification theory. The principal criticisms relevant here are (a) that the basis of power is ill-defined and thus class formation and power are confused and (b) that the state does not create social divisions but may develop existing ones.

The central claim of Parkin's thesis is that certain groups use exclusionary closure in order to maintain their privileged positions. Thus the power to exclude is central to the formation of a dominant class. If, as he also asserts, this power is based on the state sanctioning the power of the dominant group via credentialism, the education system, etc., we might legitimately ask which occurs first. How can the dominant group become dominant without the sanction of the state and simultaneously already be a group capable of excluding subordinate groups? If a prerequisite of class formation is the power to exclude, but the state provides the means for closure, it may appear that the dominant group is able to exert power, if only over the state, before it engages in excluding others. If the dominant group has the power to influence the state – a considerable measure of power it might be thought – where does this power come from, if it is the state which sanctions credentials, etc.?

Likewise, from where does the power that subordinate groups exercising dual closure derive? Parkin does not point, as Titmuss did, to the division of labour or control over the labour process, but suggests that it is the state which legally defines particular groups as inferior. Leaving aside for the moment whether this is correct, the problem remains of what resources are used by those exercising dual closure in order to usurp the position of dominant groups. Although industrial action, strikes and picketing may all be consumed within a general theory of 'life chances', this tends to miss the specific feature of this form of challenge. It is not simply a coincidence that those groups who are able to exercise dual closure are industrially based. Nor is it very helpful to be told that the state defines some subordinate groups as inferior and simultaneously defines the actions of those who exclude these groups as unlawful. If legislation is a precondition for exclusion, by both the dominant group and the subordinate class, how is it that dual closure can involve measures of dubious legality, and not be punished, whereas excluded groups are consistently penalized by the law?

Murphy (1988) has attempted to resolve some of these problems by suggesting that all forms of social closure involve power being used. The very fact that excluded groups exist within the working class means, for Murphy, that power is being exerted against them. However, not only does this detract from one of the most interesting aspects of Parkin's thesis (namely, that in the process of challenging dominant groups others are excluded), but it also confuses the means used with the subsequent effects. Moreover, certain groups who use dual closure are clearly far more successful than others. A closed shop agreement, for example, does not in itself provide success, or even the possibility of a usurpatory challenge. As Barbalet (1982, p.489) notes:

> The major difficulty with Parkin's argument lies in the assumption that class formation is a consequence of group power relations. Power relations between class competitors can and do change without changes in the nature or formation of classes themselves. Contrary to Parkin's assumption, class power and class formation are independent phenomena; a change in one will not necessarily be reflected in variation in another.

Power may be a necessary condition in the formation of classes and intraclass divisions, but it is not, as Parkin suggests, a sufficient condition of class formation. Success in the competition over scarce resources does not, in itself, amount to exploitation. Competition is, as Murphy (1988, pp.55–6) notes, an organizing feature of capitalism, but he is mistaken to equate the successful competitor with those who successfully exploit the myriad groups who compete.

Nor is it possible to accept Parkin's claim that the state always provides the criteria for exclusion within the working class. It may do so, although this is very much a 'chicken and egg' question, but the evidence in the earlier historical chapters suggests that the state responds to existing divisions and does not create them. The New Poor Law of 1834, for example, was shown to have been an extremely divisive measure, but it simply built on the existing SDW. More recently, the 'Right to Buy' legislation widened consumption cleavages within the working class but the Conservatives did not invent owner-occupation. Ironically, in giving the state such a central role, Parkin moves very close to those structural Marxists from whom he is most keen to distance himself. The strength of Parkin's account remains the emphasis he places on the form and direction of class struggle. When engaged in usurpatory struggles, dual closure will often be a consequence and this will serve to promote intra-class divisions.

Summary

The Weberian concern with class, status and power has been reflected in many of the accounts we have looked at in this chapter. Although this was not the perspective from which Murray wrote his polemic, it has to be admitted that the retort to Murray is polemical and, perhaps, a little too dismissive. Nevertheless, it has been the link between the stratification system and the distribution of resources which has been the principal concern of this chapter. Accounts which simply take the distribution of a particular resource as an indicator of class location have been examined and found wanting. Housing classes and social security classes, because they rely on distributive networks and contentious typologies, are seen to be inadequate. However, the notion of life chances, which lie behind many of the consumption-based concepts, have certain attractions. The work of Dunleavy is seen to be especially interesting and the use of 'consumption cleavages' seductive. However, in some respects, the idea suffers from the same taxonomic problems associated with the concept of housing classes. The consumption variables – the number of different resources that have to be weighted – are too much like a score card and do not provide an explanation of social divisions. Nor can it be accepted that post-Second World War developments can be taken to show that consumption cleavages are a new phenomenon. A more historically informed account would go some way to resolving these shortcomings and might provide further insights into the role of consumption in the development and practice of capitalism.

Next, the idea of a dual labour market as the motor of social divisions was considered. Once again there is a problem of cause and effect – whether labour market distinctions are the result, or the cause, of social division. The validity of the argument is also undermined by a lack of empirical evidence to support the claims of segregation. Moreover, the theory does not adequately explain why discrimination is consistently directed towards specific groups. Nor, when we want to explain the development of the SDW, is the dual labour market theory of value, since it relies on a perverse circularity to account for the growth of occupational welfare. These problems, it was argued, can also be seen in many of the accounts of post-Fordism.

Finally, social closure theory was considered and the concept of dual closure was especially interesting. This aspect of Parkin's account has been accepted without taking on board the rest of his analysis. In so far as dual closure highlights the form and direction of class struggle and how this can serve to reinforce social divisions, it is felt to be a useful approach. Unfortunately, the basis of power and the role of the state are seen to be problematic in social closure theory.

All the accounts considered in this chapter are non-Marxist. They have provided over the last 20 years or so some significant insights into social divisions in Britain. Nevertheless, the weakness of these accounts has been their reluctance to see social divisions in the context of a class society. However, this criticism should not detract from the considerable challenge these approaches have mounted to the economic determinism and functionalism of some Marxist accounts. It is to Marx and his legacy that we shall turn to next.

seven

Reserves and surplus populations?

Finally, the lowest sediment of the relative surplus population dwells in the sphere of pauperism. Apart from vagabonds, criminals, prostitutes, in short the actual lumpen proletariat . . . (Marx, 1976, p.797).

In this chapter, I want to look at how Marx discussed the poorest section of the working class and to question the way that Marxists have adopted his work. I shall take a critical look at what Marx wrote, what he did not say, the language and concepts he used, the inconsistencies in his account, and how all these have influenced Marxists when they discuss the poor. The reader should be aware that underpinning many of my criticisms there lies a hostility to Leninism and structural Marxism. Marx will be shown to have been a middle-class Victorian patriarch who propagated a number of negative stereotypes of the poor. These have been accepted too readily by subsequent Marxists. Perhaps it is because Marx himself took, such a negative view of the poor that Marxists have been rather coy about discussing the relationship between the poorest stratum of society and the rest of the working class. The role of welfare and the functions of the poor within the political economy of capitalism are more often the focus of attention. The poor, it is implied, lack the self-discipline of the horny handed sons, and more recently daughters, of toil, and this is one of the reasons why Marxists have only rarely articulated their interests. Instead, there is often a moralistic and judgemental attitude to the poor which mirrors that of the lower middle classes.

Criminals, prostitutes and vagabonds

Marx was not, as it is sometimes thought, the champion of the very poor. Like many other middle-class observers in Victorian Britain, he looked to the industrial working class and those relatively privileged sectors of the artisan class for his inspiration. While he acknowledged that even the most industrious and thrifty member of the nineteenth-century working class could fall into pauperism, he tended to discuss the poor in less than flattering terms. It should not be necessary to point out that Marx was a product of his time, and his language and tone were similar to many of his contemporaries. As we saw in Chapter 3, there was virtually a consensus among middle-class observers in the nineteenth century that the poor were a hopeless class. Certainly, the language and tone of many Victorian commentators, and Marx has to be counted among them, illustrated the breadth of opinion in the nineteenth century which observed a clear division within the working class.

Nor was Marx consistent in his views of the very poor. They are at different times described as the lumpen-proletariat, the reserve army of labour and the relative stagnant (or surplus) population. Contained within these concepts are a host of perjorative and highly subjective assertions about the nature and behaviour of the poorest members of a capitalist society. Some of these have been used subsequently by Marxists as terms of abuse or to dismiss the poor as politically insignificant, as Marx and Engels did in the Communist Manifesto:

> The lumpen-proletariat, this passive putrefaction of the lowest strata of the old society, is here swept into the movement by a proletarian revolution, but in accordance with all its conditions of life is more apt to sell itself to reactionary intrigues (1848, p.53; cited in Bovenkerk, 1984).

The idea of the poor as *putrefying* has been less popular in recent years, but that they may be 'passive' and 'reactionary' has often been asserted by groups on the Left (Trotsky, 1975; Friend and Metcalf, 1981, pp.42–5). In the 1970s, for example, it was claimed that reactionary groups within the lumpen-proletariat provided the muscle for the National Front and other neo-Fascist organizations. Not that recent Marxist writings on 'the welfare state' portray the poor as a reactionary force. Where the poor are discussed, and it is remarkable how many Marxists have been able to write lengthy tracts on the role of state welfare in a capitalist society without discussing the poor, they are usually set within an environmental context. Few today, though, would wish to be too closely identified with Engels' (1958, pp.144–5) account of the environmental school of thought:

> Apart from over-indulgence in intoxicating liquors, the sexual immorality of many English workers is one of their greatest failings. This too follows from the circumstances in which this class of society is placed. The workers have been left to themselves without the moral training necessary for the proper control of their sexual desires. While burdening the workers with numerous hardships the middle classes have left them only the pleasures of drink and sexual intercourse. The result is that the workers, in order to get something out of life, are passionately

devoted to these two pleasures and indulge in them to excess and in the grossest fashion. If people are relegated to the position of animals, they are left with the alternatives of revolting and sinking into bestiality . . . [and] . . . If the demoralisation of the worker passes beyond a certain point then it is just as natural that he will turn into a criminal... as inevitably as water turns into steam at boiling point.

Before any impressionable young Marxist rushes off to get a working-class job in the hope of experiencing this cycle of depravity, they ought to query the validity of the claim. Only right-wing writers like Murray (1990) would agree with this sensational view today, and he is a most unlikely bedfellow for Engels.

Another difficulty is that many of the terms used by Marx and Engels to describe the poorest stratum of the working class are very unclear. The concept of a lumpen-proletariat, for example, is riddled with confusion. Frank Bovenkerk (1984) has identified five different definitions of the lumpen-proletariat used by Marx and Engels:

1 That this social group is a historical remnant of an earlier society. It survived from pre-industrial society into the industrial age like reptiles in Darwin's theory of evolution.
2 Its members are simply social degenerates.
3 They are a sub-stratum of the general proletariat, but threaten the interests and cohesion of the proletariat as a whole, either because of their politically reactionary nature, or because they could be used to replace organized labour.
4 Following on from the previous definition it is possible to see another similar idea which suggests that at least some of the lumpen-proletariat are peripheral to the capitalist system of production. Thus 'From whore to pope, there is a mass of such rabble. But the honest and "working" lumpen proletariate belongs here as well' (Bovenkerk, 1984, p.20).
5 If these definitions are not confusing enough, Bovenkerk points out that there are also a number of other miscellaneous definitions which do not rest easily in the first four categories. Nor, however, do these warrant close or serious attention, since they often appear to be rather careless and casual remarks.

The degenerate 'lumpen'

The idea that the poor, or at least significant numbers of them, can be portrayed as lacking in the moral fibre required of socialists, was echoed by Lenin. Leninism has demanded self-sacrifice and 'iron proletarian discipline' in order to attain the revolutionary goal. The pursuit of pleasure is portrayed as a form of bourgeois decadence or of 'lumpen' inclinations. The implication is that a lack of self-control is partly to blame for the condition of the poor. Thus a patronizing and moralistic attitude can pervade the work of some Marxists. Stedman-Jones (1984, pp.337–49), for example, seems to have a distaste for the politics of the street, the drinking and sexual proclivities of the 'residuum' in nineteenth-century London. Others have suggested that the lumpen-proletariat has now virtually disappeared and that, anyway, it was all very different in the nineteenth century (Corrigan and Leonard, 1978, pp.85–7). There is no dispute with Marx and Engels' portrayal of the lumpen-proletariat; it is simply that with the development of capitalism, this stratum has been reduced to a few problem cases for social workers. Corrigan and Leonard claimed in 1978 that with a more buoyant labour market the lumpen-proletariat were treated as potential workers by social workers. With long-term mass unemployment a constant feature of the 1980s, are we to conclude that the lumpen-proletariat has re-emerged?

It might be argued that the context within which Marx's theory of a lumpen-proletariat has to be located is his general theory of class formation. If so, one of the key questions would be whether Marx might have designated the poor a separate place in the class system. There are some grounds for believing he would have done. Quite often, when discussing Marx's definition of class, the following quotation is cited:

> In so far as millions of families live under conditions of existence that separate their mode of life, their interests and their culture from those of other classes and put them in hostile opposition to the latter, they form a class. In so far as there is merely a local inter-connection . . . and their interests begets no community, no national bond, no political organisation amongst them, they do not form a class (Marx, 1969 p.278).

From this it is possible to conclude that in certain circumstances the poor/lumpen-proletariat do constitute a class. Like more recent commentators, it might be claimed that Marx provides the possibility of identifying some sort of underclass. However, Marx does not treat the poor as a class and Marxists have tended not to do so. The main reason lies in the second part of the quotation. The poor are not seen to have formed a community, national bond or political organization. This point is debatable, but we shall return to the political marginalization of the poor shortly. Whatever the truth in the idea of the poor as passive, unorganized and undisciplined, these characteristics, it needs to be remembered, are in contrast to those of the true proletariat. Usually the poor, in so far as they are discussed at all, are a necessary stratum which enables a capitalist economy to function properly. They are still portrayed as a rather conservative force, but there is a significant shift in emphasis away from the personal traits of the poor and their behaviour to the functions performed within a capitalist system of production.

A Reserve Army of Labour?

In contrast to Marx's ideas on the lumpen-proletariat, the Reserve Army of Labour (RAL) thesis has a considerable measure of academic respectability.

In *Capital*, Marx (1976, p.792) explains in a relatively straightforward manner how the industrial reserve army of labour operates:

> The industrial reserve army, during periods of stagnation and average prosperity, weighs down the active army of workers; during the periods of over-production and feverish activity, it puts a curb on their pretensions.

The RAL performs these functions at different times, depending on whether there is a slump or boom in trade. During periods of downturn or slump, the RAL can be expelled from employment. Not only does this provide a means for employers to dispose of labour, it also creates fear in the minds of those still employed. The threat of being thrown out of work, and into the reserve army, or the possibility that, unless employees cooperate with management they might force the enterprise out of business, is reinforced by the expulsion of the RAL. On the other hand, when the enterprise is booming, an employer can threaten to substitute workers with members of the RAL if they begin to think that, since the firm is prospering, they ought to share in the prosperity. Thus the RAL is seen to exist as a pool of labour that can either be poured back into, or drained from, when it suits Capital.

However, it would be possible for this pool of labour to be exhausted but for two other features of 'The General Law of Capitalist Accumulation' (Marx, 1976). Both features, it should be noted, are also related to the labour process. Capitalists can either introduce new working practices or simply increase the rate of exploitation. As the active army of labour becomes more combative and presses for improvements in pay and conditions, the employer seeks new methods of production. New forms of machinery and new ways of organizing production enable the capitalist to either dispose of labour, thereby adding to the RAL, or to increase the productivity of labour, thereby increasing the rate of exploitation. If the latter course is pursued (an increase in the rate of exploitation and production), the individual capitalist is looking to gain an advantage over competitors. If this strategy succeeds, other capitalists will be forced to follow suit – which in time will lead to a crisis of over-production and mass unemployment in that industry – or to replace the more expensive workers with cheaper labour. The cheaper worker is likely to be recruited from sources previously untapped by industrial capitalism, such as rural and/or immigrant labour, the very young or women.

Marx (1976, pp.781–94), makes it quite clear that the existence of a RAL is at once both a necessary condition of capitalist production and, simultaneously, a brake on the combativity of the working class. Thus the RAL thesis is central to Marx's critique of the political economy of capitalism. Numerous scholars have used the RAL thesis when explaining the persistence of poverty and unemployment in capitalist societies. Ginsburg, for example, states that: 'Hence it is suggested here that the social security system is concerned with reproducing a reserve army of labour, the patriarchal family and the disciplining of the labour force' (Ginsburg, 1979, p.2; see also Gough, 1979, p.52; Alcock, 1987, p.11; Novak, 1988, pp.77-80).

Despite the centrality of the RAL to Marxist theory, it has hardly been revised since first proposed by Marx. Although there has been an analysis of the part played by the state in developing income maintenance schemes and other social policies that assist capital in sustaining the RAL, these observations have added to, rather than modified substantially, the general thesis of a RAL. For Bowles and Gintis (1976), the education system assists in the reproduction of the RAL. Castles and Kosack (1972) have argued that immigrant workers from Southern Europe and the Third World '. . . can be imported as the interests of the capitalist class dictate'. Socialist-Feminists, with varying degrees of enthusiasm and reservation, have similarly claimed that women form a part of the RAL. There has also been some considerable discussion regarding which women, at what specific historical times and in which types of industry, operate as a RAL (Beechey, 1978; Anthias, 1980; Barrett, 1980; Humphries, 1983; Walby, 1986). Braverman (1974) relies on the RAL thesis to explain the pressure exerted on trade unions to modify their demands and on employers to introduce new technology. In short, the RAL thesis has been invoked to support many claims, but there are a number of issues that have not been adequately addressed.

There are a number of difficulties with the RAL thesis, although not everyone who uses the concept reproduces all of them. I intend to run through them briefly and then outline them in more detail shortly. The first point to note is that the RAL thesis is closer to the political economy school of thought within Marxism than it is to an approach based on class struggle analysis. The RAL is discussed in terms of the functions and structural requirements of capital accumulation, rather than those of class conflict. The active agents of history are neglected in favour of the impersonal forces of capitalism. This is not to say that class struggle is absent from accounts of the functions of the reserve army, but the members of the RAL are all too easily discussed as if they were simply a liquid contained within the structural confines of capitalism. The oft-quoted analogy with a stagnant pool, in and out of which they are poured whenever it suits capital, implies they are a passive social group. The effect can be to deny the history the poor themselves have made. It confirms a negative stereotype similar to the idea of the passive (putrefying was Marx's term) mass who are prepared to support the status quo. Thus it also blames the victims, in part, for their predicament. The state is portrayed as having played an executive role for the capitalist class and/or having ensured that the functioning of the labour market, social policy etc., conform to the needs of a capitalist mode of production. In addition, the form and direction that class struggle has taken – a divided working class often engaged in divisive and economistic struggles – is neglected. Consequently, a romanticized view of 'the' working class can be maintained and Marxism fails to engage even with that class. Nor is it clear who the members of the RAL are and why they, rather than others, are assigned to the reserves. Finally, Marx confuses the reader in his definition of the RAL and this confusion is not satisfactorily resolved by those who subsequently use the concept. These are criticisms which some may find hard to accept and it is worth illustrating them more fully.

First, the history of resistance, organization and conflict which the poorest members of the working class have engaged in is 'hidden from history', to borrow Rowbotham's (1973) phrase. The importance of the earlier historical chapters of this book in illuminating part of that history is emphasized by the implicit denial of it by Marxists who simply rely on the RAL thesis. Whether confronting the Guardians of the Poor Law in the 1830s, rioting in the 1880s, occupying the offices of the Guardians in the 1920s, marching in the 1930s, occupying DHSS offices and empty buildings in the 1970s, or rioting in the 1980s, the poor have hardly been passive. Like the rest of the working class, the poor, migrants, the single parent and the unemployed, were present at their own 'making'. What is more, they were present at the various 're-makes' as well. They might not always have been the most influential of the characters present, but to deny them a place in their own history is dangerously misleading. The danger arises from the fact that intra-class divisions are too easily seen to be due to the reserves' failure to get onto the field of play, rather than their exclusion from it. Thus the RAL is treated as if it is a conservative force within the working class. By contrast, recent work on the political organization of the poor and the unemployed suggests that they are no more or less 'conservative' than the bulk of the working class (Bagguley, 1991). Indeed, there is a strong case for arguing that, however we define them, members of the RAL have been some of the most active agents of resistance in recent years.

Secondly, it is not clear that it is the state that creates the RAL and divides the working class (Ginsburg, 1979; Gough, 1979; Jones, 1983). State social policies may reinforce social divisions, but, as we have seen in earlier chapters, they are more usually responding to existing divisions. For commentators such as Ginsburg (1979) and Novak (1988), the state performs a key function for capital. Novak (1988, pp. 159–61) does give the state a measure of autonomy but this is '*ultimately* constrained within the parameters of capitalist production' (emphasis added).

Like the length of a piece of string, the degree of autonomy that the state possesses seems to be difficult to measure or define. However, we do need to unravel the state's overbearing power from its functions for capital if we are to assess the possibilities of eradicating social divisions. Let me make it absolutely clear that I am not suggesting that the state does not enact legislation which is socially divisive, for it has done so on numerous occasions. My argument is that it builds on existing divisions, exploits fractures and fissures within the working class, and develops policies which give some sections of the working class an interest, albeit perhaps short-term, in supporting capitalism. The state does not invent social divisions because it is incapable of doing so. On the contrary, it seeks the views of middle-class observers, examines the practices of specific sections of the working class and, usually in a distorted form, represents these in so far as they can be made to fit within the parameters of capitalism. Moreover, by assigning the state the key role, Marxists have neglected one of Marx's most perceptive observations when he discussed the RAL; namely that the labour process generates social divisions.

For Marx, the development of new technology and changes in the organization of work are tied to the role of the RAL. The most interesting aspect of this view of how the RAL is used emphasizes the relative strength of some sections of the working class in resisting increased exploitation at work. If the ability of some to influence the production process were given a more central place in the account, while the supposed role of the state was relegated, the RAL thesis might provide more interesting insights into intra-class divisions. Such an approach would, however, be closer to Parkin's social closure model, discussed in the previous chapter. The focus would shift away from the structural requirements of capital and towards an examination of the conditions which enable some sections of the working class to resist the introduction of 'reserves'.

Thirdly, the empirical evidence is more ambiguous than the RAL thesis assumes. Thus it is by no means clear that the RAL substitutes for the most expensive labour. There appears to be a stronger case for seeing the RAL acting as a brake upon itself, rather than upon the more expensive and better organized sections of the working class (Cockburn, 1983; Walby, 1986, pp.74-80). The reason why the RAL does not act as a brake on the active army of labour is that the trade unions and employers can influence the operation of the labour market. As we saw in Chapter 6, dual labour market theories may not explain why discrimination takes place, but they do demonstrate that the labour market does not operate according to perfect market principles. Social closure and discrimination are key factors in excluding specific people.

Following on from the point above, it is important to acknowledge who does what to whom. Does the RAL really threaten the well-organized and most powerfully placed sections of the labour movement? If the RAL is being accused of threatening – in effect if not in practice – the relatively more secure workers, we must consider the evidence for the defence. Previous chapters provide ample evidence of the exclusion of the poor, women, Irish, the unskilled, Jewish migrants, black workers and 'roughs'. One measure of success for organized labour has always been its ability to resist management attempts at 'substitution' and the imposition of reserves. If the reserve army is charged with threatening behaviour, any jury would surely have to conclude that the organized working class got its retaliation in first. The proletariat may have been intent on challenging the ruling class, but in the ensuing melee they have also aimed a few blows at some of the weakest members of their own class.

Finally, the question 'Who constitutes the RAL?' poses further difficulties. On the one hand, the reply brings forth the moralism and language of middle-class Victorian England. For, despite the colder discourse of the economic needs of the system of production, the concept of a RAL retains all its perjorative language and associations. It is difficult to use the term without encountering a language problem (Friend and Metcalf, 1981; Byrne and Parson, 1983). On the other hand, it is necessary for advocates of the RAL thesis to explain why some, rather than others, are consistently located within the RAL (Barrett, 1980).

Marx makes it particularly difficult to ascertain who is a member of the RAL. He confuses the reader by introducing the term 'relatively surplus population' and by subdividing this group into a number of further classifications. He starts by pointing out that every worker belongs to the Relative Surplus Population (RSP) during periods of unemployment or partial employment. He goes on to point to three elements that the RSP always possesses: '. . . the floating, the latent and the stagnant' (Marx, 1976, p.794).

The floating RSP is that stratum which is in and out of employment, depending on the needs of capitalist production. He cites the example of young men who are dismissed once they reach the age of maturity because they warrant a full wage. The latent RSP are primarily those who work in agriculture, but are likely to be drawn into either the urban manufacturing areas or into pauperism. The stagnant population:

. . . forms a part of the active labour army, but with extremely irregular employment. . . . It is characterized by a maximum of working time and a minimum of wages. . . . It is constantly recruited from workers in large scale industry and agriculture who have become redundant, and especially from those decaying branches of industry where handicraft is giving way to manufacture, and manufacture to machinery (Marx, 1976, p.796).

Marx (1976, pp. 796–7) goes on to state that this stagnant population:

. . . forms at the same time a self-reproducing and self-perpetuating element of the working class, taking a proportionately greater part in the general increase of that class than the other elements. In fact, not only the number of births and deaths, but the absolute size of families, stands in inverse proportion to the level of wages. . . . This law of capitalist society would sound absurd to savages, or even to civilized colonists. It calls to mind the boundless reproduction of animals individually weak and constantly hunted down.

Having stated that the RAL/RSP consists of three groups, Marx introduces a fourth: 'Finally, the lowest sediment of the relative surplus population dwells in the sphere of pauperism.' He then divides this fourth group into four groups: First, the vagabonds, criminals and prostitutes mentioned earlier; secondly, the unemployed; thirdly, orphans and pauper children; and the fourth group within the lowest sediment are:

. . . the demoralized, the ragged, and those unable to work, chiefly people who succumb to their incapacity for adaptation, an incapacity which results from the division of labour; people who have lived beyond the worker's average lifespan; and the victims of industry, . . the mutilated, the sickly, the widows, etc. (Marx, 1976, p.797)

On the very next page, Marx (1976, p.798) reveals that the terms relative surplus population and industrial reserve army are interchangeable. Unfortunately, this does not assist the reader, since elsewhere he appears to distinguish between the two. Even if we leave aside this point, it remains the case that with initially three groups, subsequently expanded to include a fourth, and with this fourth group then divided into four further categories, Marx leaves the reader more than a little confused.

It seems that even some of the most interesting and original thinkers are drawn into taxonomic invention when confronted with intra-class divisions. The confusion is compounded by the fact that Marx links economic, social and psychological issues to the pathology of individuals and social groups. Most disappointing of all, however, is the language and tone of Marx's discussion.

Even allowing for the late Victorian period, the terms 'stagnant', 'floating', 'latent' and 'lowest sediment' suggest an unsympathetic stance. When he asserts that certain sections of the RAL breed more rapidly (with just a hint of Social Darwinism apparent) and 'succumb to their incapacity for adaptation', while others are part of some criminal class, Marx reproduces the prejudices of the Victorian middle classes. It could be argued that Marx simply took an unromantic view of the poorest members of nineteenth-century society. Certainly, it should be remembered that Marx never divorces the conditions of the poor from the demands of the capitalist system of production. However, there is no need to take too generous a view of Marx's account and it may be more useful to acknowledge the flaws.

The principle difficulty with Marx's analysis of social divisions is that it enabled subsequent Marxists to ignore or dismiss the political and social significance of the poor. Moreover, the specific reasons for certain groups being over-represented in the RAL are inadequately addressed. Racism and patriarchy within the working class are conveniently neglected in favour of seeing the RAL as the unfortunate (at best) or reactionary (at worst) elements within the working class. This, in turn, has tended to marginalize the politics of the poor.

Marginalization

Marxists have tended to dismiss the poor by adhering to Marx's views. Thus the very poor are effectively marginalized even by those scholars who focus upon them. Stedman-Jones, for example, whose account is undoubtedly the most sustained and sensitive attempt to investigate the ideological and political relations between classes in late nineteenth-century London, reproduces the view that the very poor were politically conservative. He suggests that:

Unlike the artisans, the unskilled and casual poor were ignorant,

> inarticulate and unorganized. . . . Similarly, in the absence of any
> broader consciousness of class, the political attitudes of the metro-
> politan poor were most likely to reflect the attachments to the real or
> imagined privileges of some particular occupation (Stedman-Jones,
> 1984, p.341).

Yet Stedman-Jones provides ample evidence in his own work of resistance
by the poor. At the same time, we might ask if the new industrial proletariat
were so very different? Can we be so confident that the 'real' working class
was so much more dynamic and sympathetic to the aims of socialism? As we
saw in Chapter 3, in the discussion of the 'labour aristocracy', numerous
Marxists have pointed to precisely the same lack of revolutionary zeal on
the part of the skilled and organized working class. Likewise, the 'attachment' to the privileges of particular occupations is as common, if not more
so, amongst skilled workers as the unskilled. Moreover, Stedman-Jones
(1984, p.345) bemoans the fact that the factory proletarians failed to provide the vanguard of the revolution:

> Unfortunately, however, the crowds who gathered to hear the revolu-
> tionary message were not the factory proletarians described in the
> Communist Manifesto but the traditional casual poor of the metropo-
> lis; and their hunger and desperation resulted not in the disciplined
> preparation for socialist revolution but in the frenzied rioting of Feb-
> ruary 1886.

Bad luck it would appear for the Marxists of the SDF that, despite their
efforts, it was the 'residuum' rather than the proletariat proper that took to
the streets. The attacks on the clubs of the rich and the riots are dismissed,
and the poor are characterized as more conservative than 'the respectable'
working class who stayed at home. It is somewhat ironic that the RAL is
seen to be a conservative and reactionary force, holding back the aspirations
of the true proletarian vanguard. On the other hand, when they, rather than
the 'disciplined factory proletarians', do take action, they are described as a
mob, rabble or 'frenzied rioters', who are alienating the respectable working
class with their hooligan behaviour.

It may be true to argue that the exclusion of the poor from the formal
channels of power – trade unions, Parliamentary politics, and pressure groups
– has prevented them from mounting a sustained political movement.
However, it seems a little unfair to blame those who are excluded for their
isolation. Moreover, the needs of the poor require immediate solutions, not
the gradual and piecemeal reforms organized labour has pursued. Consequently, long-term objectives are set aside in favour of demonstrations of
anger and frustration. But, given that Marxists have regarded the reformism,
economism and gradualism of the British working class as the major obstacles
to socialist transformation, it is peculiar that the poor are berated for taking
more direct and unconstitutional action. Besides, there is rarely any evidence
that the poor are more conservative than the rest of the working class.

The political marginalization of the poor is an issue which Miliband (1974) has also addressed:

> The simple fact of the matter is that the poor enter the pressure [sic] market, where they enter it at all, from the weakest possible position: that of course is one of the main reasons, if not THE main reason, why they remain poor.

A little further on the reader is informed that:

> They are, as I have suggested earlier, an integral part of the working class: but many of them constitute its inactive part, and are *self excluded* from the defence organisations which organised labour has brought into being, and which have helped to improve its bargaining position (Miliband, 1974, pp.187–8: emphasis added).

Far from excluding themselves, the poor have been excluded by others, most notably for our purposes by organized labour, a fact that is gradually being acknowledged. Novak (1988, p.147), for example, has suggested that the active endorsement by organized labour of racist and sexist practices has 'played a large part in allowing such divisions to be perpetuated'.

Alongside the portrayal of the poor as essentially passive, conservative and unorganized, there has been a neglect of the actions that the poor have taken. While Marxist historians have examined how the mob, the Lazerati, the anti-Poor Law rioters, the anti-UAB rioters and the Luddites asserted their interests, these activities, and more recent expressions of social discontent, are forgotten when discussing the politics of the poor. Riot and social disorder may not be sustainable forms of political pressure, but they give the lie to the idea of the poor as passive. When the poor have formed their own defence organizations, such as the NUWM and claimants unions, trades councils have either refused to recognize them or marginalized them by bestowing 'observer status'. When unemployed groups have retained their union branches, these have come under pressure from the union hierarchy for putting forward sectional demands and have frequently been closed down. When 'drop in' centres for the unemployed were established, the TUC was quite clear that these were intended to head off any 'extreme' organization of the unemployed. The definition of extremism was soon extended, under pressure from local authorities (mostly Labour controlled) and the MSC, to include posters protesting at unemployment (see Bagguley, 1991).

Nor has the Left always been attentive to the struggles of the poorest sections of the working class. Claimants unions and centres for the unemployed have usually been seen as providing new recruits, but not as viable organizations in their own right. Likewise, the 'workerism' of many Left groups has compelled them to support economistic and sectional struggles by various trade unionists. Although they have diligently tried to persuade workers to go beyond trade union consciousness to class consciousness, as

Lenin prescribed, there are few successful examples of this happening. The effect is often to exclude the issues and interests of the poor in the headlong rush to attract a romanticized working class.

The point here is not that social disorder is the most effective or desirable form of political expression, but that it is the form that politically marginalized groups have taken. Throughout this study, evidence of resistance, challenge and struggle has been provided. Indeed, one of the principal reasons for providing the historical background to the SDW was to counterbalance the picture of the poor as passive victims. The fact that defeat, exclusion, repression and sheer exhaustion may have overcome the attempts by the poorest and weakest members of the working class to change their lot, ought not to obscure the challenges they have mounted. As has been argued elsewhere (Mann, 1986), to dismiss or neglect the political expressions of those who are marginalized only serves to reinforce the marginalization process.

Social reproduction and surplus populations

The focus of this chapter thus far has been on the spheres of production/industrial relations and politics in maintaining social divisions. Until quite recently, Marxists tended to regard these as the principal features of poverty, whereas Weberians, as we saw in the previous chapter, focus on labour markets and life chances. However, it is misleading to suggest that Marxists only discuss political and production issues and Weberians only consider labour markets and consumption. In reality, of course, there is considerable overlap between the different spheres.

It is in the concept of 'social reproduction' that some overlap between the different spheres, and between the interests of Marxist and non-Marxist scholarship, can be observed. The 'welfare state' has been portrayed by a number of Marxists as one means by which the consumption needs of labour are organized (Ginsburg, 1979; Gough, 1979; Offe, 1984). Whereas Marxists like Offe (1984) discuss the part played by welfare in maintaining and meeting the needs of Capital, Saunders (1986) discusses consumption in the context of choice and the end of class antagonism (see also Saunders and Harris, 1990). Interestingly, Offe (1984) concluded that the welfare state was not necessarily functional for Capital. Nevertheless, his discussion is primarily concerned with the relationship between 'the welfare state' and the economic well-being of capitalism. This distinction between viewing consumption as, on the one hand, a requirement of the system of production and, on the other, a question of choice albeit under certain restraints, was one with which Marx was familiar.

Marx suggested that capitalism, like any other social form, had to reproduce its requirements in order to avoid becoming obsolete. He wrote:

> A society can no more cease to produce than it can cease to consume. When viewed, therefore, as a connected whole, and in the constant

flux of its incessant renewal, every social process of production is at the same time a process of reproduction (Marx, 1976, p.710).

Marx goes on to outline how in many cases these requirements can be taken as straightforward, e.g. capital investment, new markets for goods and the raw materials used in production. Less obvious, and more difficult to guarantee, are those requirements which are socially produced and reproduced, e.g. a sharp fall in the birth rate might lead to labour shortages. Marxism has tended, therefore, to portray various social policies as assisting capital in reproducing itself and the social values it requires.

Capitalism, it is argued, requires an educated workforce. Education in this instance does not simply mean a workforce trained to a particular level of skill, knowledge and dexterity, but also – and vitally – educated to accept the regime of a capitalist system of production. School leavers, for example, who did not know that they had to defer to managers, or that they would have to assist in making the enterprise as profitable as possible, would be of little value to an employer. Nor do employers expect to have to teach these 'social skills', although schemes like the Youth Training Scheme (YTS) and school students on 'work experience' might be seen to be getting them to do so. In general, employers are content to let the state make the long-term plans for social reproduction. That does not mean that they do not try and influence policy, for they clearly do, but on a day-to-day basis their concern is with profit maximization. Thus in the main, it is anticipated by individual capitalists that social reproduction will largely be left to the state, which in turn looks to the family and the individual (see O'Connor, 1973; Ginsburg, 1979; Gough, 1979; Novak, 1988).

There is no argument here with this general picture that Marxists have painted, but it is important to examine it in so far as it bears on social divisions and welfare. Once again it will be shown that by following too closely in Marx's footsteps we can get a little lost. The most significant point Marx makes, as far as this discussion is concerned, is that it does not matter whether the consumer enjoys the process of social reproduction or not:

> The fact that the worker performs acts of individual consumption in his [sic] own interest, and not to please the capitalist, is something entirely irrelevant to the matter. The consumption of food by a beast of burden does not become any less a necessary aspect of the production process because the beast enjoys what it eats (Marx, 1976, p.718).

By focusing on the need for social reproduction, and treating consumption as a mere necessity for capitalism, Marx makes three related errors. Some of these have subsequently been incorporated into the work of Marxist scholarship.

First, the attention is once again on the requirements of capitalism and away from the working class. The part played by the working class in establishing the form that consumption takes is ignored. Previous chapters have shown that the SDW arises, in part, as a consequence of the form and direction of class struggle. Indeed, most examples of class struggle touch on the nature of consumption. The demand for 'a fair day's pay', for example, has not been static. In the 1990s, for many workers the idea of what is 'fair' may well include the 'need' to pay the mortgage, have a holiday, a 'good' Christmas, possibly even running a car. To suggest that these activities simply expand the capitalist market and reproduce labour power fails to appreciate the contested nature of these 'needs'. It can also neglect the *raison d'être* behind many wage struggles.

The neglect of agency has a second consequence, however, which further reinforces the marginalization of the poorest sections of the working class. Individual workers make choices, however restrained these may be by 'ideology', and have particular conceptions of their 'needs'. By expressing these – purchasing houses, joining company pension schemes, profit sharing and share participation schemes – they are enjoying goods and services denied to many others. To ignore this simple fact is to ignore the effects of consumption on social divisions. Furthermore, the political consequences of some sections of the working class being in a relatively more privileged position in terms of consumption than others, may actually widen social divisions further. If the best-placed sections of the working class are able to escape the most stigmatizing aspects of public welfare, then the political constituency for improving these services is diminished. It is not just that some individuals are excluded from the consumption patterns enjoyed by others, although that might be significant in itself, but also the pattern of exclusion that is produced. It is the systematic exclusion of some groups, and the systematic reliance on others to provide the services, that deserves to be highlighted.

The third problem with Marx's view of consumption is his neglect of the sexual division of labour. Without engaging in a prolonged discussion of this issue it is not possible to do it justice (for a more sustained and specific review of social reproduction in the family, see Walby, 1990). However, the reader ought to be aware of some of the key questions that go unanswered if we accept Marx's assertion about the irrelevance of whether the individual consumer enjoys the process of consumption or not. Once again Rose's question 'Who cooks the dinner?' ought to remind us that consumption, as an aspect of social reproduction, has played a major part in promoting sexual divisions, divisions which are reflected in the SDW. The family is obviously a major provider of the services which reproduce labour. Whether it is child care, cooking, cleaning, sexual gratification or rest, women within families are overwhelmingly responsible for ensuring that their partner has his needs met. Even when these services are not provided at home by family members, it will still be women who, in the vast majority of cases, will provide them. The sexual division of labour ensures that the services associated with social reproduction are provided for men, by women who are themselves excluded from these services by their poverty or their sex.

As we saw in the previous chapter, one of the strengths of the consumption-based approach was that it did not reduce the behaviour of the state to a function of capital. Despite the drawbacks, the consumption model does ensure that the working class is a thinking class, one which, however restrained, makes choices and in so doing can make visible social divisions. Moreover, this type of work has been mirrored by, or it could be argued, prompted by, a more sensitive approach from some Marxists.

Consumption in space

Byrne and Parson (1983), for example, try to emphasize that the working class plays a major role in setting consumption patterns. They link the changes that are occurring within the working class to changes in the labour process. It is the differential abilities these changes have bestowed upon, or removed from, sections of the working class that Byrne and Parson regard as significant. Massey (1984) has similarly argued that the labour process is a vital factor in the creation of spatial divisions. She approaches the social divisions of the 1980s from the position of a Marxist geographer but, like Byrne and Parson, considers the labour process to be centrally important. Massey (1984, pp.211–13) points out, for example, that when companies relocate, they tend to substitute women workers for men. She is also sensitive to the conflicts this can generate within the working class and the labour movement.

Likewise, Byrne and Parson (1983) argue that an analysis of social divisions within Britain in the 1980s has to consider social reproduction as a focus of class struggle. Thus they state that:

> Housing is not only history in bricks and mortar; the variation in its quality is the key to spatial management of the S.R.A. [Stagnant Reserve Army], to the use of space as a mechanism for differentiating and dividing the working class in Britain today (Byrne and Parson, 1983, p.139).

In stark contrast to non-Marxist writers on consumption like Saunders, they identify a direct relationship between changes in production and changes in social reproduction. The recreation of a RAL coincides, they argue, with the 'ghettoization' and spatial segregation of the reserve army. There are also many similarities between Byrne and Parson's claims and those of Friend and Metcalf (1981). In both cases, social policies are regarded as highly significant in maintaining and reproducing social divisions. There is also agreement on the fact that the reserve army is not a politically passive force, and that intra-class divisions are crucial to an understanding of contemporary capitalism.

The major weakness in the work of Friend and Metcalf, and Byrne and Parson, is the unnecessary adherence to Marx's perjorative language. Friend and Metcalf point out that Marx's language poses problems because it tends to stigmatize the poor. Byrne and Parson in turn take issue with Friend and Metcalf for using the term 'surplus population' and point out that the 'surplus' is in fact vital for social reproduction and cannot be seen as inactive – which the term 'surplus' implies. Consequently, they prefer the term 'Stagnant Reserve Army'. They proceed to state:

> Our point is this – we must think of reproduction as class struggle; that means we need an active definition of those involved and Reserve Armies, even if stagnant, sound more active than surplus populations. We really need a new term (Byrne and Parson, 1983, p.136).

Indeed we do, for in their last but one sentence Byrne and Parson (1983, p.151) refer, albeit not as a serious concept I hope, to the Victorian concept of the 'residuum'. Once again, it appears that the discussion of social divisions is haunted by Victorian ghosts.

Nevertheless, there are a number of attractive features in an approach which takes spatial divisions and social reproduction into consideration. Once we jettison the baggage of Marx's language, there is much to be said for linking consumption/social reproduction, labour process and spatial segregation. In some respects, these concerns mirror those of non-Marxists interested in residualization (Forrest and Murie, 1983; Flynn, 1988). Furthermore, Harrison (1986) has made a persuasive argument for using Titmuss's SDW thesis as the basis for an analysis of consumption. It may be that, as Harrison suggests, the SDW could set a common agenda for Marxists and non-Marxists. Although the approach here differs in many ways from these reproduction/consumption in space accounts, they do provide an interesting alternative to the reductionism and functionalism often encountered within Marxism.

In summary

In this chapter, the focus has been on Marxist approaches to social divisions. It has been argued that Marx himself used a language that was probably inappropriate in his own day, and which is certainly not appropriate today. The various definitions and terms used by Marx and subsequently by Marxists have served, at best, to assign the poorest stratum of society within capitalism a functional role or, at worst, to simply confirm middle-class prejudices of the poor.

The concept of a lumpen-proletariat has been dismissed entirely. The view of the poor as incapable, reactionary and immoral has no place in an analysis that looks at society from the bottom up. Nor can the poor be treated as victims. They are politically active and, through social disorder and even as a 'social problem', provide a constant challenge to an economic system that tries to conceal their existence.

Nor has Marx's concept of the RAL been very useful. If the RAL thesis has any validity, it is in pointing to the way that the reserves serve as replacements for the weakest and worst paid and not, as Marx implies, as replacements for the most expensive labour. The idea that the RAL was created by the state on behalf of capital has been questioned. Although there are examples where the state has sought cheap labour, it has not been used to replace the best organized and most expensive. The effects of employer and trade union practices interfering in the operation of the labour market must also be borne in mind. The main problem with the RAL thesis, however, is its lack of clarity. The functions and economic significance of the RAL are taken for granted while the question of why some rather than others are consistently reserves is neglected.

It has also been suggested that the problem for the poor is their political exclusion from the labour movement and not their supposed reluctance to engage with it. Despite the language used by Byrne and Parson, and Friend and Metcalf, their analyses do at least focus on agency. They acknowledge the part played by the working class in continuing to make and re-make itself in the process of class struggle. Despite some attractive features, these accounts remain partial and are still inclined to unthinkingly mimic Marx. There is also some overlap with non-Marxist work which addresses consumption patterns and residualization. However, the possibility of a shared research agenda for the future seems unlikely.

One of the points to emerge from this chapter, although it is unlikely to be accepted by the faithful, is that the poor have had a raw deal from Marxism. They are condemned for their backward and conservative attitudes, they are potential strike-breakers, a pool of labour threatening to flood the labour market, the foot soldiers for counter-revolution, or, alternatively, they are the passive victims of a cruel society who must wait until the true proletariat – those noble and disciplined class warriors just waiting for the right moment – seize power and institute socialism.

*eight*_____

Stepping forward

The title of this chapter could easily have included the words 'nervously' or 'tentatively'. For there should be no doubt that in presenting a redefined theory of the SDW, a measure of nervousness is appropriate. Many of the ideas presented in this chapter have been touched upon earlier. The task here is to make them explicit and to present them in a systematic fashion.

It will be argued that the first feature of the SDW to note is the requirement that workers sell their labour power. This creates a nominally free labour market which ensures the dependence of working-class men and women. Competition between workers for work is reinforced by the divisive effects of the labour process. It is argued that the increasing specificity of labour is a peculiarly capitalist phenomenon. Alienation arises as a consequence of both the sale of labour power and the divisive affects of the detailed division of labour. Moreover, alienation further promotes sectionalism and social closure by segregating workers from one another. Class struggle, therefore, will be seen to be restrained as workers both challenge the dominant classes and exert social closure against members of their own class. Those who are excluded are observable and this provides evidence of a divided working class which middle-class observers report and is built into social policy. Thus the form and direction class struggle has taken influences the SDW. A further ingredient in the recipe for the SDW is inherited from pre-industrial, and arguably pre-capitalist, social relations. Patriarchy and racism have been passed on from one generation to the next. There have, of course, been changes in the way these have been expressed. Racism today is both a legacy of our imperial past and the longer history of excluding 'outsiders' – rural migrants in the feudal period, the Irish and Jews in the nineteenth century – while patriarchy in the last decade of the twentieth century does not take the same forms as it did a century ago.

I go on to suggest, rather mischievously it should be admitted, that if academics and other middle-class observers must use a term to describe a stratum within the working class, that the one I shall propose is as useful as any other. The chapter concludes with some speculative comments on the

SDW in the future. The prospects for unity and the likelihood of further social divisions are considered. Such crystal-ball gazing is a dangerous activity, but one which I feel academics have a responsibility to engage in.

Depending on wage slavery

In Chapter 2, it was shown that for Titmuss the SDW hinged on the socially divisive effects of the division of labour and the manner in which industrial societies promoted needs and dependencies. Although his approach to the division of labour was seen to be flawed, the premise that there is a relationship between needs, dependencies and the social division of labour has been accepted. However, if states of dependency are produced, not by industrialization as Titmuss claimed, but by capitalist social and production relations, it is necessary to explain how capitalism promotes dependency. We saw in Chapters 3, 4 and 5 that changes in social divisions have been related to changes in the labour process. However, the labour process does not make workers dependent in the first place. It reinforces dependency, increases their sense of worthlessness and constantly redefines sectional cleavages within the working class, but it does not, of itself, ensure dependency. For an account of how capitalism ensures that workers are in a state of dependence, we need to return to Marx.

For Marx, the key moment in the creation of dependency is when workers have to sell their labour power in order to subsist. He points out that workers are told that they are 'free' to leave and seek employment with any employer they wish. Simultaneously, of course, capitalism created a mass of workers all desperate for employment who, if they did actually leave one employer, would simply have to find another. Consequently, when capitalists proudly boast that if it were not for them workers would starve, they are stating boldly the reality that confronts workers in the early period of capitalism. In order to subsist, workers need to sell their labour and this is, therefore, the first stage in the creation of dependency and a competitive labour market (Novak, 1988, pp.13–23). Without a wage, and sometimes even with one, workers can at best struggle to keep themselves in food, shelter and clothing. This dependence of the worker upon Capital Marx called 'wage slavery' because workers are, in effect, chained to their employer. But the great paradox of capitalism is that in reality capital is dependent upon labour. It is only because the means of production are privately owned, and society is arranged to protect and perpetuate the private ownership of the means of production, that labour is dependent on capital. It is in this context, as will be seen shortly, that changes in the labour process and the organization of work are vitally important. It is the constant reorganization of work that enables capitalists to compete with one another and, vitally, to ensure that they rarely become dependent on particular workers.

A good example of how capitalism in its earliest phase promotes dependence was the 1834 Poor Law Amendment Act. In contrast to many of the systems of relief operating throughout the country, which until that time accepted some responsibility for the poor, the 1834 Act insisted that the-able-bodied poor could not expect relief. If the able-bodied poor were to be assisted, the intention was to ensure they were treated less favourably than even the lowest paid worker. The Poor Law Commissioners sought to make the poor self-reliant. They wanted to break the ties of obligation and duty on the part of the rich to assist the poor. They were quite explicit that the individual had a responsibility to make provisions for him or herself and to anticipate the prospect of unemployment or sickness. Seen in this light, the Act of 1834 is simply one aspect of the move towards a nominally free labour market which implies an independent working class. In Chapter 3, it was shown that the Friendly Societies were thought to provide the means by which the poor could protect themselves and that the 1834 Act did indeed encourage many workers to join a society. Thus the state, using the 1834 Act, tried to exploit existing divisions and to promote 'self-help'. Neverthe-less, it was only those workers in the best paying forms of employment who could hope to become 'society men'. The fear of the workhouse was deliber-ately generated and the intention was to make the poor feel vulnerable (Thompson, 1968, p.295). In the main, this intention was fuelled by the desire to reduce the cost of poor relief, not by a divide-and-rule strategy. Nevertheless, the Friendly Societies served as evidence to the middle classes that it was possible for workers to insure themselves. The language of self-help was translated into dependence on wage labour.

The point that needs to be emphasized, therefore, is that dependency was a precondition of a capitalist labour market. This was not an accident which happened to accompany industrialization, as Titmuss implies, but a major factor in the successful and early development of capitalism in Britain. Simultaneously, it has to be acknowledged that the degree of dependence capitalism creates, and workers experience, is not uniform. As we have seen in previous chapters, it is possible for labour to exercise a measure of control over the labour market if a particular trade, or workers in an indus-try, confront the employers as a collective. Moreover, those workers who have been able to make some provisions for themselves could do so only because they succeeded in exerting a degree of social closure. This in turn generated intra-class divisions – between women and men, Irish and English, one part of the country and another, skilled and unskilled.

Gaining access to the type of employment which provides some protec-tion against the dependencies capitalism creates is, therefore, a major con-cern for workers joining the labour market. Thus many young working-class men will be advised by their parents, who are aware of the harsh realities of work, that they should 'get a trade'. The apprenticeship system may serve to restrict the opportunities of certain groups within the working class but it also, of course, provides a route out of complete dependence for others. Making and keeping their labour scarce, by restricting entry to the trade and refusing to pass on the required skills to those who have not undertaken an apprenticeship, were the means employed by organized workers to escape abject poverty. Their objective was to avoid the worst effects of dependency and poverty. By organizing they were simultaneously challenging the rules which governed the labour market and excluding members of their own class. These points are crucially important and illustrate the manner in which capitalism promotes dependency and competition between workers for the most rewarding forms of wage labour.

Marx's account of 'wage slavery' and dependency creation has to be qualified, however, by pointing out that there are forms of dependency which cannot be reduced to a capitalist system of production. There are 'natural dependencies', as Titmuss suggested, which would occur in any society. There are also social changes which, although occurring most often within the context of capitalism, may promote needs independently of that mode of production. Urbanization, for example, has produced particular needs. It would be unreasonable to expect any mode of production to anticipate every eventuality in the move from a rural to an urban society. There are also needs which are less tangible than housing or food and it would be difficult to predict or plan for them all. The need for close social networks, for example, is not something which could easily be met by planning. Even in the nineteenth century, some employers tried to fulfil this need by building churches and establishing sports and social clubs – the Mechanics Institutes would be one example. Although we always need to treat such generosity with a hefty dose of scepticism, it does illustrate a widespread recognition of such needs. However, these too could often reinforce social divisions. The exclusion of women, the Irish and the 'unskilled' from clubs and other organizations has, as we have seen, a very long history. In addition, the most intimate of human needs would, arguably, be problematic in any social order. For example, the need and pursuit of pleasure, a perfectly rational objective, is not something which Marxists choose to address, despite the central place this has always had in working-class culture. As was demonstrated in the previous chapter, the pursuit of pleasure within capitalism is often seen by Marxists to be an irrelevance, since it is merely assisting in the reproduction of labour power. Instead, these needs tend to be discussed under the heading of commodity fetishism, which resounds with the language of Calvinistic abstinence (Elster, 1985, pp.68-72).

Likewise, Marxists have been slow to acknowledge the difficulties of satisfying those needs associated with sexuality and affection. These may have been left off the agenda because there are no easy answers. However, in meeting these needs, social divisions are reinforced. The most obvious example here would be the way that sexual divisions are replicated. It is surely no accident that the caring and 'personal services' are overwhelmingly provided by women. Similarly, the needs of those who are victims of sexual harassment, rape, incest and 'domestic violence' have only recently been acknowledged. These forms of diswelfare are perpetuated by their absence from the political agenda, an absence which as Lukes (1974) has made plain, reinforces powerlessness. Patriarchal values must, therefore, be treated as independent influences on social divisions (Walby, 1990).

The crucial point about the creation of dependency is that, however it may arise, it is not perpetuated by accident. Dependency, whether it is directly due to capitalism or not, remains one of the vital conditions for a competitive market economy and the patriarchal family. Powerful groups organize to protect their privileges and in so doing exclude others. The response of workers to the chaos of the market and its failure to meet their most basic needs for decent food, housing and health was similar to their response to the dependency generated at work. The social effects of capitalism were mitigated for workers who were able to form collectivities. Cooperative societies, Friendly Societies and, to a lesser extent, building societies provided sections of the working class with a measure of independence. Such organizations enabled their members to enjoy better food, welfare and housing than was available to other members of their class. It is in these 'defence organizations of the working class' (Miliband, 1974, p.188) that intra-class divisions were often manifest. Unable to sustain an overt class war, as seemed possible in the second quarter of the nineteenth century, workers tried to resolve their particular needs as best they could. Thus wage slavery and the prospect of abject poverty prompted a response from workers, but this was distorted by the experience of work and defeat in a capitalist economy.

Alienation

Titmuss, it will be recalled from Chapter 2, suggested that sectionalism arose in response to the promotion of individualism within advanced industrialized societies. If society encourages individualism and promotes anomie, the result will be, he argued, the pursuit of self-interest at the expense of social cohesion. In contrast, a Marxist perspective might be expected to point to the concept of alienated labour. Unfortunapely, Marx's theory of alienauion is under-developed and currently unfashionable. Moreover, the theory, which is outlined in Marx's earlier writings, is very general and abstract. A further problem, according to Elster (1985, pp.68–92), is that Marx's theory of alienation has an implicit model of human nature. Human beings are assumed to have essential and natural inclinations towards their labour. I share many of Marx's assumptions but simply stating this does not resolve the difficult philosophical issues attached to the concept of alienation. Developing a more coherent account of the relationship between alienation and needs will provide an interesting challenge for the future.

The attraction of the alienation thesis, and the reason for introducing it at this stage, is that it places the wage/labour exchange at the heart of an explanation of needs. Moreover, it will be shown how the concept of alienation ties in with the organization of work, the labour process and individuation to promote sectionalism and economism. There are various forms that alienation may take, of which four types are the most significant. Workers are alienated from (1) their own labour, (2) the products of their labour, (3) their species being and (4) their fellow human beings.

The twin elements of alienation from the products of one's labour and alienation from the process of performing the tasks are, perhaps, the closest of Marx's concepts to those used by Titmuss. The increasingly specialized and limited activities required of workers by the detailed division of labour, combined with their knowledge of only one fragment of the labour process, severely restricts the exercise of human potential. For Marx, productive activity was a basic element of human nature and, he argued, capitalism diminishes human beings. Since the worker is alienated from what he or she does – to the point where, for example, workers frequently state that they 'simply switch off' when they are working – Marx claims that an essential part of what it is to be human is lost. Unlike animals, which respond to instinct, human beings are capable of planned productive labour. In effect, capitalism cuts out that part of human nature which makes productive activity a rewarding and worthwhile exercise. Instead, workers experience their activity as something alien, controlled by another force, i.e. capital.

Leaving aside the question of human nature, and the implied claim that deskilling is the principal feature of the labour process, there is ample evidence to support Marx's view that workers are distorted by their work. The literally mind-numbing experience of 'killing time' and 'clock watching' is matched by the physical distortion of the body. However, it is in the experience of one's own labour as an alien activity that Marx sees human nature being perverted (Ollman, 1976, pp.136-40). Linked to the alienation of human beings from their activities is the alienation of human beings from the products of that activity. Given that Marx considers productive activity as an essential, if not *the* essential, prerequisite of human life, it is hardly surprising that he should also consider the significance of the product/object of that activity. Of course, all the products of human labour are transformed into objects, irrespective of the type of society in which they are produced. It is only human labour that can turn nature into object; thus clay is transformed into a jar, iron ore into tools, etc. However, capitalism sets out to alienate the producer from the product. The worker is physically prevented from using or consuming the product of his or her labour. Indeed, any employee who attempts to take home, or to use, the product/object of his or her labour is liable to be imprisoned for the theft of the very thing they made.

This alienation of the producer from the product is reinforced by the worker's ignorance as to what happens to the product. Since the organization of work has become highly specialized, workers rarely know, and often do not care, what happens to the product of their labour. Once the worker has completed the tasks required of him or her, the object of this labour is literally removed to wherever the employer dictates. This appears so natural a process it is only by considering how humans feel when they do not have the product of their labour torn from them that it is possible to appreciate Marx's point. When we produce, for example, a good crop of vegetables, or make some clothes, cook a delicious meal or restore a vintage motorcycle, we are close to the product/object of our labour. We see these products as almost a part of ourselves. Anyone who has ever produced something of value to them, will testify to the satisfaction they received from their labours. If, having completed their product, it was snatched from them, the producers would invariably protest. Yet this is, in effect, what happens to workers on a daily basis. Not only can it be illegal to protest, but workers do not expect to protest at this theft. The relationship between the producer and the product/object has been inverted. The object of their labour is explicitly divorced from the producers the moment they become wage slaves. It is because human beings derive so much meaning for their lives from their productive activities that the effects of alienating the producer from the product are so appalling.

Once the object of production has been removed from those who produce it, the next stage is for it to be seen as alien. The object of labour takes on a life of its own, a thing, the subject of the worker's frustrations and, once the capitalist releases it onto the market, the object of desire. For instead of the active subject (the worker) producing objects, capitalism reverses the relationship. The object is presented back to the producer as a desirable commodity. The worker becomes an object of production and is confronted by commodities which appear to have a life of their own. Consider for a moment the presentation of commodities in advertisements: breakfast cereals come alive, cars choose their own oil, robots discuss the merits of their product, detergents clean without any apparent human labour, and so on. The effect is, as Marx suggested, to give commodities human qualities while simultaneously dehumanizing and commodifying people (Ollman, 1976).

Following on from the above point, Marx proposes that individuals within capitalism are alienated from their species. In brief, Marx proposes that human activity in a capitalist society is so far removed from what is natural, that humans lose sight of what it is to be human. Only humans can plan, cooperate and labour for a purpose. It is the ability of human beings to construct the world as they choose and for their mutual benefit which separates us from the animal. A bee, for example, may have an apparently complex social network and build remarkable hives, but it can never conceive its achievements. It cannot decide to build the hive differently or redistribute tasks among the hive's inhabitants. Only human beings are capable of such behaviour, but under capitalism it is precisely these abilities that are frustrated. We are therefore alienated from those qualities which distinguish us as human beings. The significance of this point will be emphasized when we consider the manner in which the labour process negates the human qualities of cooperation.

The final element to Marx's theory of alienation, which further illustrates the manner in which capitalism promotes dependency, is the alienation of human beings from their fellow humans. Initially, capitalism promotes two opposing classes. One class owns and controls the means of production, whereas the other class is compelled to sell its labour power. The capitalist needs to keep labour costs as low as possible, while the worker wants as high a wage as possible. These two mutually hostile classes have such diverse interests that they are incapable of appreciating their common interest in transforming society. Marx, it may surprise some, felt that, despite the benefits capitalism bestowed upon the capitalist class, individual capitalists were also victims of the system from which they largely benefited. They too were trapped in a constant round of competition and fear. Not that Marx devoted a great deal of time to the alienation of the capitalist class and it need not concern us here.

Far more interesting for our purposes is the alienation that divides the working class. Having created a nominally free class of labourers, they are immediately compelled to compete with one another:

> Among the proletariat, competition first rears its head at the factory gate where some are allowed in and others not. Inside the factory, workers continue to compete with each other for such favors as their employer has it in him [sic] to bestow, especially for the easier and better paying jobs (Ollman, 1976, p.207; Marx and Engels, 1977, p.79).

Competition continues in the race for better housing, commodities, a place at a 'good' school, through the exam system for a place at university, and over virtually every other resource. Because capitalism dictates that competition, rather than planned cooperation, is to establish the distribution of resources workers must either confront one another, or confront the system that issues the diktat. Selfishness is justified, exploitation legitimate, callousness understandable and mistrust essential once the philosophy and practice of capitalism is accepted. Consequently, when workers do form collectivities, cooperate, care for members of their class and promote socialist ideals, they are mounting a direct challenge to the ethos of capitalism. Despite the challenges that are mounted, it is more usual for workers to pragmatically accept the ground rules of capitalism.

The point is that alienation from other human beings ensures the dependence of individual workers upon capitalism. They are fragmented from one another and while capital hails this as independence the reality is that the worker has to rely upon his or her ability to compete within, and manipulate, the rules laid down by capital. Thus even when a measure of unity and cooperation is apparent, it will frequently be expressed in sectional terms or will pursue economistic ends. This last point is clearly illustrated in Chapter 3 in respect of the 'labour aristocracy'. Only by combining could the 'labour aristocrat' escape the clutches of poverty which were constantly threatening the rest of the working class. Paradoxically, these combinations flouted the ethic of 'self-help', because they relied on a form of collectivism, but the mutualism they embodied was simultaneously exclusive. The 'society man' was compelled, by the actuarial principles of the market, to restrict entry to the society. Sectionalism and exclusion, therefore, smothered cooperation and mutualism in their infancy.

The process dividing labour

One other strand of a revised theory of the SDW needs to be unravelled and, like the wage/labour exchange and alienation, it is most closely associated with Marxism. Labour process theory, despite some reservations, is vitally important in understanding the basis of dependency within capitalism. Marx (1976, p.473) states:

> Since the production and circulation of commodities are the general prerequisites of the capitalist mode of production, division of labour in manufacture requires that a division of labour within society should have already attained a degree of development. Inversely, the division of labour in manufacture reacts back upon that society, developing and multiplying it further. With the differentiation of the instruments of labour, the trades which produce these instruments themselves become more and more differentiated.

This quotation illustrates three crucial points:

1 That the development of capitalism depends upon a pre-existing division of labour, a point that was clearly illustrated in Chapter 3.
2 That the development of the division of labour is subsequently intensified as capitalist competition itself intensifies, as demonstrated in Chapters 3–5.
3 That 'the trades themselves become more differentiated'. This final point has also been commented upon throughout Chapters 3–5.

The first of these points should require no further elaboration. However, it may be as well briefly to outline the second two in more detail.

Changes in the labour process are frequently prompted by employers who want to increase their control at the expense of their employees. With more control, the employer can improve his or her competitive position. There are two principal tactics open to employers when they are attempting to break the hold of a particular group of workers. First, they can introduce technology which does away with the need for the workers concerned. Secondly, they can attempt to change the way that work is performed in order to diminish or bypass the need for the troublesome employees. Often the effect of one strategy includes the introduction of the other. Both strategies may involve conflict and neither guarantees success. For the employer who correctly judges that the circumstances are such that he or she can attempt one or other strategy, the rewards are high. The stakes are also high since a prolonged dispute will be extremely costly and might even result in closure. Employers will also only gain a brief advantage since the success of one will almost certainly encourage competitors to follow suit (Edwards, 1979; Littler, 1982). Edwards, (1979) has proposed a third form of control which is used in small firms and is literally the employer telling, on a day-to-day basis, the employee what to do. However this is a fairly uncontentious claim and can be set to one side.

The labour process has been described and illustrated in every chapter of this book. The importance of the labour process is emphasized by its role as both a focus and a rough measure of class struggle. Moreover, weakness or failure in the contest over the labour process will reinforce dependency, whereas success can breed sectionalism and further segregation within the working class. Consequently, the labour process is the site of contests both between and within classes. The intensity of the contest has varied during different periods, with the introduction of scientific management techniques representing a management offensive and the 'restrictive practices' of the 1960s a period of relative success for organized labour. The contest has, however, been a constant feature of the irreconcilable clash of two opposing classes. It needs to be added that this contest is not necessarily related to new technology, and that new technology does not necessarily result in changes in the labour process. There have been changes to the labour process which have not involved any technological innovation (McLoughlin and Clark, 1988). Change in these circumstances may well be prompted by the employer's desire to increase productivity by, for example, simply sub-dividing tasks. There are also other reasons why an employer may change the organization of work which are not necessarily intended to increase profitability *per se* (e.g. it may be prompted by a need to conform to health and safety requirements). Whatever the reason it has to be acknowledged that change may provoke conflict and resistance by workers. Moreover, in time, the changes introduced, whether they are due to the immediate desire to extend management control over the labour process or not, may well be made to conform to this requirement. From a class struggle perspective, however, the point is that the contest is never over, and it can never be won by management or workers. Even where control appears to have been lost, workers and management will exercise their imaginations and develop new means to assert their interests in the future.

Now this claim is central to my whole argument and commentators on the labour process have disagreed over the degree to which workers can exert control, and if they can, how long that might last. Armstrong, in a spirited defence of Braverman, argues that even changes which are not immediately prompted by a desire to exert control over the labour process may come to serve that purpose. He points out that the ability of workers to retain control, or to resist management when they are seeking to extend their control, is severely restrained. Thus the 'restrictive practices' of the 1960s and 1970s were swept aside in the 1980s (Armstrong, 1988, pp.152-7). However, this is surely a consequence of the constant changes in the balance of forces between classes, a point Armstrong (1988, p.154) seems to accept, and not simply a short-term advantage. Of course, when a group of workers is able to exert a measure of control, they need to try and anticipate management's response. If they fail to do so, they may find they only had a 'short-term' advantage as Armstrong claims. Indeed, and as I have argued throughout this book, it is a feature of working-class life that poverty, due to redundancy, unemployment, injury, ill-health, etc., haunts every home. A measure of control over the labour process will make it less likely that the ghost of poverty will appear, but there is no guarantee. Irrespective of the constant threat of failure and the consequences which may accomopany it, this does not mean that success is always only a short-term phenomenon, unless Armstrong's definition of a term is much longer than most. The tool-maker and the printer, for example, resisted changes in the labour process for decades.

Edwards (1979), in contrast, claims that the labour process is always 'contested' and that workers resist management attempts at deskilling. He argues that, historically, class struggles manifest in the workplace have often focused upon issues of control. As we saw in Chapter 3, the labour aristo-crat – for want of a better term – derived his privileged position from the control held over the labour process. Likewise, in Chapter 5, it was shown how organized labour on the shop floor exerted a measure of control over the labour process in the 1950s and 1960s. Both management and workers seek control and both will use overt and covert methods to achieve it (Beynon, 1973; Brown, 1977).

In this context, Therborn's (1983) conditions for success, the degree of autonomy available to workers in the labour process and their homoge-neity, are vitally important. Following Therborn, and as argued in Chapter 5, these two conditions have meant that even unskilled workers can contest the labour process. Their success will not be permanent; indeed, it is likely to be challenged as soon as other conditions allow employers to embark on a counter-offensive. Moreover, it is a complex matrix of conditions which enables some, and not others, to be less dependent, but one of the key variables will be their location at a particular time. Indeed, 'being in the right place at the right time' is recognized by workers as one of the vagaries of working-class life. Redundancy, changes in the ownership of the firm, technological innovation, the international conditions for the industry, the buoyancy of local labour markets, demographic change and a host of other factors will either provide or restrict opportunities. The ability to organize effectively will, therefore, hinge on a number of variables beyond the day-to-day influence of workers. Defeat and failure constantly threaten, but as far as the workers are concerned the strategy has to be to try and exert some measure of control in the circumstances in which they find themselves.

The second of Marx's insights was that changes in the labour process served to differentiate trades from one another. Titmuss was correct to point to the increasing specificity of labour as a dependency-creating cir-cumstance (see Chapter 2). However, this is not inevitable but one of the consequences of the contest over the labour process. This also relates to the previous discussion of alienation and the pressure on workers to pursue sectional benefits. Changes in the organization of work and technological change demonstrate the vulnerability of all workers. It is also something which most workers are only too well aware of and in part explains their hostility to changes in working practices. The points made previously re-garding the dependence of workers upon the sale of their labour to capital are given further weight by this constant vulnerability. In order to avoid being in the most vulnerable trades, workers combine and in so doing exclude members of their own class.

At this point, it is necessary to reintroduce Parkin's notion of dual closure (see Chapter 6). The usefulness of Parkin's concept of dual closure is that it makes sense of exclusion and discrimination within the working class in the context of class struggle. The actions of workers in excluding certain social groups are presented as rational, within a particular frame of reference. It is ironic that Parkin (1979), who sets out to provide a 'bourgeois critique' of Marxism, should be more sensitive to the form and direction that class struggle frequently takes than those Marxists who point towards ideology or false consciousness. As we saw in Chapter 6, discriminatory practices, exclusion and dual closure can serve the interests of certain sections of the working class. Similarly, Hindess (1982) has argued that it is simply not possible to 'read off' the interests of the working class irrespective of the form these interests have to take. Thus economistic and sectional struggles by trade unions have to be explained in the context in which they arise. For example, struggles to maintain wage differentials may objectively reinforce divisions within the working class. For socialists, such divisions make the possibility of working-class unity more difficult and can be seen to be against the 'objective' interests of the working class. However, for those workers capable of squeezing higher wages from an employer, their immediate interests are best served by improving the size of their wage packet. Besides, they have no guarantee that a more unified working class is likely to develop or that, if it does, it will prove to be especially beneficial to them. Moreover, workers do not have to be social historians to be aware that broader-based class struggles have not been overly successful. Consequently, this pragmatic acceptance of the parameters of capitalism, which arises from the material constraints of everyday life, promotes sectionalism and economistic strategies. These in turn will be reflected in differential access to welfare. Moreover, the intention may be to achieve precisely this goal. As we saw in Chapter 6, the changes that have occurred in consumption patterns in the past 10–20 years have often been as a result of workers deciding, quite sensibly, to seek occupational and fiscal welfare at a time when cuts in public welfare have increased the vulnerability and dependence of the poor.

The constant in this sea of change are the features of those who are successful, and they tend to be white males. This should not be taken to mean that it is the same workers who have historically been able to maintain their privileges. Nor are the most privileged elements of the SDW provided exclusively for white males. There will always be some women and some black workers who gain access despite the dominant patterns of closure. Nevertheless, for white males, access will be much easier. The fact that these two characteristics (being white and male) are so often associated with the best placed sections of the working class needs, however, to be stressed. Each round in the contest over the labour process has been influenced by the preceding round. The contestants, as we saw in Chapters 3–5, insist on bringing the baggage of history into the ring. That baggage contains a set of racist and patriarchal ideas which serve to prevent some engaging in the easier, and therefore more successful, contests.

A new term?

But what are we to call those at the bottom of the class structure? Excluded groups, marginalized groups, underclass, residuum, the poor, reserve army of labour, housing and social security classes, stagnant reserve army, relative surplus population and the lumpen-proletariat are all terms that have been used to describe a layer within, or beneath, the working class. It was the confusion produced by these disparate terms and concepts that was mentioned at the very beginning of the introduction. At other points, specific groups have been identified as the constituents of a fragmented and rejected stratum within the working class. The unorganized, the unskilled, the Irish, Jews, the low paid, ethnic minorities and the elderly have all, at various points, been linked to the SDW's least rewarding element, i.e. public welfare. There is a strong case for developing a new term which does not denigrate the poorest sections of the working class, recognizes their combativity and acknowledges their vulnerability.

Having thus far criticized the terms and concepts used by others it is, perhaps, appropriate that an alternative be put forward. However, it is vitally important that there should be no confusion between the general terms used to cover the disparate groups that are pigeon-holed and the specific features of each group. Moreover, any term would have to take account of the social processes and activities which exclude and the responses of the excluded. A further, and perhaps more important, obstacle to proposing any new term is a subjective one. It simply appears pretentious to do so. New terms are not put forward very often and when they are accepted it is usually because they come from some highly respected, or detested, figure. Without being able to claim the former, it may be a little foolhardy to risk the latter.

The term favoured here to cover all those who are cast aside is 'lapilli'. My 1975 edition of *Chambers Dictionary* defines the word thus: 'small fragments of lava ejected from a volcano'.

First, it has the advantage of being a geological term with all the associations of stratum and layers. Lapilli are thrown out by volcanoes and this seemed to be a good metaphor for the experience of all those who are dependent on public welfare. Simultaneously, lapilli are active and potentially dangerous, since they can set the surrounding area ablaze. Thus lapilli are both the product of more powerful forces and also active themselves. Until they are expelled, lappilli are indistinguishable from the volcano and this too was an attractive feature of the term. For those excluded from the best jobs, housing, etc., are also part of the broader working class.

Despite the advantages of the term over others, there is little point in promoting any 'label' simply because it is new and therefore untainted. Moreover, the energy invested in the promotions exercise may dissipate the enthusiasm needed to promote unity. Nor would I want the reader to be distracted by such a mischievous invention, particularly if the more serious points of this study were overlooked. Finally, it has to be admitted that the term is somewhat arbitrary. Since there are an abundance of terms already being proposed, I could see no reason why I too should not indulge myself. Besides, the term 'lappilli' is as good as any and better than others, although it may be a little while before the term finds its way into everyday usage or the pages of the *Sunday Times*.

Prospects for the future

At the time of writing, two of the more obvious questions regarding the future are whether the Conservatives will soon be winkled out of power and, if they are, what difference will it make? If the Labour Party were to be elected, there would almost definitely be a wave of disputes because workers would hope to restore parity with other groups, restore differentials and exert control over working practices. Despite the decline in membership in the 1980s, trade unionism is deeply embedded in British culture. Any review of trade union history would show that during periods of upswing in the economy, or when political conditions are favourable, people look to a trade union to improve their living standards. If the leadership failed to lead, then the shop stewards' movement would get a new lease of life. In either case, it would be all too easy to degenerate into the kind of sectionalism of the past. Moreover, a shift in the balance of power *between* classes need not reduce divisions *within* the working class. As Parkin shows it is possible for groups to be more exclusive towards members of their own class if they are attempting to challenge the dominant class. The affect of dual closure may enable well-placed workers to improve wages, consumption patterns and occupational welfare benefits, but will do little for the poor. Without massive injections of cash for training and rigorously policed affirmative action policies, it is difficult to imagine single parents, the long-term unemployed or disaffected black youth being offered jobs in the most lucrative trades and industries.

Alternatively, it may be that organized labour will try and represent a broader constituency. This rather more optimistic scenario could point to efforts made by some unions to recruit part-timers and short-term contract staff. The TUC's support for equal opportunities and sustained criticism of racial discrimination might add weight to this view. There have already been some serious attempts at extending occupational welfare to part-time workers (Mann and Anstee, 1989). A return to the low levels of unemployment associated with the 1950s and 1960s would be a fairly major achievement in the next few years but, again, not one which would necessarily assist the poor. Trade unionists would be inclined to ask for additional perks and these might be extended to some groups of low-paid workers. At the same time skilled workers would be likely to ask for further improvements, and with the possibility of labour shortages employers might be inclined to offer such benefits. In such circumstances, the more locally orientated negotiations associated with the 1980s would encourage regional variations in pay and income. Geographical divides could widen and government would be asked to 'interfere' in the market, something Labour has said it is reluctant to do.

When organized labour has mounted a more coherent challenge to capital, it has done so through reformist social democratic channels. Despite the language of universalism and the existence of a coherent section of the labour movement pressing for socialist policies, the specific interests of women and ethnic groups are pushed aside. Social democracy is not simply the shell within which corporatism develops (Jessop, 1979), but also the golden egg which the poor are prevented from sharing. Thus a dynamic working class may improve public welfare provision but specific social groups will still be relatively poorer within it.

Policies that might reduce intra-class divisions would require the organized labour movement to sacrifice some of its power, something trade unionists and Labour Party leaders are reluctant to do. If organizations of the poor – not the pressure groups for the poor – were given a political voice, change might be possible. The reason for wanting the poor to be involved in the political process is that they can see more clearly than anyone the obstacles they confront. Whether the Labour Party, trade unions and trade councils would let claimants, black organizations, and single parents affiliate as separately organized groups is doubtful. It would require a measure of bravery on the part of the current labour movement leadership which seems to be absent. If any attempts were bolstered by a transformative vision for the twenty-first century, there would be the possibility of reducing social divisions. However, it is difficult to be optimistic.

The most likely scenario is that the political constituency for maintaining the SDW in its present form will ensure that any truly redistributive policies will be suppressed. Currently, public debate on the poor seems to be moving closer to seeing them as some sort of underclass, with all the implications this has for authoritarian and selective social policies. With middle-class observers focusing on lone parents, the long-term unemployed, street crime and the homeless, the possibility of public welfare being 'reserved for the poor' is increasingly likely. Mortgage interest rates, a buoyant labour market, a good pension, holidays and enjoying the benefits of access to fiscal and occupational welfare, are the concerns of the bulk of the working class. Improvements in the provision of public welfare, with possibly the exception of the NHS and education which have a large middle-class clientele, are unlikely in the face of such a strong demand from a larger constituency for occupational and fiscal welfare. Nor am I condemning such pragmatic concerns when the alternative is so uncertain and the trench of dependency threatens every member of the working class. If I were still an AEUW convenor, I would be looking forward to the return of a Labour government, not because it would transform society, but because I would be able to press for a general improvement in my members' position, which is the prime objective of trade unionism.

If Labour fails to gain office, the prospect is even more bleak. The pattern of intra-class divisions discussed in Chapter 5 will be reinforced. The possibility of unemployment benefit being abolished in favour of some sort of 'workfare' is very real. Changes in education and health policy (for example, Opting Out and Local Management of Schools) are likely to mean that 'The Growing Divide' (Walker and Walker, 1987) will be a yawning chasm by the end of the century. Labour may do little to end intra-class divisions, but the Conservatives will surely make them concrete. In order to remain in office, the Conservatives have to appeal to sections of the working class. The Conservative Party needs only to identify those relatively well-placed sections of the working class and persuade them that Labour might cut their fiscal benefits (e.g. mortgage income tax relief) or increase their tax burden by increasing public welfare, to improve their electoral chances. Alternatively, if they can improve on the current occupational welfare package by extending tax allowances, they may stay in power and widen the SDW.

Putting aside my crystal ball, it is clear that the SDW will continue to reflect changes in the production and consumption processes. Simultaneously, and as argued at various points the SDW both reinforces social divisions and promotes further fractures. In particular, the SDW makes it extremely difficult to construct political alliances over social policy issues. The Friendly Societies in the nineteenty century, the national insurance schemes in the first half of the twentieth century and occupational and fiscal welfare today, encourage the marginalization of the poor.

Divided by welfare?

This book began by highlighting the dangers of terms like 'the underclass'. There is throughout a genuine concern that the observations, or discourse as Foucault's supporters might prefer to call it, of the poor construct a particular knowledge base. These observations can then serve to reinforce the powerful and disaggregate the powerless. Sinfield (1978, p.149) was entirely correct to consider power an under-theorized element of the SDW in which the 'visibility' of public welfare makes the poor more vulnerable to exposure and punitive measures. In this context, Cook's (1989) work on the different responses to tax and benefit fraud exposes the privileges of the powerful and the punishment of the weak.

Titmuss was wrong to tie 'man-made' dependencies to industrialization, and it is alienation, rather than anomie, which is promoted by capitalism and the labour process. This point has been heavily qualified, however, and the impact of specific pre-capitalist social divisions has been emphasized throughout. The competition generated by capitalism, combined with the individuating effects of the labour process, both encourage sectionalism and increase the vulnerability of sections of the working class. It is in response to dependency that the working class 'makes' the SDW through the form and direction of class struggle.

It has been shown in Chapters 3–5 that historically the working class has formed defence organizations that were exclusive. Exclusion, or 'closure' as Parkin (1979) calls it, was based on a combination of actuarial principles, xenophobia and patriarchal logic. We have also discussed the manner in which sections of the working class combine in order to protect themselves from the worst effects of capitalist social relations. Those groups with some leverage over the labour process have been able to exert this and improve their position in the labour market. The fluidity and contested nature of the labour process ensure that different sections of the working class are able to exert leverage at different moments. There are, however, some groups who are constantly excluded.

Racism and patriarchy have been recurring themes in the promotion of intra-class divisions, even if skill has been a more fluid concept. Changes in technology and the labour process, the composition of available labour, and the overall balance of forces between capital and labour, have all affected the ability of different sections of the working class to establish a measure of security within an insecure economic system. The reassertion of market principles that has taken place in the 1980s has, as we saw in Chapter 5, encouraged both workers and management to pursue their needs through the occupational and fiscal systems of welfare. Or, rather more often, to obtain occupational welfare benefits which are also underpinned by fiscal policy.

The stark reality is that those who can gain access to occupational and fiscal welfare almost invariably receive more benefits and a better service. Quite sensibly, socialists have not refused to join pension schemes or profit-sharing arrangements, accept transport allowances, take cheap mortgages, and so on. The only significant 'benefit' that has been rejected on principle has been private health insurance. Indeed, it is because occupational and fiscal welfare benefits and services are 'better' that they are socially divisive. If the occupational and fiscal welfare systems were simply different, rather than being inequitable, we might applaud the choice and variation they provided. Supporters of a 'mixed economy of welfare', or 'welfare pluralism', fail to acknowledge that it is because occupational and fiscal welfare systems are more attractive that they exist (Beresford and Croft, 1984; Bosanquet, 1984; Donnison, 1984). If there really were equity between the different systems of welfare, there would be little point, for the beneficiaries, in pursuing occupational and fiscal welfare.

The development of occupational and fiscal welfare has not benefited the poor. The most notable feature in the changing landscape of welfare provision in recent years has been the growth in social divisions which are reinforced by the SDW. Part-time workers, the unemployed, single parents, the irregularly employed, the elderly, the physically handicapped and the low paid are still essentially dependent upon public welfare. They have to rely upon the most visible and stigmatized benefits which provide the least security. Public welfare also often serves to reinforce exclusion from the patterns of consumption that accompany occupational and fiscal welfare. Despite the changes that have occurred since Titmuss wrote his original essay on the SDW, it remains the case that for all those who have no alternative but to turn to public welfare when they are in need, the fall into the trench of dependency is more likely, and the climb out of it more difficult.

The struggle to be the well-placed workers of tomorrow is always taking place today. It is significant that the services and benefits that trade unions offer are seen by some commentators as an important aspect of the inter-union jostling for position (Bassett, 1986; Leadbeater, 1987). If the unions and staff associations representing white-collar and supervisory staff press for occupational welfare – cheap mortgages, low interest loans, travel and car allowances and a host of other 'fringes' – the manual unions who are able to do so will follow suit. Similarly, there is already widespread support for fiscal welfare, e.g. tax relief on mortgages, which will make it hard for any government radically to alter current fiscal policy in favour of the poor. As the number of people who rely on public welfare declines, so too will the political constituency for improvements in it. As the gap widens between those who have access to fiscal and occupational welfare and those who have to rely on public welfare, there is a temptation for middle–class observers to identify an 'underclass'. It is a temptation which has to be resisted if the process of 'making' an underclass is not to be built into new state policies. Otherwise, the impact on intra-class divisions and the SDW could well be to recreate the sort of distinctions, between those at the top and those at the bottom of the working class, which existed in Victorian Britain.

Bibliography

Abercrombie, N., Hill, S. and Turner, B. (1980). *The Dominant Ideology Thesis*. George Allen and Unwin, London.

Addison, P. (1975). *The Road to 1945*. Cape, London.

Aglietta, M. (1987). *A Theory of Capitalist Regulation: The U.S. Experience*. Verso, London.

Alcock, P. (1987). *Poverty and State Support*. Longman, London.

Alexander, S. (1976). Women's work in nineteenth century London: A study of the years 1820–1850. In Mitchell, J. and Oakley, A. (eds), *The Rights and Wrongs of Women*. Penguin, Harmondsworth.

Althusser, L. (1969). *For Marx*. Penguin, Harmondsworth.

Anderson, P. (1980). *Arguments Within English Marxism*. Verso, London.

Andrzejewski, S. L. (1954). *Military Organisation and Society*. Routledge and Kegan Paul, London.

Anthias, F. (1980). Women and the Reserve Army of Labour: A critique of Veronica Beechey. *Capital and Class*, 10: 50–63.

Armstrong, P. (1988). Labour and monopoly capital. In Hyman, R. and Streek, W. (eds), *New Technology and Industrial Relations*. Basil Blackwell, Oxford.

Arnott, H. (1987). Second class citizens. In Walker, A. and Walker, C. (eds), *The Growing Divide: A Social Audit 1979–87*. CPAG, London.

Ashworth, M. and Dilnot, A. (1987). Company cars taxation. *Fiscal Studies*, 8 (4): 24–38.

Atkinson, J. (1984). Manpower strategies for flexible organisations. *Personnel Management*, August, 18–21.

Atkinson, J. and Gregory, D. (1986). A flexible future. *Marxism Today*, April, 12–17.

Audit Commission (1986). *Managing the Crisis in Council Housing*. HMSO, London.

Bagguley, P. (1989). *The Post-Fordist Enigma: Theories of Labour Flexibility*. Lancaster Regionalism Group, Working Paper No. 29, February.

Bagguley, P. (1991). *From Protest to Aquiescence: Political Movements of the Unemployed*. Macmillan, London.

Barbalet, J.M. (1982). Social closure in class analysis: A critique of Parkin. *Sociology*, 16 (4): 484–97.

Barnett, C. (1986). *The Audit of War; The Illusion and Reality of Britain as a Great Nation*. Macmillan, London.

Barrett, M. (1980). *Women's Oppression Today: Some Problems in Marxist Feminist Analysis*. New Left Books, London.

Barron, R.D. and Norris, G.M. (1976). Sexual divisions and the dual labour market. In Barker, D.L. and Allen, S. (eds), *Dependence and Exploitation in Work and Marriage*. Longman, London.

Bassett, P. (1986). *Strike Free: New Industrial Relations in Britain*. Macmillan, London.

Beechey, V. (1978). Women and production: A critical analysis of some sociological theories of women's work. In Kuhn, A. and Wolpe, A. (eds), *Feminism and Materialism: Women and Modes of Production*. Routledge and Kegan Paul, London.

Belchem, J. (1985). English working class radicalism and the Irish, 1815–1850. In Swift, I. and Gilley, R. (eds), *The Irish in the Victorian City*. Croom Helm, London.

Beresford, P. and Croft, S. (1984). Welfare pluralism: The new face of Fabianism. *Critical Social Policy*, 9: 19–39.

Best, G.F.A. (1972). *Mid-Victorian Britain 1851–1875*. Shoken, New York.

Beynon, H. (1973). *Working for Ford*. Penguin, Harmondsworth.

Black, D. (1980). *Inequalities in Health*. Report of a Research Working Party chaired by Sir Douglas Black. DHSS, London.

Blackburn, R. and Mann, M. (1979). *The Working Class and the Labour Market*. Macmillan, London.

Blackburn, R. and Mann, M. (1981). The dual labour market model. In Braham, P., Rhodes, E. and Pearn, M. (eds), *Discrimination and Disadvantage in Employment: The Experience of Black Workers*. Harper and Row/Open University Press, London/Milton Keynes.

Booth, A. (1989). *Raising the Roof on Housing Myths*. Shelter, London.

Bosanquet, N. (1984). Is privatisation inevitable. In Le Grand, J. and Robinson, R. (eds), *Privatisation and the Welfare State*. George Allen and Unwin, London.

Boston, S. (1980). *Women Workers and the Trade Union Movement*. Davis-Poynter, London.

Bovenkerk, F. (1984). The rehabilitation of the rabble: How and why Marx and Engels wrongly depicted the lumpen-proletariat as a reactionary force. *The Netherlands Journal of Sociology (Sociologicia Neerlandica)*, 20 (1): 13–42.

Bowles, S. and Gintis, H. (1976). *Schooling in Capitalist America*. Basic Books, New York.

Bradley, H. (1986). Change and the development of gender-based job segregation in the labour process. In Knights, D. and Wilmott, H. (eds), *Gender and the Labour Process*. Gower, Aldershot.

Braverman, H. (1974). *Labor and Monopoly Capital*. Monthly Review Press, New York.

Braybon, G. (1981). *Women Workers in the First World War: The British Experience*. Croom Helm, London.

Braybon, G. and Summerfield, P. (1987). *Out of the Cage: Women's Experiences in Two World Wars*. Pandora/Routledge and Kegan Paul, London.

Briggs, E. and Deacon, A. (1973). The creation of the Unemployment Assistance Board. *Policy and Politics*, 2 (1): 43–62.

Brown, G. (1977). *Sabotage*. Spokesman Books, Nottingham.

Building Societies Association (1989). *Housing and Saving*. BSA, London.

Burgess, K. (1980). *The Challenge of Labour*. Croom Helm, London.

Buswell, C. (1987). Training for low pay. In Glendinning, C. and Millar, J. (eds), *Women and Poverty in Britain*. Wheatsheaf, Brighton.

Byrne, D. and Parson, D. (1983). The state and the reserve army: The management of class relations in space. In Anderson, J., Duncan S. and Hudson, R. (eds), *Redundant Spaces in Cities and Regions: Studies in Industrial Decline and Social Change*. Institute of British Geographers Special Publication No.15. Academic Press, London.

Campling, J. (1990). Social policy digest. *Journal of Social Policy*, **19** (1): 93–112.

Castells, M. (1978). *City, Class and Power*. Macmillan, London

Castles, F.G. (1985). *The Working Class and Welfare*. George Allen and Unwin, London.

Castles, S. and Kosack, G. (1972). The function of labour immigration in Western European capitalism. *New Left Review*, **73**: 3–21.

Castles, S. and Kosack, G. (1973). *Immigrant Workers and Class Structure in Western Europe*. Oxford University Press, Oxford.

Charles, L. and Duffin, L. (eds) (1985). *Women and Work in Pre-Industrial England*. Croom Helm, London.

Clark, J. (1988). *The Process of Technological Change: New Technology and Social Choice in the Work Place*. Cambridge University Press, Cambridge.

Clarke, S. (1977). Marxism, sociology and Poultanzas' theory of the state. *Capital and Class*, Summer, 1–31.

Coates, K. and Topham, T. (1986). *Trade Unions and Politics*. Basil Blackwell, Oxford.

Cockburn, C. (1983). *Brothers: Male Dominance and Technological Change*. Pluto Press, London.

Cohen, S. (1985). Anti-Semitism, immigration controls and the welfare state. *Critical Social Policy*, **13**: 73–92.

Cole, G.D.H. and Postgate, R. (1961). *The British Common People 1746–1946*. Methuen, London.

Cook, D. (1989). *Rich Law, Poor Law: Different Responses to Tax and Supplementary Benefit Fraud*. Open University Press, Milton Keynes.

Corrigan, P. and Leonard, P. (1978). *Social Work Practice Under Capitalism: A Marxist Approach*. Macmillan, London

Cousins, C. (1987). *Controlling Social Welfare: A Sociology of State Welfare, Work and Organisation*. Wheatsheaf, Brighton.

Crompton, R. and Jones, G. (1984). *White Collar Proletariat: Deskilling and Gender in Clerical Work*. Macmillan, London.

Cronin, J.E. (1979). *Industrial Conflict in Modern Britain*. Croom Helm, London.

Cronin, J.E. (1984). *Labour and Society in Britain 1918–1979*, Batsford, London.

Crossick, G. (1978). *An Artisan Elite in Victorian Society*. Croom Helm, London.

Crouch, C. (1979). *The Politics of Industrial Relations*. Fontana/Collins, Glasgow.

Crouch, C. (1982). *The Logic of Collective Action*. Collins, Glasgow.

Crowther, M.A. (1978). The later years of the workhouse 1890–1929. In Thane, P. (ed.), *The Origins of British Social Policy*. London, Croom Helm.

Crowther, M.A. (1981). *The Workhouse System 1834–1929: The History of an English Social Institution*. Batsford, London.

Dahrendorf, R. (1988). *The Modern Social Conflict*. Weidenfeld and Nicholson, London.

Deacon, A. (1976). *In Search of the Scrounger: The Administration of Unemployment Insurance in Britain 1920–31*. Occasional Papers in Social Administration, No. 60. Social Administration Research Trust, London.

Deacon, A. (1977). Concession and coercion: The politics of unemployment insurance in the twenties. In Briggs, A. and Saville, J. (eds), *Essays in Labour History*, Vol. 3. Croom Helm, London.

Deacon, A. (1981). Unemployment and politics since 1945. In Showler, B. and Sinfield, A. (eds), *The Workless State*. Martin Robertson, Oxford.

Deacon, A. (1984). Was there a consensus? Social policy in the 1940s. In Jones, C. and Stevenson, J. (eds), *Yearbook of Social Policy in Britain 1983*. Routledge and Kegan Paul, London.

Deacon, A. and Bradshaw, J. (1983). *Reserved for the Poor*. Basil Blackwell, Oxford.

Doeringer, P. and Piore, M. J. (1971). *Internal Labour Markets and Manpower Analysis*. Heath, Lexington, Mass.

Donnison, D. (1979). Social policy since Titmuss. *Journal of Social Policy*, 8 (2): 145–57.

Donnison, D. (1982). *The Politics of Poverty*. Martin Robertson, Oxford.

Donnison, D. (1984). The progressive potential of privatisation. In Le Grand, J. and Robinson, R. (eds), *Privatisation and the Welfare State*. George Allen and Unwin, London.

Dow, J.C.R. (1964). *The Management of the British Economy 1945–1960*. Cambridge University Press, Cambridge.

Drake, B. (1984). *Women in Trade Unions*. Virago Press, London.

Dunleavy, P. (1980). *Urban Political Analysis*. Macmillan, London.

Dunleavy, P. (1986). Sectoral cleavages and the stabilization of state expenditures. *Environment and Planning: Society and Space*, 4: 128–44.

Durkheim, E. (1933). *The Division of Labour in Society*. Free Press, New York.

Edwards, R. (1979). *Contested Terrain: The Transformation of Work in the Twentieth Century*. Heinemann, London.

Elster, J. (1985). *Making Sense of Marx*. Cambridge University Press, Cambridge.

Elster, J. (1986). *Karl Marx: A Reader*. Cambridge University Press, Cambridge.

Engels, F. (1958). *The Condition of the Working Class in England*. Basil Blackwell, Oxford.

EOC (1985). *Model of Equality*. A consulting actuary's report on the methods and costs of equalising the treatment of men and women in occupational pension schemes. Prepared by Duncan C. Fraser and Co. for the Equal Opportunities Commission.

Esping-Andersen, G. (1990). *The Three Worlds of Welfare Capitalism*. Polity, Cambridge.

Field, F. (1981). *Inequality in Britain*. Fontana, Glasgow.

Field, F. (1989). *Losing Out: The Emergence of Britain's Underclass*. Basil Blackwell, Oxford.

Field, F. (1990). Britain's underclass. In Murray, C., *The Emerging British UNDERCLASS*. IEA Health and Welfare Unit, London.

Fitzgerald, R. (1988). *British Labour Management and Industrial Welfare 1846–1939*. Croom Helm, London.

Flynn, R. (1988). Political aquiescence, privatisation and residualisation in British housing policy. *Journal of Social Policy*, 17 (3): 289–312.

Forrest, R. and Murie, A. (1983). Residualisation and council housing: Aspects of the changing social relations of housing tenure. *Journal of Social Policy*, 12 (4): 453–68.

Forrest, R. and Murie, A. (1986). Marginalization and subsidized individualism: The sale of council houses in the restructuring of the British Welfare State. *International Journal of Urban and Regional Research*, 10 (1): 46–66.

Forrest, M. and Murie, A. (1989). Fiscal reorientation, centralization and the privatization of council housing. In McDowell, L., Sarre, P. and Hamnett, C. (eds),

Divided Nation: Social and Cultural Change in Britain. Hodder and Stoughton, London.

Foster, J. (1974). *Class Struggle and the Industrial Revolution*. Methuen, London.

Fox, A. (1985). *Man Mismanagement*. Hutchinson, London.

Fraser, D. (1984). *The Evolution of the British Welfare State*. Macmillan, London.

Friend, A. and Metcalf, A. (1981). *Slump City*. Pluto Press, London.

Fry, V.C., Hammond, E.M. and Kay, J.A. (1985). *Taxing Pensions: The Taxation of Occupational Pension Schemes in the U.K*. Institute of Fiscal Studies, London.

Fryer, P. (1984). *Staying Power: The History of Black People in Britain*. Pluto Press, London.

Galbraith, J.K. (1967). *The New Industrial State*. Penguin, Harmondsworth.

Gamble, A. (1974). *The Conservative Nation*. Routledge and Kegan Paul, London.

Gamble, A. (1985). *Britain in Decline: Economic Policy, Political Strategy and the British State*. Macmillan, London.

Giddens, A. (1973). *The Class Structure of the Advanced Societies*. Hutchinson, London.

Giddens, A. (1978). *Durkheim*. Fontana/Collins, Glasgow.

Giddens, A. (1980). Classes, capitalism and the state. *Theory and Society*, 9: 877–90.

Ginsburg, N. (1979). *Class Capital and Social Policy*. Macmillan, London.

Glendinning, C. and Millar, J. (eds) (1987). *Women and Poverty in Britain*. Wheatsheaf, Brighton.

Glyn, A. and Harrison, J. (1980). *The British Economic Disaster*. Pluto Press, London.

Golding, P. (ed.) (1986). *Excluding the Poor*. CPAG, London.

Golding, P. and Middleton, S. (1982). *Images of Welfare*. Martin Robertson, Oxford.

Goldthorpe, D., Lockwood, J., Bechhoffer, F. and Platt, J. (1968). *The Affluent Worker: Industrial Attitudes and Behaviour*. Cambridge University Press, Cambridge.

Goodin, R.E. and Le Grand, J., with Dryzek, J., Gibson, D.M., Hanson, R.L., Haveman, R.H. and Winter, D. (1987). *Not Only the Poor: The Middle Classes and the Welfare State*. Allen and Unwin, London

Gosden, P.H.J.H. (1961). *The Friendly Societies in England, 1815–1875*. Manchester University Press, Manchester.

Gosden, P.H.J.H. (1973). *Self-help Voluntary Associations in the 19th Century*. Batsford, London

Gough, I. (1979). *The Political Economy of the Welfare State*. Macmillan, London.

Government Actuary Report (1983). *Seventh Survey*. HMSO, London.

Gray, R. (1976). *The Labour Aristocracy in Victorian Edinburgh*. Oxford University Press. Oxford.

Green, F., Hadjimatheou, G. and Smail, R. (1984). *Unequal Fringes: Fringe Benefits in the United Kingdom*. Low Pay Unit, London.

Gregg, P. (1976). *Black Death to Industrial Revolution: A Social and Economic History of England*. Harrap, London

Groves, D. (1987). Occupational pension provision and women's poverty in old age. In Glendinning, C. and Millar, J. (eds), *Women and Poverty in Britain*. Wheatsheaf, Brighton.

Halevy, E. (1961). *History of the English People in the Nineteenth Century*, Vols 5 and 6. Benn, London.

Hall, S. and Schwarz, B. (1985). State and society 1880–1930. In Langan, M. and Schwarz, B. (eds), *Crises in the British State 1880–1930*. Hutchinson, London.

Halsey, A.H. (1989). Social trends since World War II. In McDowell, L., Sarre, P. and Hamnett, C. (eds), *Divided Nation: Social and Cultural Change in Britain*. Hodder and Stoughton, London.

Hannah, L. (1986). *Inventing Retirement: The Development of Occupational Pensions in Britain*. Cambridge University Press, Cambridge.

Hannington, W. (1973). *Unemployed Struggles 1919–1936*. E.P. Publishing, East Ardsley.

Hansard (1908). Vol. 190, 4th Series, June 1908, Cols 565–566, 580.

Hansard (1921). Vol. 138, Feb.–March 1921, Col. 1199.

Hanson, D.G. (1972). Welfare before the welfare state. In *The Long Debate on Poverty*, I.E.A. Readings, No. 9. IEA, London.

Harris, J. (1972). *Unemployment and Politics 1886–1914*. Oxford University Press, Oxford.

Harris, J. (1977). *William Beveridge: A Biography*. Oxford University Press, Oxford.

Harrison, M.L. (ed.) (1984). *Corporatism and the Welfare State*. Gower, Aldershot.

Harrison, M.L. (1986). Consumption and urban theory: An alternative approach based on the social division of welfare. *International Journal of Urban and Regional Research*, 10 (2): 232–42.

Harrison, R.J. and Zeitlin, J. (eds) (1985). *Divisions of Labour: Skilled Workers and Technological Change in Nineteenth Century England*. Harvester, Brighton.

Hay, J.R. (1975). *Origins of the Liberal Welfare Reforms 1906–1914*. Macmillan, London.

Hay, J.R. (1977). Employers and social policy in Britain: The evolution of welfare legislation, 1905–1914. *Social History*, 4: 435–55.

Heath, A. and McDonald, S.K. (1989). Social change and the future of the Left. In McDowell, L., Sarre, P. and Hamnett, C. (eds), *Divided Nation: Social and Cultural Change in Britain*. Hodder and Stoughton, London.

Henriques, U. (1979). *Before the Welfare State; Social Administration in Early Industrial Britain*. Longman, London.

Hills, J. (1987). What happened to spending on the welfare state? In Walker, A. and Walker, C. (eds), *The Growing Divide: A Social Audit 1979–87*. CPAG, London.

Himmelfarb, G. (1984). *The Idea of Poverty*. Faber and Faber, London.

Hindess, B. (1982). Power, interests and the outcomes of struggles. *Sociology*, 16 (4): 498–511.

Hinton, J. (1983). *Labour and Socialism 1867–1974*. Wheatsheaf, Brighton.

Hobsbawm, E.J. (1959). *Primitive Rebels: Studies in Archaic Forms of Social Movement in the 19th and 20th Centuries*. Manchester University Press, Manchester.

Hobsbawm, E.J. (1968). *Labouring Men*. Weidenfeld and Nicholson, London.

Holloway, J. and Picciotto, S. (eds) (1978). *State and Capital: A Marxist Debate*. Arnold, London.

Humphries, J. (1983). The emancipation of women in the 1970s and 1980s: From the latent to the floating. *Capital and Class*, 20: 6–28.

Hunt, E.H. (1981). *British Labour History 1815–1914*. Weidenfeld and Nicholson, London.

Inland Revenue (1990). Cmnd 1021, Chapter 21. HMSO, London.

Jessop, B. (1979). Corporatism, parliamentarism and social democracy. In Schmitter, P.C. and Lehmbruch, G. (eds), *Trends Toward Corporatist Intermediation*. Sage, London.

Johnson, N. (1987). *The Welfare State in Transition: The Theory and Practice of Welfare Pluralism*. Wheatsheaf, Brighton.

Jones, C. (1983). *State Social Work and the Working Class*. Macmillan, London.

Jordan, B. (1973). *Paupers: The Making of the Claiming Class*. Routledge and Kegan Paul, London.

Kaye, H.J. (1984). *The British Marxist Historians: An Introductory Analysis*. Polity, Cambridge.

Kelly, J. (1988). *Trade Unions and Socialist Politics*. Verso, London.

Kincaid, J. (1984). Richard Titmuss. In Barker, P. (ed.), *Founders of the Welfare State*. Heinemann, London.

Kingsford, P. (1982). *The Hunger Marchers in Britain, 1920–39*. Lawrence and Wishart, London.

Knights, D. and Wilmott, H. (eds) (1986a). *Gender and the Labour Process*. Gower, Aldershot.

Knights, D. and Wilmott, D. (eds) (1986b). *Managing the Labour Process*. Gower, Aldershot.

Knott, J. (1986). *Popular Opposition to the 1834 Poor Law*. Croom Helm, London.

Korpi, W. (1978). *The Working Class in Welfare Capitalism: Work Unions and Politics in Sweden*. Routledge and Kegan Paul, London.

Langan, M. (1985). Reorganizing the labour market: Unemployment, the state and the labour market. In Langan, M. and Schwarz, B. (eds), *Crises in the British State 1880–1930*. Hutchinson/CCCS, London/Birmingham.

Langan, M. and Schwarz, B. (eds) (1985). *Crises in the British State 1880–1930*. Hutchinson/CCCS, London/Birmingham.

Layton-Henry, Z. and Rich, P.B. (eds) (1986). *Race, Government and Politics in Britain*. Macmillan, London.

Leadbeater, C. (1987). Unions go to Marxism. *Marxism Today*, September, 22–7.

Leadbeater, C. (1989). In the land of the dispossessed. In McDowell, L., Sarre, P. and Hamnett, C. (eds), *Divided Nation: Social and Cultural Change in Britain*. Hodder and Stoughton, London.

Lee, P. and Raban, C. (1988). *Welfare Theory and Social Policy: Reform or Revolution?* Sage, London.

Leeson, R.A. (1980). *Travelling Brothers*. Granada, St. Albans.

Le Grand, J. (1982). *The Strategy of Equality*. Allen and Unwin, London.

Le Grand, J. (1987). The middle class use of the British social services. In Goodin, R.E. and Le Grand, J. (eds), *Not Only the Poor*. Allen and Unwin, London.

Le Grand, J. and Robinson, R. (eds) (1984). *Privatisation and the Welfare State*. Allen and Unwin, London.

Lewenhak, S. (1977). *Women and Trade Unions*. Benn, London.

Lewis, J. (1986). *Labour and Love: Women's Experience of Home and Family 1850–1940*. Basil Blackwell, Oxford.

Lewis, J. and Piachaud, D. (1987). Women and poverty in the twentieth century. In Glendinning, C. and Millar, J. (eds), *Women and Poverty in Britain*. Wheatsheaf, Brighton.

Liddington, J. and Norris, J. (1978). *One Hand Tied Behind Us: The Rise of the Women's Suffrage Movement*. Virago, London.

Littler, C.R. (1982). *The Development of the Labour Process in Capialist Societies: A Comparative Study of the Transformation of Work Organisation in Britain, Japan and the U.S.A.* Heinemann, London.

Littler, C.R. (ed.) (1985). *The Experience of Work*. Gower, Aldershot.

Lodge, D. (1988). *Nice Work*. Penguin, Harmondsworth.

Lonsdale, S. (1985). *Work and Inequality*. Longman, London.

Lonsdale, S. (1987). Patterns of paid work. In Glendinning, C. and Millar, J. (eds), *Women and Poverty in Britain*. Wheatsheaf, Brighton.

Lowe, R. (1986). *Adjusting to Democracy: The Role of the Ministry of Labour in British Politics, 1916–1939*. Clarendon Press, Oxford.

Lukes, S. (1974). *Power: A Radical View*. Macmillan, London.

Lynes, T. (1976). Unemployment Assistance Tribunals in the 1930s. In Adler, M. and Bradley, A. (eds), *Justice, Discretion and Poverty*. Professional Books, Oxon.

MacGregor, S. (1981). *The Politics of Poverty*. Longman, London.

MacNicol, J. (1987). In pursuit of the underclass. *Journal of Social Policy*, 16 (3): 293–318.

Mandel, E. (1978). *Late Capitalism*. New Left Books, London.

Mann, K. (1984). Incorporation, exclusion, underclasses and the unemployed. In Harrison, M. L. (ed.), *Corporatism and the Welfare State*. Gower, Aldershot.

Mann, K. (1986). The making of a claiming class – the neglect of agency in analyses of the Welfare State. *Critical Social Policy*, 15: 62–74.

Mann, K. and Anstee, J. (1989). *Growing Fringes: Hypothesis on the Development of Occupational Welfare*. Armley, Leeds.

Marwick, A. (1968). *Britain in the Century of Total War*. Bodley Head, London.

Marx, K. (1976). *Capital*. New Left Books/Penguin, London/Harmondsworth.

Marx, K. (1979). *Early Texts* (edited and translated by D. McLennan). Basil Blackwell, Oxford.

Marx, K. and Engels, F. (1956). *Selected Correspondence*. Lawrence and Wishart, London.

Marx, K. and Engels, F. (1969). *Basic Writings on Politics and Philosophy* (edited by L.S. Feuer). Collins/Fontana, London.

Marx, K. and Engels, F. (1971). *Articles on Britain*. Progress Publishers, Moscow .

Marx, K. and Engels, F. (1977). *The German Ideology* (edited by C.J. Arthur). Lawrence and Wishart, London.

Massey, D. (1984). *Spatial Divisions of Labour: Social Structures and the Geography of Production*. Macmillan, London.

McDowell, L., Sarre, P. and Hamnett, C. (eds) (1989). *Divided Nation: Social and Cultural Change in Britain*. Hodder and Stoughton, London.

McGoldrick, A. (1984). *Equal Treatment in Occupational Pension Schemes*. Equal Opportunities Commission, London.

McLoughlin, I. and Clark, J. (1988). *Technological Change at Work*. Open University Press, Milton Keynes.

Middlemas, K. (1979). *Politics in Industrial Society since 1911*. Andre Deutsch, London.

Middlemas, K. (1986). *Power, Competition and the State*. Macmillan, London.

Middleton, C. (1979). The sexual division of labour in feudal England. *New Left Review*, 113–114: 147–68.

Middleton, C. (1985). Women's labour and the transition to pre-industrial capitalism. In Charles, L. and Duffin, L. (eds), *Women and Work in Pre-Industrial England*. Croom Helm, London.

Middleton, L. (ed.) (1977). *Women in the Labour Movement*. Croom Helm, London.

Miles, R. (1989). Racism and class structure. In McDowell, L., Sarre, P. and Hamnett, C. (eds), *Divided Nation: Social and Cultural Change in Britain*. Hodder and Stoughton, London.

Miliband, R. (1973). *The State in Capitalist Society*. Quartet Books, London.

Miliband, R. (1974). Politics and poverty. In Wedderburn, D. (ed.), *Poverty, Inequality and Class Structure*. Cambridge University Press, Cambridge.

Mishra, R. (1984). *The Welfare State in Crisis: Social Thought and Social Change.* Wheatsheaf, Brighton.

Moorhouse, H.F. (1978). Marxist theories of the labour aristocracy. *Social History,* 3: 61–82.

Morris Committee (1929). Minutes of Evidence, Second Day, para.763.

Murphy, J.T. (1972). *Preparing for Power.* Cape, London.

Murphy, R. (1988). *Social Closure: The Theory of Monopolization and Exclusion.* Clarendon Press, Oxford.

Murray, C. (1990). *The Emerging British UNDERCLASS.* IEA Health and Welfare Unit, London

Musson, A.E. (1976). Class struggle and the labour aristrocracy. *Social History,* III: 335–56.

Newman, O. (1981). *The Challenge of Corporatism.* Macmillan, London.

Nottingham, C. (1986). Recasting bourgeois Britain? The British State in the years which followed the First World War. *International Review of Social History,* xxxi (3): 227–47.

Novak, T. (1988). *Poverty and the State: An Historical Sociology.* Open University Press, Milton Keynes.

O'Connor, J. (1973). *The Fiscal Crisis of the State.* St Martins Press, New York.

Offe, C. (1981). The attribution of public status to interest groups: Observations on the West German case. In Berger, S. (ed.), *Organising Interests in Western Europe.* Cambridge University Press, Cambridge.

Offe, C. (1982). Some contradictions of the modern welfare state. *Critical Social Policy,* 12 (2): 7–16

Offe, C. (1984). *Contradictions of the Welfare State* (edited by J. Keane). Hutchinson, London.

Ollman, B. (1976). *Alienation: Marx's Conception of Man in Capitalist Society.* Cambridge University Press, Cambridge.

Orwell, G. (1970). *Collected Essays, Journalism and Letters.* Penguin, Harmondsworth.

O'Tuathaigh, M.A.G. (1985). The Irish in nineteenth century Britain: Problems of integration. In Swift, R. and Gilley, S. (eds), *The Irish in the Victorian City.* Croom Helm, London.

Pahl, R. (1970). *Patterns of Urban Life.* Longman, London.

Pahl, R. (1975). *Whose City.* Penguin, Harmondsworth.

Pahl, R. (1984). *Divisions of Labour.* Basil Blackwell, Oxford.

Panitch, L. (1981). The limits of corporatism: Trade unions in the capitalist state. *New Left Review,* 125: 21–43.

Parkin, F. (1979). *Marxism and Class Theory: A Bourgeois Critique.* Tavistock, London.

Pearson, G. (1983). *Hooligan – A History of Respectable Fears.* Macmillan, London.

Pelling, H. (1958). *The British Communist Party.* Black, London.

Pelling, H. (1965). *The Origins of the Labour Party 1880–1900.* Clarendon Press, Oxford.

Pelling, H. (1968). *Popular Politics and Society in Late Victorian Britain.* Macmillan, London.

Phizalklea, A. (1983). *One Way Ticket Migration and Female Labour.* Routledge and Kegan Paul, London.

Piachaud, D. (1987a). The growth of poverty. In Walker, A. and Walker, C. (eds), *The Growing Divide: A Social Audit 1979–1987.* CPAG, London.

Piachaud, D. (1987b). Problems in the definition and measurement of poverty. *Journal of Social Policy,* 16 (2): 147–64.

Pimlott, B. (1977). *Labour and the Left in the 1930s*. Cambridge University Press, Cambridge.

Piore, M. and Sabel, C. (1984). *The Seond Industrial Divide: Possibilities for Prosperity*. Basic Books, New York.

Piven, F.F. and Cloward, R.A. (1977). *Poor People's Movements*. Pantheon, New York.

Piven, F.F. and Cloward, R. (1982). *The New Class War: Reagan's Attack on the Welfare State and its Consequences*. Pantheon, New York.

Pond, C., Field, F. and Winyard, S. (1976). Trade unions and taxation. *Studies for Trade Unionists*, 2 (6).

Pope, R., Pratt, A. and Hoyle, B. (eds) (1986). *Social Welfare in Britain 1885–1985*. Croom Helm, London.

Poster, M. (1984). *Foucault, Marxism and History: Mode of Production vs Mode of Information*. Polity, Cambridge.

Potter, S. (1986). Car tax concessions: Perk or problem. *Town and Country Planning*, 55 (6): 169–70.

Preteceille, E. (1986). Collective consumption, urban segregation, and social classes. *Environment and Planning, Society and Space*, 4: 145–54.

Preteceille, E. and Terrail, J.P. (1985). *Capitalism, Consumption and Needs* (translated by S. Mathews). Basil Blackwell, Oxford.

Price, R. and Bain, G.S. (1983). Union growth: dimensions, determinants and destiny. In Bain, G.S. (ed.), *Industrial Relations in Britain*. Basil Blackwell, Oxford.

Priestley, J.B. (1934). *English Journey*. Heinemann, London.

Prosser, T. (1981). The politics of discretion: Aspects of discretionary power in the supplementary benefits scheme. In Adler, M. and Asquith, S. (eds), *Discretion and Welfare*. Heinemann, London.

Ramdin, R. (1987). *The Making of the Black Working Class in Britain*. Gower, Aldershot.

Reddin, M. (1982). Occupation, welfare and social division. In Jones, C. and Stevenson, J. (eds), *The Year Book of Social Policy in Britain 1980–81*. Routledge and Kegan Paul, London.

Redmayne, R. (1950). *Ideals in Industry*. Petty and Sons, Leeds.

Rex, J. (1971). The concept of housing classes and the sociology of race relations. *Race*, 12: 293–301.

Rex, J. (1973). *Race, Colonialism and the City*. Routledge and Kegan Paul, London.

Rex, J. and Moore, J. (1967). *Race, Community and Conflict*. Oxford University Press, Oxford.

Rex, J. and Tomlinson, S. (1979). *Colonial Immigrants in a British City: A Class Analysis*. Routledge and Kegan Paul, London

Richter, D.C. (1981). *Riotous Victorians*. Ohio University Press, London.

Rose, H. (1981). Rereading Titmuss: The sexual division of welfare. *Journal of Social Policy*, 10 (4): 477–502.

Rowbotham, S. (1973). *Hidden from History*. Pluto Press, London.

Rude, G. (1980). *Ideology and Popular Protest*. Lawrence and Wishart, London.

Ryan, P. (1978). Poplarism 1894–1930. In Thane, P. (ed.), *The Origins of British Social Policy*. Croom Helm, London.

Sabel, C.F. (1982). *Work and Politics – The Division of Labour in Industry*. Cambridge University Press, Cambridge.

Sandford, C., Pond, C. and Walker, R. (eds) (1980). *Taxation and Social Policy*. Heinemann, London.

Saunders, P. (1981). *Social Theory and the Urban Question*. Hutchinson, London.

Saunders, P. (1986). Comment on Dunleavy and Preteceille. *Environment and Planning, Society and Space*, 4: 155–63.

Saunders, P. and Harris, C. (1990). Privatisation and the consumer. *Sociology*, 24 (1): 57–74.

Saville, J. (1975). The welfare state: An historical approach. In Butterworth, E. and Holman, R. (eds), *Social Welfare in Modern Britain*. Fontana/Collins, Glasgow.

Seccombe, W. (1986). Patriarchy stabilized: The construction of the male breadwinner wage norm in 19th century Britain. *Social History*, 11 (1): 53–80.

Shaw, C. (1987). Eliminating the yahoo, eugenics, Social Darwinism and Five Fabians. *History of Political Thought*, VIII (3): 521–44.

Sherman, M. (1985). 'It is not a case of numbers': A case study of institutional racism, 1941–1943. In Lunn, K. (ed.), *Race and Labour in Twentieth Century Britain*. Frank Cass, London.

Sinfield, A. (1978). Analyses in the social division of welfare. *Journal of Social Policy*, 7 (2): 129–56.

Sinfield, A. (1981). *What Unemployment Means*. Martin Robertson, Oxford.

Sinfield, A. (1986). Poverty, privilege and welfare. In Bean, P. and Whyne, D. (eds), *Barabara Wooton: Essays in Her Honour*. Tavistock, London.

Sivanandan, A. (1982). *A Different Hunger: Writings on Black Resistance*. Pluto Press, London.

Sked, A. and Cook, C. (1979). *Post-War Britain: A Political History*. Penguin, Harmondsworth.

Smith, D. (1982). *Conflict and Compromise*. Routledge and Kegan Paul, London.

Smith, D.J. (1977). *Racial Disadvantage in Britain – the PEP Report*. Penguin, Harmondsworth.

Smith, G. (1987). *When Jim Crow Met John Bull: Black American Soldiers in W.W. 2 Britain*. I.B. Tauris, London.

Social Trends (1983). Vol. 13. HMSO, London.

Social Trends (1986). Vol. 16. HMSO, London.

Social Trends (1987). Vol. 17. HMSO, London.

Social Trends (1988). Vol. 18. HMSO, London.

Social Trends (1991). Vol. 21. HMSO, London.

Soldon, N.C. (1978). *Women in British Trade Unions, 1874–1976*. Gill and Macmillan, Dublin.

Stark, D. (1982). Class struggle and the transformation of the labour process. In Giddens, A. and Held, D. (eds), *Classes, Power, and Conflict: Classical and Contemporary Debates*. Macmillan, London.

Stedman-Jones, G. (1983). *Languages of Class*. Cambridge University Press, Cambridge.

Stedman-Jones, G. (1984). *Outcast London*. Oxford University Press, Oxford.

Stevenson, J. (1977). *Social Conditions in Britain between the Wars*. Penguin, Harmondsworth.

Stevenson, J. and Cook, C. (1977). *The Slump: Society and Politics During the Depression*. Jonathan Cape, London.

Swift, I. and Gilley, R. (eds) (1985). *The Irish in the Victorian City*. Croom Helm, London.

Taylor, B. (1983). The men are as bad as their masters. In Newton, J.L., Ryan, M.P. and Walkowitzt, J.R. (eds), *Sex and Class in Women's History*. Routledge and Kegan Paul, London.

Taylor-Gooby, P. (1981). The empiricist tradition in social adminstration. *Critical Social Policy*, 1 (2): 6–21.

Taylor-Gooby, P. (1985). *Public Opinion, Ideology and State Welfare.* Routledge and Kegan Paul, London.

Thane, P. (1975). The working class and state welfare 1880–1914. *Society for the Study of Labour History.* Bulletin 31.

Thane, P. (1978). *The Origins of British Social Policy.* Croom Helm, London.

Thane, P. (1982). *Foundations of the Welfare State.* Longman, London.

Thane, P. (1984). The working class and state welfare in Britain, 1880–1914. *The Historical Journal,* **27** (4): 877–900.

Therborn, G. (1983). Why some classes are more successful than others. *New Left Review,* **138**: 37–56.

Thomis, M.I. (1976). *Responses to Industrialisation: The British Experience 1780–1850.* David and Charles, Newton Abbot.

Thompson, E.P. (1968). *The Making of the English Working Class.* Penguin, Harmondsworth.

Thompson, E.P. (1978). Peculiarities of the English. In *The Poverty of Theory and other Essays.* Merlin, London.

Thompson, E.P. (1980). *Writing by Candlelight.* Merlin, London.

Thompson, E.P. (1984). Mr Attlee and the Gadarene Swine. *The Guardian,* 3 March.

Titmuss, R.M. (1958). *Essays on the Welfare State.* Allen and Unwin, London.

Titmuss, R.M. (1959). *The Irresponsible Society.* Fabian Society, London.

Titmuss, R.M. (1962). *Income Distribution and Social Change: A Study in Criticism.* Allen and Unwin, London.

Titmuss, R.M. (1970). *The Gift Relationship – From Human Blood to Social Policy.* Allen and Unwin, London.

Townsend, P. (1979). *Poverty in the United Kingdom.* Penguin, Harmondsworth.

Townsend, P. (1987). Poor health. In Walker, A. and Walker, C. (eds), *The Growing Divide: A Social Audit 1979–87.* CPAG, London.

Treble, J.H. (1968). The Place of Irish Catholics in the Social Life of the North of England 1829–51. Unpublished PhD thesis, University of Leeds.

Treble, J.H. (1979). *Urban Poverty in Britain, 1830–1914.* Batsford, London.

Trotsky, L. (1975). *The Struggle Against Fascism in Germany.* Penguin, Harmondsworth.

Walby, S. (1986). *Patriarchy at Work: Patriarchal and Captalist Relations in Employment.* Polity, Cambridge.

Walby, S. (1990). *Theorizing Patriarchy.* Basil Blackwell, Oxford.

Walker, A. (1984). The political economy of privatisation. In Le Grand, J. and Robinson, R. (eds), *Privatisation and the Welfare State.* George Allen and Unwin, London.

Walker, A. and Walker, C. (eds) (1987). *The Growing Divide: A Social Audit 1979–1987.* CPAG, London.

Walker, R. and Lawton, D. (1989). Social assistance and territorial justice: The example of single payments. *Journal of Social Policy,* **17** (4): 437–76.

Ward, J.T. and Fraser, H. (1980). *Workers and Employers: Documents on Trade Union and Industrial Relations in Britain since the 18th Century.* Macmillan, London.

Ward, S. (1981). *Pensions.* Pluto Press, London

Ward, S. (1985). The financial crisis facing pensioners. *Critical Social Policy,* **14**: 43–56.

Warde, A. (1990). Introduction to the sociolgy of consumption. *Sociology,* **24** (1): 1–4.

Webb, B. and Webb, S. (1916). *The Prevention of Destitution.* Longman, London.

Webb, B. and Webb, S. (1920). *History of Trade Unionism*. Longman, London.
Weber, M. (1968). *Economy and Society*. Bedminster Press, New York.
Wetherly, P. (1988). Class struggle and the welfare state: Some theoretical problems considered. *Critical Social Policy*, **22**: 24–40.
White, J. (1982). 1910–1914 reconsidered. In Cronin, J.G. and Schneer, J. (eds), *Social Conflict and the Political Order in Modern Britain*. Croom Helm, London.
Whitehead, M. (1987). *The Health Divide: Inequalities in Health in the 1980s*. Health Education Council, London.
Whiteside, N. (1980). Welfare and the unions in the First World War. *The Historical Journal*, **23** (4): 857–74.
Wilensky, H.L. (1976). *The New Corporatism, Centralization and the Welfare State*. Sage, London.
Wilkinson, F. (ed.) (1981). *The Dynamics of Labour Market Segmentation*. Academic Press, London.
Williams, N.J., Sewel, J.F. and Twine, F. (1986). Council house sales and residualisation. *Journal of Social Policy*, **15** (3): 273–92.
Willman, P. (1986). *Technological Change, Collective Bargaining and Industrial Efficiency*. Oxford University Press, Oxford.
Wilson, E. (1977). *Women and the Welfare State*. Tavistock, London.
Wilson, H. (1974). *The Labour Government 1964–70*. Penguin, Harmondsworth.
Wilson, W.J. (1987). *The Truly Disadvantaged: The Inner City, The Underclass and Public Policy*. University of Chicago Press, Chicago.
Wilson, W.J. (ed.) (1987). *The Ghetto Underclass*. Special edition of the Annals of the American Academy of Political and Social Science. Sage, London.
Winyard, S. (1987). Divided Britain. In Walker, A. and Walker, C. (eds), *The Growing Divide: A Social Audit 1979–1987*. CPAG, Bath.
Wook, S. and Windolph, P. (1987). *Social Closure in the Labour Market*. Gower, Aldershot.
Wraithe, R.E. and Hutcheson, P. (1973). *Administrative Tribunals*. Allen and Unwin, London.
Wright, S. (1985). Churmaids, Huswyfes and Hucksters. In Charles, L. and Duffin, L. (eds), *Women and Work in Pre-Industrial England*. Croom Helm, London.
Yeo, S. (1979). Working class associations, private capital, welfare and the state in the late nineteenth and twentieth centuries. In Parry, N., Rustin, M. and Satyamurti, C. (eds), *Social Work, Welfare and the State*. Arnold, London.

Index